She's Mad Real

She's Mad Real

*Popular Culture and
West Indian Girls
in Brooklyn*

Oneka LaBennett

NEW YORK UNIVERSITY PRESS
New York and London

NEW YORK UNIVERSITY PRESS
New York and London
www.nyupress.org

References to Internet websites (URLs) were accurate at the time of writing.
Neither the author nor New York University Press is responsible for URLs
that may have expired or changed since the manuscript was prepared.

Library of Congress Cataloging-in-Publication Data

LaBennett, Oneka.
She's mad real : popular culture and West Indian girls in Brooklyn /
Oneka LaBennett.
p. cm.
Includes bibliographical references and index.
ISBN 978-0-8147-5247-0 (hardback) — ISBN 978-0-8147-5248-7 (pb) —
ISBN 978-0-8147-5312-5 (e-book)
1. African American girls—New York (State)—Brooklyn. 2. Minority youth—
New York (State)—Brooklyn. 3. West Indians—New York (State)—Brooklyn—
Social life and customs. 4. Consumer behavior—New York (State)—Brooklyn.
I. Title.
HQ1439.N6L33   201
305.235'20899697290747275—dc22   2011005520

New York University Press books are printed on acid-free paper,
and their binding materials are chosen for strength and durability.
We strive to use environmentally responsible suppliers and materials
to the greatest extent possible in publishing our books.

Manufactured in the United States of America
c   10 9 8 7 6 5 4 3 2 1
p   10 9 8 7 6 5 4 3 2 1

Contents

Acknowledgments

Because this project developed over the course of a decade, I had to rely on generous support from many people without whom I could not have completed this book.

My greatest thanks goes to the adults and youth in Brooklyn who shared their stories and experiences with me. I owe a debt of gratitude especially to the Museum Team interns and staff at the Brooklyn Children's Museum, who welcomed me and allowed me to hang out with them. I hope this book enables readers to hear their voices and to appreciate their vitality and resilience in the face of popular representations and policy discourses that are not attuned to the complexity of their subjectivities.

As an undergraduate student, the world of academia mystified me, and I was fortunate to connect with Elizabeth Traube, Ann duCille, Lydia L. English, and Steven Gregory, brilliant professors who initially sparked my interest in anthropology and who continue to serve as intellectual(s) heroes.

My advisers at Harvard University, Mary M. Steedly, James L. Watson, J. Lorand Matory, and Mary C. Waters, animated and guided me.

Early on, I received a faculty research grant from College of the Holy Cross, and I thank my former colleagues from that time, especially Daniel Goldstein, Susan Cunningham, and James Manigault-Bryant.

This project came to fruition after I joined the faculty at Fordham University, and I am grateful for the faculty research grant and the faculty fellowship I received from Fordham. My colleagues in the Department of African and African American Studies each offered immeasurable assistance in the form of friendship, feedback, and professional support; my sincerest appreciation goes to Mark Chapman, Jane Edward, Amir Idris, Claude Mangum, Fawzia Mustafa, Mark Naison, Carina Ray, Irma Watkins-Owens, and Noël Wolfe, and to everyone with whom I have worked under the auspices of the Bronx African American History Project (BAAHP). I am also indebted to Glenn Hendler in American Studies, Allan Gilbert in Sociology and Anthropology, Arnaldo Cruz-Malavé in Latin American and Latino Studies, and my Fordham students who have advocated for my courses.

At crucial junctures I benefited greatly from critical commentary and reassurance generously provided by O. Hugo Benavides, Daniel HoSang, and Raymond Codrington, whom I owe tremendous thanks. I would also like to acknowledge colleagues whose kindness bolstered me and whose work invigorated me: Elizabeth Chin, Deborah A. Thomas, Jacqueline Nassy Brown, and Jennifer Tilton.

I am extremely thankful to Jennifer Hammer, my editor at NYU Press, for her commitment to this project and for her invaluable suggestions, which sharpened the book's readability considerably; to Andrew Tiedt, who devoted his expertise to my demographic statistics; to Danielle Jakubowski, who meticulously transcribed interviews; and to anonymous reviewers, whose insightful criticism, coupled with a keen awareness of my project's vision, enlivened and enhanced this work.

My friends and family have sustained me through numerous challenges. Thank you, David Drogin, Nicole Davis, Dominique Kim, Enas Hanna, and Melissa Woods for years of friendship, and thank you, Mom, Ray, and Don, for your love.

Finally, my deepest love and thanks to my husband, Shawn McDaniel, whose devotion, patience, and loving encouragement fortified me. You were a constant source of inspiration, a ready ear, and a willing proofreader whose presence simultaneously soothed and motivated me. Our years together have been my happiest even amid struggle and hard work. You and Mr. B bring joy to my life!

Consuming Identities

Toward a Youth Culture–Centered
Approach to West Indian Transnationalism

China takes the A train to the Fulton Street/Broadway Nassau stop to get to her job as a sales clerk at a clothing store near Ground Zero, one of two after-school jobs China holds. It is just after 4 p.m. on a Friday in August, and, on this particular afternoon, China rides the train with her best friend, Nadine, and two other friends, Neema and Mariah.[1] The subway car is full of businesspeople leaving early from Wall Street jobs, vacationing tourists, and a few local New Yorkers of varying ethnicities. The businesspeople are mostly White and dressed in suits. The tourists, dressed in shorts and tee shirts with cameras swinging from their necks and purses held close, are also White. Both the tourists and the businesspeople appear to be uneasy sharing such close quarters with the Black teenage girls. China and Nadine wear jeans, tight tee shirts, and sneakers, while Neema and Mariah wear cotton shorts with matching tank tops, and inexpensive, trendy sandals. The four girls are acutely aware of how the other commuters regard their presence on the subway car. The girls seem to spontaneously react to and feed the avoidance and the silent disapproval of the White passengers by yelling loudly across the subway car, taking up more seats than they need, and laughing boisterously. China, whose hair is dyed the same shade of gold as that of her idol, the R&B/hip-hop singer Mary J. Blige, is listening to her iPod. She sits on the opposite side of the subway car, facing the other girls. China sings loudly over the divide, entertaining her friends (who are in hysterics at her poor singing) and visibly annoying the other commuters around her.

CHINA: [singing melodramatically] Another lesson learned! Better know your friends! Or else you will get burned! Gotta count on me! 'Cause I can guarantee that I'll be fine. . . . No more pain, no more pain, no more drama in my life, no one's gonna hurt me again.

China is severely off-key as she belts out the Mary J. Blige ballad "No More Drama," from the album of the same name. Hamming it up, arms flailing, China does her best impersonation of Blige's performance in the song's music video, as her friends' laughter and the stares of the other passengers intensify. Although the Blige song is about the pain of a broken heart, sung from the perspective of a woman looking back on her youth, the lyrics seem especially relevant to China's life. At seventeen, she has already experienced prolonged separation from her mother, who initially left China in Barbados before reuniting with her when China was ten. China has come to rely heavily on her best friend, Nadine, a first-generation Trinidadian, who moved in with China's family after Nadine's mom took a job in a southern city during Nadine's senior year in high school. Like many West Indian children and adolescents, even before immigrating to the United States, these girls were accustomed to being cared for by extended kin. Nadine's and China's experiences of being raised by grandmothers in the Caribbean for several years before reuniting with their mothers is a common practice of "child fostering," a Caribbean kinship solution to the rifts accompanying immigration.[2] Both girls know the heartache of such separation, and the self-reliance they learned in their parents' absence continues to shape their lives; they use their own hard-earned money for luxuries like iPods, cell phones, and professionally manicured false nails, in addition to necessities like food and clothes. China's life story parallels Blige's song in terms of both the hardship of parental separation and the "drama" that characterizes life for children in the Caribbean who learn to be independent at young ages and who face daily challenges and dangers, including tending to younger siblings and walking to school without adult supervision. To attend school, these children journey alongside speeding cars on poorly paved roads where pedestrians are routinely struck and killed.

China identifies with the adversity Mary J. Blige has overcome, as illustrated both in her music and in the performer's personal narrative. Asked why Blige is her favorite singer, China responded:

> She's *mad* real. She don't front for nobody. If you listen to her music you learn stuff about her life and how she struggled to get where she is. She's not just singing about how she's out at the club. She's *mad real.*

While Blige's personal struggles, which include overcoming poverty and drug addiction, resonate with China, her subway performance is less about China's own "drama" and more an action staged in defiance of her surroundings.[3] Unlike the many child performers, such as break dancers and candy sellers who earn a living on the subway, China's mini-performance is improvised and not intended to please anyone other than herself and her friends. She negotiates the public space of the subway as if on the attack and uses her poor singing as an affront to the other riders. China and her friends are accustomed to adults, especially White adults, regarding them suspiciously in public settings. When they shop for clothes, salespeople and other shoppers observe their every move, certain that they are shoplifters. At school, asserting a West Indian identity can sometimes put China in the good graces of teachers, but in settings such as the subway and retail stores, China is stereotypically marked by her age, gender, and race.

Placing Black Youth

China and Nadine are among the West Indian teenage girls you will get to know in this book. While China's raucous rendition of Blige's song took place on a New York City subway, Black teenage girls are overwhelmingly represented in national and global popular discourses in negative terms, either as being "at risk" for teenage pregnancy, obesity, or sexually transmitted diseases or as helpless victims of inner-city poverty and violence. Examples include the pregnant, overweight, and abused young woman depicted in the film *Precious: Based on the Novel Push by Sapphire* and the fat-lipped and scarred pictures of Barbadian hip-hop/R&B star Rihanna after famously being assaulted by her boyfriend, singer Chris Brown. Meanwhile, popular images represent their male counterparts as dangerous menaces to society or as hapless casualties of pathological family life; common portrayals of Black inner-city teenage boys include dark-faced, hooded drug dealers, aspiring rappers, and, the character Precious's male equivalent, the illiterate football player rescued by an affluent White family in the film *The Blind Side*. These representations do not fully convey the diverse, real life experiences of Black teenagers. However, such popular representations are pervasive and often portray Black adolescents' consumer and leisure culture as corruptive, uncivilized, and pathological. This book is intended to intervene and to heed the alarm that educators, policymakers, parents, and the media have sounded with regard to the negative ways in which teens in general, and Black teenage girls in particular, are being "influenced" by popular Black youth culture. *She's Mad Real* takes Black youth culture as its starting point, arguing that West Indian adolescents are strategic consumers of popular culture and that, through this consumption, they assert far more agency in defining race, ethnicity, and gender than academic and popular discourses tend to acknowledge. The consumer and leisure spheres are revealed not as unabashed arenas of pleasure and power but as dynamic sites in which marginalized Black teenage identities are produced and contested, confined and liberated. Indeed, we will see that youthful racial, gender, and nation-based identities are critically constructed in popular representations.

Popular representations of and about Black teenagers do not exist in a vacuum but, rather, are placed within local, national, and global contexts. This ethnography examines the relationship between *place* and Black youth culture, exposing the spatial construction of West Indian girls' subjectivities. China and her friends attend an afterschool program at the Brooklyn Children's Museum (BCM) in Crown Heights.[4] The museum program and her job near Ground Zero are two wage-earning positions China holds in addition to attending high school. Yet, in public places such as subway cars, movie theaters, and clothing stores, China and her friends are viewed not as hardworking citizens and valued consumers but as threats to civic decorum. This book situates West Indian girls' consumer and leisure culture within public spaces in order to interrogate the ways in which teens like China are marginalized and policed while they attempt to carve out places for themselves within New York's contested terrains.

She's Mad Real: Authenticity, Femininity and Popular Black Youth Culture

She's Mad Real paves new ground by engaging concerns about female adolescent identity formation vis-à-vis consumer culture with the social construction of West Indian notions of belonging. It addresses questions such as: What constitutes Blackness in today's global world? Are teenage girls equipped to form strong self-definitions in the face of a hip-hop culture that is largely characterized as corruptive? The pursuit of "authentic Blackness" takes center stage in youthful constructions of Black femininity, and China emphasizes this centrality when she describes Mary J. Blige as "mad real." She plainly articulates African diaspora scholars' theorizations regarding the importance of authenticity in popular Black youth cultures (Fleetwood 2005; Gilroy 1993; Gray 1995; Hall 1996; Jackson 2005; Kelley 1997; Ogbar 2009). This book puts West Indian and African American girls in dialogue with scholars who have analyzed the paradoxes attached to notions of Black authenticity. The West Indian and African American girls you will meet strive to identify "*real* Black people" among the contradictory media images routinely offered to them. This is, of course, a tangled and precarious exercise. For West Indian youth in particular, "realness" is contingent and deeply problematic—they struggle to negotiate "authentic" West Indian selves while sometimes simultaneously identifying with African Americans. The quest for authenticity also has significant implications for the youths' gender identities. For China and her friends, calling a performer like Mary J. Blige "mad real" is the highest compliment they could bestow because it connotes a feminine style that confronts and circumvents mainstream racialized and classed notions of beauty. Thus, being "mad real," "really for real," and "keepin' it real" reemerge throughout this text as a central trope.

The anthropologist John L. Jackson Jr. has critiqued how authenticity functions in contemporary academic discourses, charging that a reliance on authenticity "explains what is most constraining and potentially self-destructive about identity politics" (Jackson 2005: 12). Jackson follows philosopher Kwame Anthony Appiah in highlighting the shortcomings of social authenticity, arguing that this form of collective identity formation relies heavily on "scripts," or narratives "that people use in shaping their life plans and in telling their life stories" (Appiah 1996; Jackson 2005: 12). Jackson writes:

> These scripts provide guidelines for proper and improper behavior, for legitimate and illegitimate group membership, for social inclusion or ostracism. We use these scripts as easy shorthand for serious causal analysis, and scholars who invoke "racial authenticity" usually do so to talk about how such scripts delimit individuals' social options—describing how racial identity can be made to function a lot like social incarceration, a quotidian breeding ground, claims Paul Gilroy, for even more brutal forms of fascism (Gilroy 2000; Jackson 2005: 13).

Rather than interrogating authenticity to "delimit individuals' social options," in this book we will come to see girls' reliance on "being mad real" as central to their subjectivity formations as critical social actors. While a number of scholarly analyses interpret the pursuit of realness as serving to essentialize Black people and limit Black youths' chances for success by situating them outside White mainstream America, *She's Mad Real* reveals how girls use invocations of realness to (re)write their own social scripts (Fleetwood 2005; Gilroy 1993).

Instead of seeing Black girls' invocations of "being for real" as a form of objectification that obscures agency and denies humanity (Jackson 2005), we can interpret attempts at identifying and claiming authenticity or "realness" as critical responses to popular and public policy discourses that ignore the complex realities of their lives. China's subway performance is a clamorous demand to be heard, and her identification with Blige signals her determination to overcome daily challenges. For China and her peers, finding authenticity in consumer culture and claiming public space are contradictory exercises marked by crossing perilous boundaries between the private and the public spheres, between consumption and production, and between work and leisure. As they navigate these boundaries, youth of color are often misunderstood, viewed as criminals, or rendered invisible. Compare the description of China and her friends with one of some subway performers on the same train line: "Show time! Show time! It's show time folks! Show time!" Any frequent rider of the New York City subway in recent years recognizes this prompt. It marks the beginning of a familiar scene. When the uptown A trains stops at Canal Street, most seats on the train are occupied. Three brown-skinned children enter. There are two boys; one appears to be about thirteen years old, and the other one, who is much taller and who is carrying a boom box, looks to be about sixteen. The smallest child is a skinny little girl who cannot be more than ten years old. Setting the boom box down next to the doors, the taller boy delivers the "It's show time!" cue. Seeing that a performance is about to ensue, a few people seated closest to the group move further away. As Michael Jackson's "You've Got Me Working Day and Night" plays on the boom box, the little girl starts to move, with the boys flanking her, their backs against the subway doors. As the train careens forward, the little girl does back flips, cartwheels, and handstands. Michael Jackson's voice soars: "You got me workin', workin' day and night . . . And I'll be workin', from sun-up to midnight!" The little girl is fazed neither by the screeching abrupt stops of the train nor by the protruding feet and shopping bags of commuters. Some tourists look on in amazement, cheering the little girl on, while others appear annoyed by the impending threat of limbs flying through the air. Wearing cotton shorts and a dirty tee shirt, the girl looks fragile as she contorts herself, deftly avoiding the subway car's center pole. Seasoned straphangers have seen this show before and continue reading their books and their copies of the *Daily News*. Next, the tallest boy begins his routine, consisting of more sophisticated break-dancing moves. The boy's muscles bulge as he spins on one hand, then spirals on his head, his legs somehow managing not to hit poles and people. The last boy is the most talented. He works the subway car pole in a move that oddly resembles a stripper's routine, but, when he flips his body 360 degrees, his lanky legs hit the subway car ceiling with a loud thud. Passengers gasp at the sound and applaud as the little girl makes her rounds, collecting money in a black backpack. I hand her a one-dollar bill and count at least an additional ten dollars going in to her collection. A passenger comments as he hands over a dollar bill, "Look at this! Twenty dollars in ten minutes! How old are you?" The little girl smiles and says, "I'm eight." Before I get a chance to ask any questions, the group vanishes through the momentarily open subway doors. The train lurches on.

There are variations on the scene I've just sketched. Most frequently, the performers are Black or Latino and are preadolescent or teenage boys. The little girl I described is the only girl I have seen in such a performance. An alternative and perhaps more common scenario is one in which a group of three or so teens, again usually boys, enters a subway car, announcing they have candy for sale. "Candy! Get your peanut M&Ms, Snickers, Reese's Pieces! One dollar!" When I first noticed the candy sellers, years ago, the youth would proclaim, "Good afternoon, ladies and gentlemen! We're selling candy to raise money for our school trip!" More recently, however, children like these have announced, "I'm just keepin' it real. I'm not selling candy for a school trip or anything. Just trying to stay off the streets and get a little money in my pocket."

Although the Metropolitan Transit Authority (MTA) prohibits peddling on subway cars, I have never seen police officers enforce this rule in relation to young candy sellers or break dancers. That these youngsters are primarily Black and Latino both speaks to and feeds notions of racialized and age-based inequalities in New York City. Their acts of literally commandeering the public, ostensibly MTA-controlled space of the New York City subway cars can, at first glance, be read as an effort to "take back" public spaces that overwhelmingly displace and marginalize youth of color. For tourists, these youth affirm images of New York City as gritty and spontaneous, while feeding stereotypes of needy "inner-city" youth. New Yorkers wonder if this is a scam—if someone "puts these kids up to it." The fact that they all seem to speak from the same rehearsed script and that their routines share similar elements raises questions about whether they are coached by adults who might be taking the profits. Some comments on Internet blogs come from riders who regard the youth as nuisances who, in attempting to hawk their goods and talents, "bombard" commuters, while other commentators sympathize with what they assume to be needy kids. Reporters have sought to get to the bottom of these entrepreneurial activities, which, at least in the case of the candy sellers, are indeed usually orchestrated by adults. According to ABC News, about fifty thousand children nationwide are involved in candy-selling rings led by nefarious adult crew leaders with criminal records. Reportedly, the children are often either from housing projects or homeless, picked up in vans and bused to subway stops or suburban neighborhoods, where they ring bells and peddle candy (Leamy 2008: n.p.). The children are exploited, working twelve-hour shifts with no bathroom breaks and receiving pennies on what they earn (Leamy 2008). Yet, as much as the candy-crew leaders exploit these children, efforts to assign blame for their predicament echo entrenched discourses that pathologize urban children and their parents. The ABC News report, for example, states, "Parents go along with it because they don't care or don't know better" (Leamy 2008). This explanation does not allow for parents who are themselves socially and economically isolated, lacking employment, housing, and access to child care. The story seems to be more nuanced for the break-dance crews (also known as b-boy crews), some of which are composed of devoted and remarkably disciplined dancers steeped in the hip-hop dance traditions of the Bronx. Distinct from the group of child dancers described earlier, because there is less evidence of exploitation and because they hail from a Bronx tradition of the public production of hip-hop, b-boy crews regularly perform on subway platforms and in cars "making money foot over hand" according to the *New York Times* (Goodman 2009). Generally older than the youth I witnessed, members of these crews have been arrested for panhandling, but a few nights in jail have not been enough to make them abandon the pleasure and profits they garner from performing on the subways (Goodman 2009).

The complex and contradictory stories of all of these youth remain largely unknown to most casual observers. Their presence in New York's public spaces is regarded alternatively as a nuisance and as an entertaining oddity. They are avoided, pitied, or exoticized. They are either exploited pawns or crafty entrepreneurs. In the sketches of young subway dancers and candy sellers we have seen, these urban minority youth are negotiating the spheres of labor, leisure, and consumption to turn a profit and to demand the attention of a public that rarely engages with them. The examples of the candy crews and break dancers reveal that, even on the surface, minority teens are making creative, nontraditional, and dangerous efforts to earn wages in a labor market that exploits them and leaves them largely disenfranchised.

The historian Robin Kelley's term "play-labor," whereby "the pursuit of leisure, pleasure and creative expression is *labor*," can be applied to the dancers and candy sellers who, like many African American urban youth, "have tried to turn [their] labor into cold hard cash" (Kelley 1997: 45). Kelley theorizes that, for urban minority youth with few resources and unequal access to employment, the lines between play and labor become blurred, and play becomes a means to earn wages. The child performers' version of play-labor clearly fits within Kelley's framework, in the sense that dancing to hip-hop has been interpreted as a central component of urban youth's leisure or play culture, while it has also, from its inception, been a mechanism for earning money. Compared with that of the child performers and candy sellers, China's impromptu singing is a less remarkable but also disruptive form of public play that is not aimed at earning wages but that does the work of annoying, confounding, and distancing the adults around the girls. China's antics do not inspire tourists to dole out cash so much as they provoke them to hold tighter to their purses. Yet, China and the subway performers are linked in the sense that both (re)produce Black youth culture, in the form of singing or dancing and by physically co-opting public space. But the limited descriptions provided here do not give us the whole picture, even when accounting for ABC News's efforts to "dig deeper" into the candy sellers' case. Are the subway performers and peddlers representative of New York City's Black teenagers? Kelley notes that "*some* African American youth" negotiate what he sees as a hazy divide between play and labor and that, for these youth, play is more than "an expression of stylistic innovation, gender identities, and/or racial and class anger-increasingly it is viewed as a way to survive economic crisis or a means of upward mobility" (Kelley 1997: 45, emphasis added). Kelley's notion of play-labor is perfectly in line with the instances we have just considered and his own examples, including break dancing, graffiti art, the creation and commodification of hip-hop, selling drugs, and sex work, all involve youth who, like the youngsters I witnessed on the train, respond to massive unemployment and severe disenfranchisement by turning play into "an alternative to unfulfilling wage labor" (Kelley 1997: 53). And, as Kelley notes, this form of play is neither idle nor easy; it often entails hours of coaching, practice and body conditioning (Kelley 1997: 67). Although the *New York Times* article alludes to "making money foot over hand" and the subway observer surmised that the young dancers I witnessed collected "twenty bucks" (notably a more generous estimation than my count), minority youths' play-labor incomes are vastly overshadowed by the enormous profits of the film and recording companies that capitalize on Black youth culture's creative vitality. Kelley's framework also addresses the gender disparity I observed; minority boys figure more prominently among those who perform on the subway for money—girls are largely invisible in such forms of play-labor. Noting the predominance of Black boys in public examples of play-labor, Kelley asserts "controlling women's access to public space . . . and forms of play [is] central to the construction of masculinity" (Kelley 1997: 55).

Even with Kelley's extremely valuable "suggestive observations," however, questions are left unanswered about subway candy sellers and break dancers: Are these youth African American? Caribbean? African? Latino? How do their forms of play-labor compare with the practices of the majority of New York City's minority youth? And, while Kelley's theorization provides a meaningful explanation of why *some* Black youth engage in largely illegal play-labor, it does not reveal much about Black youth like China and her friends, who are neither selling candy on trains nor break dancing for their supper. Kelley is to be commended for exploring the gendered ways in which public space and play-labor are defined and negotiated, but he does not deal with how teens, Black girls in particular, whose parents, to reverse the problematic phrasing of the ABC News report, *do* care and *do* know better, might also be involved in equally creative forms of play-labor that do not fit neatly into hegemonic society's notions of Black teenagers as "at risk," "needy," and "dangerous."

How do gender, ethnicity, class, and access to education influence how Black teenagers form their subjectivities in relation to consumer culture and the city's public spaces? We can garner insights into what academics, educators, politicians, psychologists, and social workers think about urban minority girls by reading books and newspaper articles and by watching talk shows and popular films, but how can we learn about these girls from their own perspectives?

This ethnography invites its reader to take a downtown train to Brooklyn, staying on long after the candy crews, break dancers, men in suits, hipsters, and fashionistas have dwindled, to explore the lives of Caribbean immigrant and African American teens in the neighborhoods of Flatbush and Crown Heights. It is a journey you will not experience if you visit adolescents in schools, youth detention centers, or homeless shelters; it centers on "normal" teens making remarkable strides in the face of gendered and race-based discrimination not altogether different from the challenges faced by young subway peddlers and performers. This is a transnational journey that takes leisure culture and consumption as its starting point but uses them as a lens through which we can see some of the complexities of African diasporic teenage subjectivities. The soundtrack to this journey is a fusion of West Indian dancehall and hip-hop, and the next stop on the train is Kingston . . . Avenue, in Crown Heights, Brooklyn.

• • •

This book examines how Brooklyn's West Indian teenage girls articulate gender and racial identities through their immersion in consumer culture and public leisure activities. For West Indian young women and for their African American peers, the realm of leisure and consumption is a contested terrain, filled with opportunities for self-actualization but fraught with difficult choices and the pressures of racial discrimination as they confront a hegemonic culture composed of retailers, shopkeepers, fellow consumers, teachers, and policy makers. Relying on ethnographic fieldwork with first- and second-generation West Indian girls who frequented the Brooklyn Children's Museum in Crown Heights and the Flatbush YMCA in Flatbush, Brooklyn, I situate girls' uses of consumer goods and mass-mediated images within their extracurricular and leisure activities.

This volume reveals how West Indian adolescent girls' identities are mediated through a tenuous relationship between host and home countries, between adulthood and childhood, and between being Black and West Indian—all within the larger urban context of life in New York City. It expands the current transnationalism literature that centers chiefly on adults and intervenes in an academic and popular race discourse that tends to focus not on college-bound teenagers like the ones to whom we will soon be introduced but, rather, on "problem youth of color," seen, at best, as victims of "inner-city" poverty and a violent mass media. I advocate in this book for a youth culture–centered approach to West Indian transnationalism, demonstrating that teenagers are most animated when talking about consumer culture and arguing that, in fact, youthful racial, gender, and nation-based identities are predominantly constituted in popular representations.

West Indian Youth in Context

Before turning to the youth whose experiences will dominate this text, I would like to situate readers by providing an overview of West Indians within America's foreign-born Black population and by offering a brief summary of scholarly analyses relevant to this study. About three million people within the United States' Black population are foreign-born. These are primarily immigrants from the Caribbean and from Africa. Afro-Caribbeans, most commonly known as West Indians (descendants of African slaves settled in the Anglophone countries of the Caribbean), now make up 70 percent of the foreign-born Black population, about 2.1 million people (Massey et al. 2007: 245). One-third of New York City's Black population is foreign-born. In Miami, West Indians make up more than 48 percent of the Black community, and they are expected to soon outnumber the native-born Black population (Fears 2002). According to data from the 2000 U.S. Population Census and the 2008 American Community Survey (also conducted by the Bureau of the Census), a significant proportion of New York's City's rapidly growing foreign-born Black population hails from the Caribbean (33%), in particular Jamaica (8%), Haiti (7%), and the Dominican Republic (6%).[5] The rapid increase in the number of Black immigrants from the Caribbean and Africa has sparked debate and competition, with journalists theorizing that America's Black population is just as diverse as its Asian and Latino communities and with sociologists and anthropologists noting that negative stereotyping on both sides divides the foreign- and the native-born Black communities. The ongoing controversy surrounding whether President Barack Obama is legitimately African American provides a glimpse into the questions, complexities, and misunderstandings surrounding foreign-born Black immigrants and their American-born children.

This book builds on a body of scholarship focused on exploring how first- and second-generation immigrants from nations such as Jamaica, Trinidad, Barbados, Guyana, Grenada, and St. Vincent reconcile their identities with American social constructions of race. These immigrants come from ethnically diverse countries populated primarily by descendants of African slaves and East Indian indentured servants. Still, with the exception of Guyana (where East Indians constitute the majority), West Indian immigrants come primarily from nations where people of African descent are the majority. After migrating to the United States, West Indian youth, in particular, carefully negotiate their subjectivities within cultural contexts where long-held discriminatory racializations accompany black or brown skin. Drawing on research with first- and second-generation West Indian girls in Brooklyn, New York, this ethnography argues that leisure and consumer culture provides a complex and fruitful site for delineating West Indian transnationalism. Many scholars of West Indian migration who situate identity formation within the rubric of transnationalism neglect popular culture, focusing instead on the contexts of work, political activities, and the creation of social networks. Although extremely valuable, these studies have concentrated on adults and on labor, rather than on youth and leisure. This work places West Indian adolescent girls' leisure culture at the analytical center and investigates their strategic subjectivities amid contemporary discourses of Black youth culture in general, and hip-hop in particular, as a corruptive element. Hip-hop's transnational appeal, fraught with gender inequality and racialized notions of authenticity, demands serious critical analysis. Because youth are on the front lines of global processes (Maira and Soep 2005), studying popular Black youth culture presents a crucial opportunity for anthropology to address critical debates surrounding diasporic belonging.

This ethnography charts the course for a youth culture–oriented approach to Caribbean Diaspora Studies that speaks to the particularities of working with this stage in the life cycle. Even works that strive to complicate theoretical frameworks like "transnationalism" and "diasporic homelands" by emphasizing Caribbean family networks have privileged adult migrants' experiences (Olwig 2007), marginalizing the significance of youth consumer culture.[6] When immigrant youth have been studied, West Indian migration scholars have made only passing references to consumer culture, focusing instead on schools (López 2003; Ogbu 1990; Waters 1999, 2001). Recently, growing attention has been paid to second-generation immigrants and to youth culture in the broader migration literature, and in the works of scholars interested in globalized culture and African diasporic subjectivities. But this book's critical imperative is to recognize that an explicit engagement with how West Indian transnationalism is contextualized within youthful subjectivities would enhance our understandings of how transnational processes are socially constructed.

She's Mad Real unpacks the unique dynamics of conducting ethnographic fieldwork with adolescents in public leisure settings. This approach fills a void in that there is little ethnographic work on West Indian migration and consumer/leisure culture from an adolescent perspective. We can attribute this void to three factors. First, researchers often privilege adults as more legitimate informants; second, scholars favor schools and labor, rather than leisure and consumption, as more acceptable sites of inquiry; and third, ethnographic approaches have relied on traditional methodological strategies better suited to working with adults than with adolescents.

West Indian Migration Studies

Brief attention to the literature on West Indian migration allows us to address the first two factors simultaneously. Questions of ethnic identification contextualized within gender, labor, residence, and political activities have preoccupied West Indian migration scholars. Roy Bryce-Laporte described West Indians as "invisible immigrants" in a 1972 essay, framing the question that consumes the body of West Indian migration literature: What comparisons and contrasts exist between the experiences of Black West Indians and African Americans? In a thoughtful historiography of West Indian migration studies, sociologist Philip Kasinitz dates social science research on West Indian immigrants to Ira De A. Reid's 1939 study *The Negro Immigrant,* which began the trend of comparing West Indians with African Americans (Kasinitz 2001:259). Kasinitz traces the West Indian "model minority" myth to Reid and, later, Nathan Glazer and Daniel Patrick Moynihan, two social scientists and extremely influential policymakers who positioned West Indians against the "underclass" thesis that described African Americans as developing "pathological" cultural traits (Glazer and Moynihan 1970; Kasinitz 2001:259). In the deeply problematic "underclass" rhetoric, which has since been revealed as unduly influenced by negative stereotypes of African Americans, West Indians purportedly enjoyed greater employment and demonstrated a stronger work ethic, a penchant for entrepreneurialism, and a higher value for education. The "model minority" myth was taken up by Thomas Sowell in the 1980s and inspired a strident debate in West Indian migration studies (Kasinitz 2001: 260; Sowell 1981). Important corrections were offered by scholars including Constance Sutton and Elsa Chaney (1987) and Kasinitz (1992), who complicated the assimilation framework by analyzing how New York City neighborhoods were increasingly becoming Caribbeanized.

A number of other related themes have animated the work of West Indian migration scholars. Gender divisions in the labor market and women's work as domestics, as nannies, and in network-building social institutions such as rotating credit unions took center stage in studies by Nancy Foner (Foner 1978, 2001, 2005). Suzanne Model and Milton Vickerman pondered the socioeconomic accomplishments of the first generation (Model 1991, 1995; Vickerman 1999). Reuel Rogers has considered how Afro-Caribbean immigrants reconcile their political identities with those of African Americans, while Irma Watkins-Owens has studied the social networks created by West Indian immigrant women in turn-of-the-century Harlem (Rogers 2001, 2006; Watkins-Owens 1996, 2001). The vast majority of these studies were focused on adults.

Transnational and global perspectives have also received significant attention from researchers such as Linda Basch and Karen Fog Olwig, exploring the politics of national identity and global family networks respectively (Basch 2001; Olwig 2007). It is particularly useful for the purposes of this book to consider scholars who frame West Indian migration within the rubric of transnationalism but who focus on adults as the primary practitioners of transnational processes. There is a fine body of literature that fits into this category, and this study seeks to build on the valuable research done in this school. Linda Basch, who pioneered this school of thought, defines transnational social practices as "the processes by which migrants forge and sustain simultaneous multi-stranded social relations that link together their societies of origin and settlement" (Basch 2001: 118). "These relations," she asserts, "occur along the lines of family, economic and political relations" (Basch 2001: 118). Basch's research on Eastern Caribbean immigrants in Brooklyn, New York, reveals the complex ways in which adult immigrants remain politically active in their home and host countries, giving examples of New York residents who campaign for political candidates in the United States and then return to Grenada to run for political office (Basch 2001). Basch also cites immigrants who own property in Grenada and invest in businesses "back home" as examples of transnational actions. Significantly, all of these practices—owning property, maintaining dual residences, and running for political office—are activities from which youth are generally blocked due to age and financial dependency on adults. Therefore, transnationalism in Basch's framework is articulated through activities that are typically open only to adults.

Most of the research on West Indians in the United States has focused on the eastern seaboard and on New York in particular; Percy Hintzen's *West Indian in the West: Self-Representation in an Immigrant Community* is a noted exception (Hintzen 2001). Hintzen's analysis, which compares the ways in which San Francisco Bay–area and New York City–based West Indians "publicize their collective presence in different geosocial locations," shares components with *She's Mad Real* (Hintzen 2001: 5). Focusing on "carnivals, sports events, clubs, restaurants, associations and other arenas of publicizing identity" Hintzen argues that "the social geography of New York produces a social identity of West Indianness that is different from that of California and shows how location shapes the ways in which identities are organized and understood" (Hintzen 2001: 5). While Hintzen similarly emphasizes the centrality of place in producing social and individual identities, all of his respondents were over the age of eighteen (Hintzen 2001: 6), in contrast to the youth in this book, most of whom were between the ages of twelve and seventeen when initially interviewed. Moreover, the present study emphasizes subjectivity formation within leisure and public consumption, rather than within "publicizing identity."

Considering Immigrant Youth

Of course, not all West Indian migration scholars have neglected youth. Sociologist Mary Waters spearheaded a move to center attention on the children of immigrants with an impressive body of work. Waters has theorized that first- and second-generation West Indian youths' practices of identity formation can be placed in three categories: those who are "ethnic identified" and see a strong difference between themselves and Black Americans; those who are "American identified" and embrace many aspects of African American culture while downplaying their immigrant or ethnic identities; and those who are "immigrant identified," youngsters who have migrated more recently and who stress their national place of birth in defining their identities (Waters 1999: 290–302). While she allows that these three paths are fluid identities and that individuals might assert more than one at the same time, because Waters's research is centered around school and work, she is not privy to the dynamic ways in which first- and second-generation youth utilize consumer culture and leisure activities in creating more malleable transnational identities.

In describing her research and methodological approach Waters writes, "Because of the strong patterns of residential segregation in U.S. society, I believed that the workplace was the best site to capture the most diverse interactions the immigrants would have" (Waters 1999: 9). Waters interviewed fifty-nine adults and eighty-three adolescent and young-adult children of immigrants for her study (Waters 1999: 9). Including youth and adults from a range of class backgrounds, Waters also conducted participant observation in two public high schools. Using this carefully conceptualized methodological approach, Waters acquired a wealth of data on West Indian youth and avers, "Part of becoming American for these teens is to expect expensive consumer goods, such as fashionable clothes and jewelry, from parents (Waters 1999: 217). Additionally, she goes on to state, "So both the immigrant parental generation and the adolescents associate 'becoming American' with access to consumer goods and full participation in a materialist culture" (Waters 1999: 219). Waters acknowledges that West Indians negotiate becoming American within the consumer realm and that leisure culture plays a significant role in how they define themselves. Still, her references to consumer culture and to the specific ways in which youth utilize popular goods in "becoming American" are few and far between.

Waters has collaborated with Philip Kasinitz, and with John H. Mollenkopf and Jennifer Holdaway on two edited volumes devoted entirely to second-generation immigrant youth from a number of national backgrounds: *Becoming New Yorkers: Ethnographies of the New Second Generation* (2004) and *Inheriting the City: The Children of Immigrants Come of Age* (2008). The former volume returns to the old mainstays of labor and school, while the later examines immigrant youth's levels of success relative to those of native-born groups and compares achievement within and between these groups, measuring achievement in terms of education and participation in the labor force. In *Becoming New Yorkers*, Sherri-Ann Butterfield complicates Waters' three-path framework for second-generation West Indian migration in ways that support the analysis in this book. She stresses the role of New York City as a landscape, asserts the importance of context for identity development, and argues that, within New York City, identity formation among West Indian and African Americans is bidirectional, with both groups influencing each other (Butterfield 2004: 290–291). Tellingly, Butterfield suggests that the fact that reggae music and Latin music can be heard alongside rap and pop in New York's West Indian neighborhoods indicates that there is no one "black culture" (Butterfield 2004: 290). Still, while Butterfield recognizes New York City as a critical site for analysis, she neglects to theorize consumer space and youth culture as principal elements of West Indian New York. Even when respondents' accounts are grounded in consumer spheres such as markets and hair salons, Butterfield's attention is focused on schools and on categories such as gender, ethnicity, and race, and she shows little regard for how those categories come to be defined within leisure and consumption (Butterfield 2004).

The persistent trend even when youth are given specific attention has been to concentrate on labor and schools as the ideals sites of analysis, as in Nancy López's excellent study of girls' and boys' varying levels of achievement in American schools (2003). All of this research reveals that more attention has been given to adults than to youth and that when youth are considered, as in the work of Waters, Kasinitz, Mollenkopf, Holdaway, and López, schools and labor have been the "go to" sites, rather than consumer culture and leisure activities. Without a doubt, these studies reveal invaluable insights, and, certainly, the realms of work and school are critical loci of social and economic equality. However, the spheres of consumption and leisure are equally meaningful avenues for exposing social inequalities and parsing transnational youthful subjectivities, and it is regrettable that prevailing studies erect an artificial but absolute divide between the realms of work and leisure. Moreover, this seems to be an odd methodological and theoretical trend when we consider that consumer culture and leisure activities are paramount to how young people themselves conceptualize their identities.

Other Ways to Understand Youth Culture:
Globalization and African Diasporic Belonging

Why were youth largely ignored until recently, and why is consumer culture not a focal point? We can find clues toward answering this query even in studies not explicitly centered on youth. The following passage from Jacqueline Nassy Brown's pivotal work, *Dropping Anchor, Setting Sail: Geographies of Race in Black Liverpool*, underscores youth experience as a potentially rich subject for analysis and demonstrates that a call for a youth culture–centered approach to West Indian transnationalism is applicable not only to the United States but also to the Caribbean diaspora in England and elsewhere. Brown's insightful ethnography examines the complexities and contradictions of Black identity, drawing together many historical periods and bodies of literature. In the preface, Brown recounts her reasons for choosing Liverpool as a field site, relating that, when she arrived in Liverpool, one of her primary contacts took her to a Caribbean community center where she encountered a group of "kids," averaging about thirteen years old. Brown writes:

> I asked them a set of basic questions like, "Black people have been in this city for hundreds of years, so do you see yourselves as English?" The gist of the answer was "no." That term refers to White people, they said, with far more flair than I can re-create here. I asked another question having something to do with Black identity. Waxing historical, one young girl quoted Malcolm X in her response. They answered my questions with ease and great interest—except for one. Everyone—adults and children—froze when I asked these kids whether they were of Caribbean background, and whether they consider themselves Afro-Caribbean. We were in a place called the Caribbean Centre, so I thought that an ethnicity question was called for. . . . I penetrated an open wound, as I learned later. After the interview, a couple of the kids approached me with a question of their own. Could I teach them some new dance steps from America? For all of the scientific reasons there were for choosing this city as a field site, it was these kids who made Liverpool irresistible. In view of the heavy political content of their answers, I surmised that their parents must be *really* interesting (Brown 2005: xi, emphasis in original).

Brown encountered a group of adolescents who quickly proved to be wonderful "informants"—wrestling with the very issues of Blackness and English identity that she wished to interrogate. Still, while finding the adolescents to be "irresistible," she opted to interview their parents. I gather that these youngsters shared Brooklyn teens' reliance on youth culture as the language through which they articulated Caribbean diasporic identity. And their query about learning American dance moves speaks to an important point Brown herself goes on to analyze: the ways in which Caribbean peoples in both the United States and Great Britain formulate their identities in relation to American popular youth culture. Brown subsequently asks the question "Why Liverpool?" Why had she chosen Liverpool as a legitimate place to study Englishness? However, Brown's preliminary findings also prompt us to ask, "Why adults? Why not youth and youth culture?" The youth Brown encountered quickly illustrated that they were grappling with how to reconcile Black, Afro-Caribbean, and British identities and that they had much to teach an anthropologist hoping to understand how racial and ethnic identity is socially constructed.

Analyses centered on youthful global and national identity formation have come not from scholars of West Indian migration but from researchers concerned with leisure and global youth cultures more generally. Dick Hebdige offered early contributions in this vein by analyzing the significance of reggae music and of the Rasta and Rude Boy cultures in both Jamaica and England in the mid- to late 1960s and early 1970s (Hebdige 1976). Hebdige illustrates how young members of the African diaspora in England, the United States, and the Caribbean created what are now referred to as transnational identities as they channeled Black popular music, Rastafarianism, and a Black consciousness constructed in opposition to White hegemony. These identity processes were defined largely within the realms of music and popular culture, but they had implications for education, employment, and intergenerational differences. Hebdige notes that the British West Indian youth "review[ed] his [sic] position with a more critical eye than his [sic] parents" and that the older generation was less willing to relinquish the idea that England "promised a golden future" even when their lived circumstances told them the contrary (Hebdige 1976: 151). Identity formation for British West Indian youth in the 1960s and 1970s, then, was embedded in notions of Black consciousness routed through Africa, the United States, the Caribbean, and England, and expressed through music and popular culture. For Hebdige, music and leisure culture were the primary sites in which British West Indian youth formed their identities. Referring to the emergent black consciousness, he writes:

These developments were translated into specifically Jamaican terms and the men of the dreadlocks began to make an incongruous and sinister appearance once more on the grey streets of the metropolis. By 1973, McGlashan could report the bizarre conjunction of Africa and Ealing at the West London Grand Rastafarian ball, where Rastas, twice removed from the mythical homeland yearned in unison for an end to "sufferation" as giggling white girls danced to the reggae. The cult of Ras Tafari appealed at least as strongly to the black youth of Great Britain as it did to their cousins in Jamaica. If anything it proved even more irresistible, giving the stranded Community at once a name and a future. . . . *All this was reflected in and communicated through the music* which had found in Britain an even larger and more avid audience than in its country of origin (Hebdige 1976: 151–152, emphasis added).

While scholars such as Hebdige and Stuart Hall relied on British and West Indian expressive youth cultures as legitimate sites of analysis, researchers focused on West Indian migration in the United States, as we have seen, have not followed in this tradition. Hebdige emerged from the Birmingham School, an approach that prioritized youth subcultures and leisure activities while being criticized for overstating resistance and for relying too heavily on class-based analyses. These legitimate criticisms aside, the youth-centered approach of the Center for Contemporary Cultural Studies (CCCS) laid the foundation for more contemporary studies focused on transnationalism and youth culture such as anthropologist Sunaina Maira's *Desis in the House: Indian American Youth Culture in New York City*, which engages many of the theoretical and methodological points raised here (Maira 2002).[7] Maira's study of second-generation Indian American adolescents in New York City reveals the "constructedness and dynamism of ethnic identity but also suggests that Indian American youth use certain markers of what it means to be Indian in order to contest one another's performances and narrations of ethnicity and to assert their own" (Maira 2002: 14). Rooted in the Desi party scene, a dance club subculture centered around bhangra remix music (Indian folk music mixed with American dance and hip-hop genres), Maira's book explores youthful immigrant identities in New York City from her *subjects'* perspectives and within a locus that holds meaning for the youth themselves. From this *emic* approach,[8] Maira analyzes how "rhetorical gestures—of ethnic authenticity, of gendered innocence or sexual waywardness, of ritualized coolness—are linked to the particular insertion of Indian Americans into the racial and class structures of the nation-state and into the transnational flows of labor, capital, and media images in the late twentieth century" (Maira 2002: 15). Maira argues that traditionally critical arenas such as race and class structures, labor, capital, and transnational identity negotiations can and should be studied within the realms of leisure and consumption. She suggests that second-generation youth culture raises important questions about the relationships between immigrant communities and "the nation-state in which they live and the one ostensibly left behind" (Maira 2002: 21).

Maira lays the groundwork for the notion of "youthscapes" in this ethnography, a concept she and Elizabeth Soep develop further in the edited volume of the same name (Maira and Soep 2005). Borrowing from Arjun Appadurai's notions of ethnoscapes, mediascapes, and ideoscapes, Maira and Soep argue that youthful social and material relationships are created within the global channeling of labor, capital, media images, and ideologies (Maira 2002: 21; Maira and Soep 2005). Maira and Soep conceptualize "local youth practices as embedded, both in obvious and unexpected ways, within the shifts in national and global forces marking the late twentieth and early twenty-first centuries" (Maira and Soep 2005: xv). Youthscapes, then, are spheres that are at once political, geographical, temporal, and social (Maira and Soep 2005). After contending with the frameworks on which scholars have thus far relied to theorize cultural globalization—considering concepts such as "diaspora," "transnationalism," and "cosmopolitanism"—Maira and Soep resolve that the growing literature on globalization "while highly relevant to studies of youth . . . leaves key questions about an entire generation largely unanswered or in some cases, unconnected" (Maira and Soep 2005: xvii). I follow Maira and Soep in asking, "How can youth studies offer new models or methods for studying border politics and commodity cultures in an era of global capitalism and changing patterns of coerced and voluntary migration" (Maira and Soep 2005:xvii)? For these authors, studying youth culture unearths how social identities are fashioned and refashioned within transnational popular culture (Maira and Soep 2002: xvii–xviii).

Bridging the Divide: From Childhood to Youth, between Play and Labor

This book bridges the approaches of scholars who focus on contemporary youth culture and researchers who study West Indian transnationalism by recasting the divide between labor and leisure. En route to making these connections, I situate this study within the developing literature on the anthropology of children, childhood, and youth. Although West Indian migration scholarship reflects a general neglect of children in the broader anthropological literature, recently, ethnographers have adjusted their gazes to consider the quotidian experiences of children as they relate to local/global economic systems and to the politics of culture (Cole and Durham 2007; Honwana and de Boeck 2005; James and Prout 1990; Lancy 2008; Montgomery 2009; Scheper-Hughes and Sargent 1998; Schwartzman 2001; Stephens 1995).[9] In fact, a consideration of anthropological research on childhood and globalization offers an effective on-ramp for merging youth culture studies with West Indian transnationalism research. While the increasingly rapid global movement of people, commodities, and ideas has influenced how children around the world imagine and experience growing up, globalization has also "sharpen[ed] the sense of exclusion and marginality among people who cannot acquire those goods" (Cole and Durham 2007: 4). And anthropologists are progressively more in tune with the global disparities in how childhood is socially constructed and with how ever-increasing migration affects children's lived realities (Cole and Durham 2007; Honwana and de Boeck 2005; Katz 2004; LeVine and New 2008). When ethnographers began field explorations of childhood in the 1920s, studies described the differing lives of children where there were no schools (LeVine and New 2008: 1). However, even after the introduction of Western schooling, and continuing today, the majority of the world's children, located in Africa, Latin America, Asia, and the Pacific, begin working at early ages and share in the responsibilities of caring for themselves and siblings and of obtaining food and water (LeVine and New 2008: 1–7). Cross-cultural childhood researchers have noted, for example, that in Malawi and the Niger Delta, it is not uncommon for five-year-olds to sleep in separate dwellings from their mothers, to start skill training, and to learn to bathe themselves (Rogoff et al., in LeVine and New 2008). Children experience similarly early incorporations into the work world in the Caribbean, where (to borrow a section heading from LeVine and New), the lines of "work, play, participation and learning" are blurred from an early age (LeVine and New 2008). Anthropologists drawing on case studies of child-rearing practices in low-income homes in Kingston, Jamaica, describe children whose entry into domestic labor stands in marked contrast to middle-class American norms:

> At the age of four or five, children of both sexes begin doing household chores, such as sweeping, mopping, floor polishing, and caretaking for younger children. Chantelle, age seven, watched her toddler and infant siblings, did light laundry and some cooking, and ran errands (Sargent and Harris 1998: 206).

Similarly, in rural Guyanese villages, it is common for children as young as five to play significant roles in family farming, in the care of younger siblings, and in domestic chores.[10] Although childhood researchers note that early exposure to work is part of "normal" development for most of the world's children, increasingly the changes accompanying global economic restructuring have diminished local resources, transforming family life and further recasting the divide between work and play for children. Within this schema, tourism enables the state "to circumscribe boundaries around the nation while servicing imperialism," and "girls as young as seven work in the [Bahamian] Straw Market, offering songs to tourists in exchange for twenty-five cents" (Alexander 2005: 61). Girls, in particular, bear increasing burdens in countries such as the Sudan, where they must fetch water and wood, shouldering ever-widening responsibilities to help their mothers with household tasks and preventing them from attending school (Katz 2004: 7). Media coverage of the 2010 earthquake in Haiti sparked discussion about the suffering of Haitian children—the majority of whom lived in poverty even before the earthquake—with news reports giving special attention to Restavek children, youngsters sold or given away to a life of indentured labor in Port-au-Prince because their poor, rural parents could not afford to care for them.[11]

Scholars of the anthropology of childhood have problematized child rights issues outside Europe and North America by juxtaposing such examples with troublesome evidence of "hurried child" syndrome in the United States and Japan, where youngsters are "overburdened with demands to assume ever higher levels of competency and more and more skills at an ever earlier age" (Scheper-Hughes and Sargent 1998: 12). Still, "the cherished myth of child-centeredness" flourishes in contemporary Western societies, where children and adolescents are thought of as being free from the pressures of working, paying bills, saving money, and managing finances (Scheper-Hughes and Sargent 1998: 10). Such concerns are thought of as the exclusive domain of adults. Sherri-Ann Butterfield illustrates this point when she explains her methodological choice to limit her study to second-generation West Indians between the ages of twenty-two and thirty-two. Butterfield writes, "The men and women in this age bracket had come into full adulthood and were experiencing socioeconomic advantages and disadvantages, since they were now primarily responsible for their own lives" (Butterfield 2004: 291). Butterfield suggests that persons under the age of twenty-two do not "experience socioeconomic advantages and disadvantages." *She's Mad Real* complicates this approach. Readers will learn not only about how West Indian youth formulate their identities in relation to consumer culture but also about how they and their African American peers earn money. The teenagers with whom I worked held one, two, and sometimes three jobs. As noted earlier, Nadine, for example, had been separated from her mother and had been living with her best friend's family for almost a year, and China was looking for a third job, one that would provide health insurance benefits. These teens purchased almost all of the consumer goods they enjoyed, including cell phones, iPods, and the hallmark of black teenagers' "predatory consumption"—sneakers—with their own hard-earned money (Chin 2001). But they also used that money to save for college and to help buy food.

Play-Labor

Robin Kelley's concept of play-labor, mentioned earlier, which astutely "challenges the way in which work and leisure have been dichotomized in studies of the U.S. working class," provides an apt if incomplete framework for elaborating how the teens in this study approach labor and leisure (Kelley 1997: 45). As much as this book draws on a tradition of youth culture studies emanating from the Birmingham School, these scholars theorized leisure as the opposite of work. Leisure was defined as taking place at night, on the weekends, and after hours, while "work" was done on the clock, in exchange for wages and in separate spaces (Kelley 1997: 45). For the teens in this study, however, an afterschool internship at the Brooklyn Children's Museum, for which they received either minimum wages and/or service learning credits from their high schools, served as a site of play-labor. Yet, we will see that their acts of play-labor are both similar to and distinct from the working-class and underclass underground economies of which Kelley writes. Play-labor for these teens is legal and adult sanctioned, yet often framed in response to institutionalized discrimination and racial spatialization. As Black adolescents who practice play-labor in a museum, an institution commonly perceived as elitist (Hodges 1978), these teens' actions can be seen as transgressive. They claim the Brooklyn Children's Museum as "their museum" in response to global economic restructuring, urban "development," the policing of inner-city streets, and the social barriers that accompany gentrification, which have left them with few safe public spaces in which to engage in play. Especially for teens coming from "respectable" West Indian households, the city streets are viewed as dangerous places where even "good kids" are subject to police harassment and violent crime. This concern, coupled with the ever-rising criteria for college admission and the hyperscheduling of children and adolescents of all ethnicities, has meant that play-labor has become increasingly structured and organized.

Play-labor also served as an avenue to forming West Indian youths' subjectivities. As museum workers, the teens engaged in the labor of imparting knowledge about the natural sciences and about cultural diversity to younger peers. This form of work enabled them to position themselves as experts and owners of the museum space. Formulating their identities within a museum also imbued an acute sense of cultural identity. They were constantly being encouraged by museum educators to "expand their horizons" by learning about other ethnic groups and by visiting other museums. This meant that the teens' engagements with transnational popular culture were set against a backdrop of explicit cultural production.

Music and African Diasporic Youth Culture

Within this context, music constantly reemerged as the primary vehicle by which West Indian teens asserted their West Indianness, while either distancing themselves from or allying themselves with African Americanness. Stuart Hall has theorized that Caribbean identities are always constituted within, not outside, representation (Hall 1990: 222). While, in this instance, Hall was writing about how Caribbean identities are represented in film, his notion of identity as "not as transparent and unproblematic as we think" and as "a production which is never complete" is perhaps best exemplified in the ways in which West Indian youth negotiate transnational racial, gender, and ethnic identities in relation to popular consumer culture (Hall 1990). The hybrid nature of Black diasporic identity as theorized by Stuart Hall has influenced researchers such as Paul Gilroy, who situates his conceptualization of a Black Atlantic culture—shaped more by common routes than by common roots—within the realms of music and popular culture (Gilroy 1993). Gilroy echoes Hall's framework and highlights Black music as rich with questions of racialized belonging, authenticity, and nationalism. And there is perhaps no site within popular youth culture as laden with questions of authenticity, national discourses, and gender inequality as hip-hop.

Youthful subjectivities in and around the production of music have served as a point of departure for a number of critical works analyzing global youth cultures. George Lipsitz has explored identity construction in the production of musical fusions including bhangra, Algerian rai, and Puerto Rican bulgalu (Lipsitz 1994). Other studies that can inform West Indian migration research by taking us beyond the old West Indian/African American comparative framework include Juan Flores's examination of the intricate commonalities and specificities of Puerto Rican and Latino immigrant identity (Flores 2000); Murray Forman and Mark Anthony Neal's attention to African diasporic subjectivities and racial authenticity vis-à-vis hip-hop culture (Forman 2004, 2005; Neal 2004); Raymond Codrington and Rupa Huq's analyses of race, place, and postcolonial identity among Europe's African, Caribbean, and Asian immigrant hip-hop-based youth cultures (Codrington 2006; Huq 2006); Abdoulaye Niang's interrogations of the politics of hip-hop culture in African cities (Niang 2006); and Marc Perry's theorizations of hip-hop as a global Black "space" in which diasporic Blackness is creatively self-fashioned (Perry 2008). Perry's work is particularly relevant, as he argues that hip-hop is the most disseminated global image of Blackness and that Black youth use hip-hop to create notions of self that contest and resist being bound within national subjectivities (Perry 2008).

She's Mad Real draws upon these approaches and those of scholars who explore the intersection of race and gender in African diasporic youth cultures. Work of this ilk, by scholars such as Angela McRobbie, Tracey Skelton, Donna Hope, and Sonjah Stanley-Niaah, has investigated transnational music and leisure cultures as complex and contested sites for the construction of African diasporic femininities (Hope 2006; McRobbie 1999; Skelton 1996; Stanley-Niaah 2009). A common tension throughout all of the studies concerned with diasporic subjectivities emerges from an attempt to gauge how youth around the globe create specific, locally derived identities while simultaneously being influenced by and influencing a "homogenous" global youth culture writ large (Nilan and Feixa 2006). While many fear that a homogenous global youth culture reflective of American (or Western) imperialism is eclipsing local expressive and material cultures, some scholars have posited that African American hip-hop has come to embody *the* hegemonic African diasporic youth culture (Thomas and Campt 2007).

I am suggesting that closer attention to youth culture in general and hip-hop in particular can help anthropology. How can hip-hop help anthropology? Hip-hop provides us with a gateway to previously undertheorized West Indian subjectivities within heretofore neglected contexts. Waters, Kasinitz, Mollenkopf, Holdaway, and López's growing attention to the second generation is a signal that, increasingly, the children of immigrants will take center stage in our investigations of how immigrant groups negotiate national, racial, and ethnic identities. But we have little hope of ethnographically grounding the ways in which youth are key players in defining Blackness and in negotiating racialized and transnationally situated notions of belonging if we continue to ignore what for them is perhaps the most consequential sphere for the social construction of identities.

Urban Youth "At Risk"

Beyond the immigration research, much of the literature on urban youth of color focuses on teens "at risk" for social, psychological, and physical problems such as teen pregnancy, participation in gangs and violent crime, drug use, obesity, acquiring HIV/AIDS, sexual assault, rape, and various forms of domestic violence. These are legitimate problems that face urban teenagers. Jody Miller has written compellingly about the ways in which sexual harassment, sexual assault, and gang rape shape the experiences of African American young women in severely disadvantaged communities (J. Miller 2008). Miller "investigate[s] how the structural inequalities that create extreme—and racialized—urban poverty facilitate both cultural adaptations and social contexts that heighten and shape the tremendous gender-based violence faced by urban African American girls" (J. Miller 2008: 3). She underscores how extreme poverty and race and class inequalities, in conjunction with urban space, have made routine sexual violence a reality for urban Black girls and women. While most of the young women in She's Mad Real come from working-class families and some come from homes where incomes dipped below the poverty level, for the most part the core group of teens with whom I worked did not hail from extremely impoverished households. Participation in afterschool programs such as BCM and the Flatbush YMCA, the limited availability of community resources, and the watchful eyes of concerned mothers shielded the girls in this study from experiencing the systemic gender-based violence detailed by Miller. Still, as evidenced in the one case of sexual harassment I did encounter, and given that victims of such crimes are often reluctant to discuss their experiences, the girls in this study were certainly not immune to these problems.

The harsh realities of problems faced by urban minority youth notwithstanding, a growing number of scholars have began to expose the ways in which being labeled as "at risk" pathologizes these youth. This book illustrates how such essentializing public policy and social science discourse limits our understandings of the diverse, real-life experiences of urban adolescents. The West Indian and African American youth in this study were "good kids," a label their parents and educators adamantly repeated time and again, signaling a desire to distance their young charges from the "at-risk" categorization that has pathologized teens like them in educational and public policy discourses. While these predominantly working-class teens experienced the disenfranchisement and isolation that went along with living in minority neighborhoods and felt the effects of high youth unemployment, most of them graduated from high school and went on to four-year colleges. Although I learned about a few girls who got pregnant, none of my primary contacts in this study became teenage mothers. These teens did, however, have an acute awareness of the ways in which "at-risk" discourses stereotype their identities and explicitly urged me to write a book that presents their true experiences.

As I conducted my research and shared my findings at conferences and other public lectures, I began to realize that audiences, whether they were scholarly or otherwise, expected me to recount horror stories of the sort popularized on talk shows. I was expected to share explicit details of victimized youth who sold drugs, got pregnant, were arrested, dropped out of school, were physically abused by parents, and lived in squalor conditions. On one occasion, when I interviewed for a position at a college in the New York tri-state area, after giving my job-talk (a formal lecture that accompanies an academic job interview), I was pulled aside by a tenured faculty member who suggested that my work was "not political." When I asked him what he meant, he recounted an experience he had while visiting a family's home in the field: "These two children sat at their kitchen table and squashed roaches with the palms of their hands, for fun. It was a game for them." He waited expectantly, his eyes wide and beseeching, for me to offer an equally dramatic anecdote. I had none. I gathered that, in his mind, research on the hardships of poverty was more "political" than studies focused on working-class youths' consumer and leisure culture. I realized then that either my sources were exceptions or scholarly discourses had been overwhelmingly influenced by representations of urban minority youth as pathological, socially abnormal, or completely victimized by abject poverty and catastrophic social inequality. Make no mistake, the teens I studied experienced social inequalities. The fact that they also voluntarily hung out at a museum after school should not preclude us from hearing their stories. Listening to hip-hop and frequenting museums do not fit neatly together in our popular understandings of urban youth. However, the teens in this book did both.

Dispelling the Model Minority Myth

In writing a book about West Indian and African American girls who frequent a museum, who do well at school, and who "stay off the streets," I run the risk of having readers conclude that the teens in this study are "model minorities." I would like to end such considerations here. This book speaks to the diversity of urban Black girls' experiences. It does not suggest that West Indians are inherently better workers or students than their African American peers, nor does it suggest that they negotiate consumer culture in a less threatening way. The greater educational success of foreign-born Blacks has sparked debates about whether they deserve to take advantage of affirmative action programs designed to even the playing fields for descendants of slaves. However, studies focused on *how* West Indian households earn higher incomes and on *how* these immigrants measure their economic success relative to African Americans have found that the "West Indian success story" is complicated and contradictory (Model 1995; Waters 1999).

The idea that West Indians and other "voluntary minorities" have a different approach or "cultural orientation" to life in America because they entered this country voluntarily, differentiating them from "involuntary minorities" such as African Americans, and that this distinct "culture" enables them to achieve greater educational and financial success, has been interrogated in West Indian migration studies (Ogbu 1990; Waters 1999). Waters has argued that, in fact, structural differences such as the availability of social networks, immigrant status, and "a different metric for judging a job" all facilitate hiring of West Indian immigrants (Waters 1999: 140). In other words, these differences are race-neutral and do not imply cultural values distinct from those of other groups, including African Americans (Waters 1999: 140). These differences are, however, often stereotyped with cultural explanations (Hintzen 2001: 94–95; Waters 1999: 140).

A recent, important study conducted by sociologist Douglass Massey and his colleagues at Princeton and the University of Pennsylvania has sought to frame these structural explanations alongside extensive data on foreign-born Black "success" in terms of college admissions (Massey et al. 2007). Brief attention to this study here will allow us to situate the teens' negotiations of African American and West Indian stereotypes presented in this book against structural explanations. Qualitative research has revealed that Black immigrants do better than African Americans in terms of education, income, and residential segregation (Massey et al. 2007: 247). With regard to education, noted migration scholars Alejandro Portes and Rubén Rumbaut found that foreign-born Blacks have greater success than native blacks (Portes and Rumbaut 1990, 2001, in Massey et al. 2007: 245). In addition to the structural explanations offered by Waters, if we look at the massive immigration of Afro-Caribbeans to the United States after 1965, when immigration restrictions were loosened, we see that the majority of those who came were from the skilled middle class, rather than from a cross-section of West Indian populations (Massey et al. 2007: 246). Jamaicans, for example, who represent the largest Afro-Caribbean group in the country and who also constituted the largest group among the teens at the Brooklyn Children's Museum, are "the most class selective of all immigrant streams, and second-generation Jamaican immigrants perform very favorably compared with Black natives across a range of social and economic outcomes in the United States" (Massey et al. 2007: 246; Butcher 1994). Thus, many of those Jamaicans who emigrate arrive with greater occupational and educational capital but are subsequently compared to the general African American population.

According to the Princeton/University of Pennsylvania study, 40 percent of Black students at Ivy League colleges are either first- or second-generation immigrants (Massey et al. 2007). This issue surfaced during Barack Obama's presidential campaign, sparking debates about whether we could speak about a "singular Black experience" when it appeared that African and Caribbean immigrant Blacks were outperforming African Americans. Citing Massey et al., *The Wall Street Journal* reported:

> Black immigrants, on the whole, fare far better economically than native-born blacks. A quarter of foreign-born blacks have bachelor's degrees, vs. 16% of those born in America . . . The median income for African-immigrant households is over $45,000, vs. $41,000 for black Caribbean-immigrant households and just under $36,000 for U.S.-born black households. Black immigrant children are more likely than native-born black children to be raised in two-parent homes (Kaufman and Fields 2008: A1).

Massey et al. presented their study's thrust in an article titled "Black Immigrants and Natives Attending Selective Colleges and Universities in the United States." Using data from the National Longitudinal Survey of Freshman (NLSF), the article offers numerous insights into the overrepresentation of Black immigrant children, especially in highly selective colleges and universities. The researchers concluded that Black immigrant children are overrepresented because they are more desirable candidates to college admissions officers (because of factors such as having higher SAT scores, having attended private schools in greater numbers or having higher high school GPAs or because they have better "soft skills," such as feeling more comfortable with Whites) and thus are admitted to highly selective colleges at a significantly higher rate than native-born African Americans. Tellingly, the study found no significant differences in socioeconomic factors such as family income. There were minor differences in the percentage that came from two-parent households, with immigrants being slightly more likely to come from such households. Still, perhaps not surprisingly, statistics on the comparative economic and social successes of Black immigrants and African Americans do not paint the complete picture. The phrasing of *The Wall Street Journal* article quoted, for example, seems to overemphasize these small differences. There were also some experiential differences; the researchers found that native Black students experienced greater levels of violence and tended to live in segregated neighborhoods more than their immigrant peers. Also, immigrant fathers tended to have higher educational degrees than native-born fathers. But, significantly, once they entered college, there was no real difference in performance between native-born and foreign-born Blacks, while White students tended to achieve higher grades than both immigrant and native-born Blacks.

Massey et al. position their findings against a controversial moment in 2004 involving prominent African American scholars Henry Louis Gates Jr. and Lani Guinier:

[They] pointed out at a reunion of black Harvard alumni that a majority of those present were of West Indian or African origin, not the descendants of African American slaves. They argued that children from black families in the country for generations were being left behind in the competition for elite education. According to Gates, "I just want people to be honest enough to talk about it" (Massey et al. 2007: 246; Rimer and Arenson 2004).

The authors cite this moment as the catalyst for controversies surrounding the overrepresentation of foreign-born Blacks in elite higher education. If the way it was summarized in *The Wall Street Journal* article is any indication, however, Massey et al.'s incisive findings, which are meant to inform this debate, have not translated into popular understandings. Popular views continue to overemphasize foreign-born Blacks' success, as evidenced in the discourses during Barack Obama's presidential campaign in which commentators debated whether or not Obama's African father and educational achievements differentiated the candidate from African Americans. These controversies run the risk of misconstruing the success of foreign-born Blacks. It should be noted that the youth with whom I conducted research experienced high levels of college admission. In focusing on West Indian and African American youth mixing in a play-labor/educational setting, this book seeks to shed light on subtle but crucial cultural practices ignored in the popular debates. Massey et al. concede that one limitation of their research is that it studies the college selection process *after the fact* and thus it cannot speak to, among other things, how unconscious stereotyping might influence college admissions officers (Massey et al. 2007: 252). This book explores cultural and racial stereotypes and directly addresses how Black teens comprehend and position their identities in relation to such stereotypes. It also complicates hard divides between "immigrant" and "native" Blacks because a number of the youth described here have both African American and West Indian parentage and because West Indian and African American identity formation is a bidirectional process that draws on both ethnic traditions, as evidenced in the increasingly blurred lines between hip-hop and West Indian dancehall music.

The Study

She's Mad Real delves into how first- and second-generation West Indian girls make sense of themselves within the contexts of leisure activities and consumer culture. Spanning over a decade, it draws on a number of methodologies and materials including in-depth interviews, participant observation, focus groups, and analyses of youth representations in educational policies, local and national newspapers and Internet blogs. My fieldwork began in 1997 with a participant observation study of a group of cheerleaders at the Flatbush YMCA in Brooklyn, New York, and continued with a group of teens enrolled in an afterschool program at the Brooklyn Children's Museum (BCM) in Crown Heights. From 1997 to 1999, I lived one block away from the YMCA in an apartment building where two of the girls in this study also resided. At the YMCA, I interviewed thirty cheerleaders who cheered for the Y's basketball team. Of these girls, twenty-five were of West Indian descent, with at least one parent coming from the Anglophone Caribbean; three were African Americans, and two were Latinas. At BCM, I initially interviewed eighteen girls, all of whom were West Indian. During the early period of my reserach, all of the girls were between the ages of twelve and seventeen. I returned to both fieldsites in 2000 and 2002 for several months of fieldwork. Between

2005 and 2006, I returned to the field again, this time focusing my research at the Brooklyn Children's Museum. I conducted one-on-one interviews with at least fifteen more girls and engaged in participant observation with the Museum Team afterschool program, in which between thirty and thirty-five teens participated. And, in 2007 and 2008, I reconnected with a number of young women who are now college students and whom I first met in 2005, when they were teenagers participating in BCM's Museum Team program.

The ethnographic material presented here draws primarily from work with BCM youth and relies most heavily on fieldwork conducted after 2005. While my study ostensibly focused on girls from the English-speaking Caribbean, the fieldwork offers insight into the ways in which African American girls and boys influence and are influenced by their West Indian peers of both genders. I spent countless hours with these teens, participating in their activities at the museum (which included leading tours, feeding animals, tutoring younger children, studying for the SATs, designing costumes, and making a book about what it means to be West Indian and Black), accompanying them on trips around New York City, attending spoken word poetry and hip-hop concerts with them, going to the movies, shopping, and frequenting local eateries. During periods when my work as a professor kept me from the field, I corresponded with a core group of girls and BCM educators via e-mail and phone conversations. While I conducted recorded interviews with more than sixty girls, this study focuses on a smaller core group of teens. I became deeply invested in the lives of the girls you will meet here; I lost sleep the night before their prom and again when China and Nadine planned to forgo college and instead move into a housing project after graduating from high school. Some of them confided fears about going to college, worries about strained relationships with their mothers, and deep concerns about body image only after they had graduated from high school and left the BCM program.

Throughout all of this fieldwork, I found that while of course the realms of school and labor were critical to how the teens formulated their gender and ethnic identities, the lines between play and work were in fact amorphous, and it was within the sphere of popular and consumer culture that the fiercest battles were fought over staking simultaneous claims to West Indianness and African Americanness. Their ideas about African American culture, about when and if they should ally themselves with African Americans and about what represented respectable femininity, were more often than not communicated within the parlance of popular youth culture.

West Indian youth used hip-hop music and culture in particular as an arena within which they developed racialized, gendered, and ethnic identities in relation to their African American peers. As Butterfield has argued, this was not always an either/or choice between identifying as West Indian or as African American but was rather a complex bidirectional process whereby African American and West Indian youth constructed racial and ethnic subjectivities conjointly and based on social settings (Butterfield 2004:291). When they wished to assert a separate West Indian ethnic identity, West Indian girls voiced their preferences for Caribbean musical artists such as Spragga Benz and Lady Saw. However, when they wanted to demonstrate their fluency in the latest American popular culture, they sang along with and knew all of the words to the latest chart-topping American hip-hop song. And, as their interactions at BCM illustrate, everyday activities involved complex cultural negotiations in which, sometimes, an either/or choice seemed necessary.

A Methodology for Studying Urban Youth

What are the particular methodological problems involved with conducting urban ethnographic fieldwork with adolescents? While most of her subjects were college-age and most of mine were still in high school, Sunaina Maira's work is useful here (Maira 2002; Maira and Soep 2005). In her volume coedited with Elizabeth Soep, Maira positions "youthscapes" as both a conceptual and a methodological tool. This term highlights the degree to which research with children and youth is different from research focused on adults. Adolescents are, in some respects, much less willing to speak freely and at length than adults, and issues of power and authority color the dynamics between anthropologist and interviewee in particular ways when the researcher is an adult and the subject is an adolescent. A host of researchers have delved into the particular methodological concerns attached to studying children and youth (Bennett, Cieslik, and Miles 2003; Best 2007; Christensen and James 2000; Fine and Sandstrom 1998; Fraser et al. 2004; Graue and Walsh 1998; Holmes 1998; Waksler 1991). Following these scholars, I was acutely aware of my positionality and of the need to respectfully employ the authority that went along with my status as an adult. As Maira and Soep and Best have noted, however, it is only recently that researchers have began to fully engage with the growing population of immigrant youth in America. Studying urban immigrant youth presents unique methodological challenges. Well aware of discourses that frame them as "at risk," such youth are at times reluctant to trust outsiders seeking to write about them. Urban dwellers in general can be less willing to invite strangers into their homes, and immigrants in particular are protective of their domestic environments. Teenagers, for whom the pursuit of "cool" is an all-consuming goal, are generally not inclined to share details about family economic hardships. For all of these reasons, the material presented here was gathered over the course of a decade during which I was able to gain the trust of a core group of girls. I situated my fieldwork within public settings, first a YMCA and later a museum, because I initially felt I could more readily gain access to these settings than to youths' homes. However, after spending years and countless hours at the Brooklyn Children's Museum, I found that for many teens the museum *was* home. And consumer culture emerged as the one realm about which teens were always eager to speak. In a number of ways, this book's methodological approach follows the tenets of New Childhood Studies, which aims to reframe adult-centered research and to represent children and youth as more than incomplete "others" in order to "provid[e] a more complex portrait of young people as meaningfully engaged, independent social actors whose activities and practices influence a variety of social contexts and settings" (Best 2007: 10).

Issues of age, class, ethnicity, race, geographic sites, and positionality (mine and the teens') make mine an uncommon ethnographic study. The fact that I was born in Guyana and moved to Flatbush when I was nearly eight years old, spending the remainder of my childhood and adolescence there, proved to be an advantage with the teens. However, when I began my initial fieldwork, in 1997, I was a Ph.D. student at Harvard, a boon with parents and educators but not exactly a point of popularity with my original group of interviewees, teenage cheerleaders at the Flatbush YMCA. In the more recent period of fieldwork, I found that my status as a college professor was a plus with the college-bound BCM teens, who relied on me for advice about selecting schools. As much as for college advising though, the girls turned to me for hair-styling and hair-care tips and for advice on how to handle overprotective mothers. Throughout my fieldwork, personal knowledge of West Indian parenting practices tempered the degree to which I pressed girls to reveal information that might get them in trouble with their mothers. Knowing that I was also interviewing many of their mothers, the West Indian cheerleaders interviewed at the Flatbush YCMA all denied having boyfriends. They were reluctant to talk about relationships, dating, and sex because they feared I would share this information with mothers. When I refocused the research around adolescents at BCM, a program where teens' parents were not present on a regular basis and one in which I spoke almost exclusively with youth and their afterschool educators, the girls were much more forthcoming about their intimate relationships.

Working with Youth

In focusing on West Indian adolescent girls, I share a primary goal with sociologist Amy L. Best, who calls for:

a serious dialogue about what might be considered the methodological, ethical, practical, and conceptual boundaries for a more critical youth studies that is attentive to the changing social realities of youth and children as they come of age in a historical moment mediated by advanced communication systems and increasingly sophisticated media, economic change, and deepening inequalities (Best 2007: 5–6).

While my nationality, ethnicity, and gender may have influenced the girls to identify with me, as an adult I remained conscious of how my age and professional status granted me greater power and authority. Power imbalances are present even when the researcher is a native anthropologist. The fact that I was barely out of my twenties when I began the research that partially informs this study helped reduce the divide between my subjects and me. Yet, I carefully and continuously renegotiated my insider/outsider status while researching this book. Scholars engaged in critical youth studies have become increasingly concerned with reducing the power imbalance between researcher and researched and with conducting nonexploitative research (Best 2007: 7). To this end, years of repeated fieldwork served me better than pressing for answers teenage girls were uncomfortable providing.

Youth researchers have increasingly sought to amplify children's voices, privilege their perspectives, and include them in the processes through which knowledge about them is created by designing collaborative or participatory research protocols (Best 2007; Cahill 2007a; Chin 2007; Fleetwood 2005). Discussing the problems with utilizing traditional anthropological methods to study children and advocating for children as native anthropologists, Elizabeth Chin writes:

The researched are often disenfranchised by a research process that excludes their active participation because they are understood as uninformed or uninitiated. Children, because they are widely thought to be developmentally incapable of really understanding the complexities of research, are further disenfranchised. Children are generally understood to be beneficiaries of the knowledge produced by the experts that later "helps" them somehow (Chin 2007: 274).

The material presented in these pages reflects more than answers to questions I asked or descriptions of observations I made. Especially with regard to popular culture, this book highlights questions the youth themselves raised. Since BCM's Museum Team program is an afterschool program with its own innovative pedagogical approaches, in many instances the youth were prompted not by me but by their educators to participate in the processes of (re)presenting West Indian and African American identity. Therefore it was not up to me as the "professional anthropologist" to create a collaborative protocol. As museum interns, the youth understood themselves as "culture experts," facilitating my aim to reveal them as "agents of knowledge about their own lives" (Best 2007: 15). For my part, I conducted a few workshops at BCM, introducing the teens to anthropological definitions of "race." And, as mentioned, I offered my services as a college adviser. I was surprised to learn that, after I completed my fieldwork, some of the questions I had raised about cultural production and the politics of representation influenced BCM educators to guide the teens in writing an ethnography about life in their Brooklyn neighborhoods. However, for the most part, I ascertained that any "help" I offered the BCM teens and their educators was positioned against a history of adults and outsiders telling them what to do. We explore the politics of help in the Conclusion. Perhaps motivated equally by a desire to control how they were represented and by the hope of becoming celebrities (my repeated attempts to explain that anthropological books had little hope of landing in Oprah's Book Club went unheard), the teens in this study, more than anything else, wanted me to *finish the book about them*.

A Note on Terms

I refrain in this book from using the word "kids" to refer to my adolescent respondents, opting instead for terms such as "youth," "teens," "teenagers," and "adolescents." The teens objected to being called "kids," and both their BCM educators and I honored this request by calling them "teens." The teens did not object to being called "girls," and so I employ this term, in addition to referring to them as "young women." The professionals who taught BCM youth are referred to by their moniker of choice, "educators." Throughout the text, there is also a conscious effort to refrain from using "informant," the traditional anthropological term for the people who share their experiences with ethnographers. Particularly because the youth in this study were suspicious of outsiders who routinely stereotyped their cultural norms and behaviors, I felt that "informant" connoted a relationship that was not true to the rapport I shared with the teens. Instead, I refer to the people, adult and youth alike, who shared their lives with me as "interviewees," although this term is also lacking in that it connotes the interlocutory relationships of journalism, not ethnography. "Interviewees," therefore, should be understood here not as people with whom I consulted briefly but as individuals with whom I shared many ethnographic encounters, including formal and informal interviews, participant observation, and, in some cases, friendships that continued for the duration of my research and beyond. "West Indian" refers to immigrants from the Anglophone Caribbean and their American-born children, "African American" refers to descendants of African slaves who have lived in the United States for generations, and "Black" refers to the broader members of the African diaspora, although this term is problematized by the West Indian teens who sometimes identified as "Black" and other times used Black to mean "African American." Last, whenever possible, I have specified interviewees' particular national origins (i.e., Jamaican, Trinidadian, Guyanese). Asserting specific national origins is a situational practice; immigrants tend to refer to themselves as "West Indians" when they are in the company of Americans but specify their national origins when they are with other West Indians. Although this was sometimes true for the teens, I also found that they formed close friendships with youth from other Caribbean nations and bonded over shared West Indian social practices.

Overview of the Chapters

In the following chapters, popular youth culture and public play-labor activities serve as the central entry points for understanding how Brooklyn's West Indian teenage girls and their African American peers articulate gender and racial identities. Chapter 2 presents an ethnographic mapping of the youngsters' journeys within and beyond the confines of the Brooklyn Children's Museum, placing West Indian immigrant youth within the racial and gender-based obstacles Black teens must traverse as they navigate New York City. Outings to a Barnes and Noble bookstore, a McDonald's restaurant and a movie theater, along with the teens' uses of cellular phones emerge as conflict-ridden sites. The chapter addresses the prominent role of consumer culture in shaping the lives of these urban dwellers and interprets the youths' extracurricular activities in and around BCM as spatializing forces that help to construct transnational racial and gender identities. Arguing that BCM is a gendered and racialized space, one in which adolescents experience the contradictions of safety and control, it explores how girls outperform boys in the internship program and relates this achievement to larger trends in educational gender disparity among urban minority youth and to Caribbean child-rearing practices. Chapter 3 uses an evening at a hip-hop concert as a springboard to interrogate the common view that hip-hop culture is largely constituted in misogyny, rampant consumerism, and male violence. West Indian girls pursue a symbolic "dual citizenship" as they construct their subjectivities and negotiate dialectic notions of authenticity within hip-hop culture. The girls voice strong preferences for female hip-hop artists and television personalities whom they define as "real." We explore their conceptualizations of authenticity and complicate their frameworks by examining the contradictory ways in which cheerleaders at the Flatbush YMCA and youth at BCM interpret American hip-hop and West Indian dancehall music. Although the mainstream versions of both genres rely on sexually explicit lyrical content and debasing portrayals of women, West Indian girls and their mothers apply a double standard, seeing hip-hop as corruptive and dancehall as "positive." I suggest that these contradictions speak to the ways in which Black consumer culture has been demonized in American society and offer my ethnographic material as a counter to popular ideas about the "breakdown" of the Black family. Chapter 4 analyzes the teens' conceptualizations of racial identity, obesity, and body image, and gendered definitions of beauty as they surface in a group conversation about a popular television program. Here, a fast-paced focus group discussion among boys and girls situates the youth as critical consumers of popular culture who cross-examine long-held stereotypes about Black female sexuality. The teens sound off on a variety of topics in this chapter, including the use of West Indian accents as opposed to African American vernacular, religiosity, homophobia in West Indian and African American communities, and representations of Blackness on reality TV programs. We contemplate these issues as they relate to notions of Black beauty and to public "role models" such as the model and TV producer Tyra Banks and First Lady Michelle Obama. Finally, chapter 5 connects the insights of the previous chapters, emphasizing the linkages that tie together spatialized definitions of race and gender, the concept of "authenticity," and the creation of transnational, youthful West Indian subjectivities. In the Conclusion, we consider how West Indian notions of success are gendered and generational, as I interrogate my own attempts to "help" the girls. I reflect on the degree to which West Indian girls' bold critiques and strategic identity assertions translate into real-life opportunities for social empowerment and economic success in the shadow of a museum threatened by economic restructuring and gentrification. I grapple with the choices, both grim and hopeful, these young women face as they transition into womanhood and into becoming Americans.

This book takes girls and young women's uses of and views on popular youth culture seriously. For adolescent girls in general and Black girls in particular, popular youth culture, constituted of daily activities such as watching television, talking on cell phones, and listening to hip-hop, has either been dismissed as trivial or judged as corrupt. By placing the actual voices of young girls at the center of this analysis, I present a much-needed correction to the general literature on adolescent identity formation and to scholarship that explores the influences of contemporary consumer culture on young women and girls. I challenge prevailing analyses that invoke images of passive girls, incapable of deciphering the misogynous, materialistic, and unrealistic definitions of femininity offered in today's omnipresent mass-mediated youth culture. Keen attention to the meanings girls themselves make of female hip-hop artists, popular television programs, and images of West Indians in the news media reveals unexpected demands for independent femininity and complex portrayals of Black characters, positioning these young women as critical social players looking to form bold political alliances. Although they have been essentially ignored in the literature on adolescent identity formation, West Indian teenage girls and their African American peers perform complex and contradictory negotiations as they make sense of themselves within American society and offer potent examples of female agency.

2

"Our Museum"

Mapping Race, Gender, and
West Indian Transnationalism

At Barnes and Noble

It was a hot July day in 2006, and, emerging from the subway station at Borough Hall/Court Street, I was relieved to enter the cool, air-conditioned space of the Barnes and Noble bookstore. I arrived to find that China, Nadine, Mariah, Amanda, and Dionne were already there. China and Nadine, the best friends we met in chapter 1, are both tall, dark-skinned girls with chemically straightened hair. Although China is from Barbados and Nadine from Trinidad, intra-island differences took a back seat for this pair, who typically dressed similarly, down to their occasional splurge for matching long, synthetic manicured false nails. While China was the more extroverted of the two, Nadine held her own. The two girls were a constant source of comedy and entertainment for their peers, with Nadine typically acting as a calming foil to China's broad gestures and sometimes bossy temperament. Mariah, a second-generation Jamaican girl, was usually a welcome third wheel to the China-and-Nadine duo. Today all three girls wore dark blue jeans with tank tops or tee shirts. Amanda and Dionne were not part of the China-Nadine-Mariah crew, and, immediately upon arriving, the girls separated into two groups. In the periodical section of the store, Amanda and Dionne, the two sixteen-year-olds, were looking at a magazine devoted to classic Barbie dolls. The seventeen-year-old girls, China, Nadine, and Mariah, were pouring over the latest editions of *People* and *US Weekly*. Seated on two benches, the girls gleefully eyed the periodicals as they chatted and laughed. They had intentionally arrived early, thrilled to peruse the bookstore since there was no Barnes and Nobles or other large bookstore in their neighborhoods. China, Nadine, and Mariah remarked on which actresses were caught on the beach looking fat, which reality TV stars' romances had ended, and who had looked beautiful at the latest premieres. Amanda, a second-generation Jamaican girl whose round face was topped by a full head of neat cornrow braids, sat shyly with Dionne, whose mother and father were from Guyana and Brooklyn, respectively. The two quickly and defensively shared that they "didn't still play with Barbies" but "liked looking at the pictures."

The girls in the Brooklyn Children's Museum (BCM) Museum Team Internship Program and I had planned this Saturday afternoon outing. Eight girls—a group of twelfth and eleventh graders—accepted my invitation; I would take them out, my treat, to a movie of their choosing and lunch anywhere they wanted to go. After much debate, they asked me to meet them at the Barnes and Noble bookstore on Court Street, at noon. From there we'd do lunch at McDonald's and see a movie at the United Artists multiplex, all on the same block in the affluent neighborhood of Brooklyn Heights.

Soon Neema, a Jamaican-descended Costa Rican, a second-generation Guyanese girl named Natasha, and Joanna, whose mother and father were from Trinidad and Jamaica, joined us. The three newest arrivals quickly settled in, and we all continued to thumb through the periodicals. With the exception of *X Men: The Last Stand*, starring Halle Berry, the summer of 2006 offered no blockbuster films featuring Black actresses, and the pages of the entertainment magazines we perused reflected this paucity. The girls commented on the numerous White female celebrities depicted in the glossy pages, including Jennifer Aniston, Angelina Jolie, and Britney Spears. When we came to a page containing a small candid photograph of the African American R&B singer Beyoncé Knowles as she casually walked along a Los Angeles street lined with high-end stores, Joanna paused, saying, "Oh, she looks good without make-up!" Sucking her teeth, China retorted, "Please! She ain't for real! That's a hair weave and I bet you anything she's wearing make-up!" For a few minutes, the girls loudly debated this issue, twisting the magazine and grabbing at it for a closer look, until the Barnes and Noble security guard, a Black man in his mid-thirties or so, walked past us for the second time. The girls continued to talk and laugh but hushed their tones when the guard approached. Having heard numerous stories in the past about how Black teens were harassed by shopkeepers who assumed they were shoplifting or were served last in pizzerias when they had been waiting far longer than White teens, I couldn't help but wonder if my presence in the Barnes and Noble was shielding the girls from these types of discrimination. The other customers around us, mostly White adult men and women (I noticed only a few Black and Latino shoppers), did not appear to make any special note of us. I observed the other shoppers, all of whom appeared relaxed, some sitting on the floor in aisles, one man clandestinely removing the plastic wrap from a sealed item; for the adult White shoppers, this was an unremarkable Saturday activity carried out in a relaxing and welcoming space. They were at liberty to enjoy the air-conditioning as long as they wished and free to sit in the aisles undisturbed. For the girls, however, this was a tenuously negotiated space and a rare Saturday activity. It was a special treat to hang out at Barnes and Noble, and they were on their "best behavior" so as to not warrant the attention of the guard. After more than half an hour in the Barnes and Noble, none of the girls bought anything. As we left, Amanda remarked that it was a waste of money to buy magazines when she could read them at the library for free.

At McDonald's

The eight teens and I walked next door to McDonald's and lined up to order. China, Neema, and Nadine were first, and I stood beside them as each placed orders for Big Macs, fries, and sodas, with Nadine opting for a chocolate shake in place of the soda. China scowled when the cashier asked me, "You payin' for all these orders together?" The question embarrassed China, not because it implied that she could not pay for her meal but because it positioned me as the adult in charge. China was used to taking care of herself and paying her own way.

As the first three girls stepped aside, Joanna approached the counter and asked me, "Can I make mine a large?" I said "yes" and repeated that they were free to order whatever they wanted. Overhearing this development, China reentered the line, asking, "We can supersize it?"[1] When I nodded, to the exasperation of the cashier, China amended her order, upping the size of each item. Joanna, Amanda, Mariah, and Dionne followed suit, ordering Big Macs, Double Quarter-Pounders with Cheese, ten-piece Chicken McNuggets, large sodas or shakes, and large fries with a few apple pies and a hot fudge sundae thrown in. Although McDonald's menu items are among the most affordable in the girls' neighborhoods, it was still unusual for them to be able to order whatever they wanted. Typically, when the girls paid for their own meals, they selected cautiously, carefully thinking about how much cash they had, when their next paycheck was coming in, if they had saved up enough money for the prom or college application fees, and so on.

Finally, it was my turn to order, and I found myself in a panic. I had not eaten at a McDonald's in years. I scanned the menu, looking for a healthy option while simultaneously considering what selection would go unnoticed by the girls. Self-preservation won out over my desire to fit in and I ordered a Caesar salad with grilled chicken and a bottle of water.

Balancing trays laden with fragrant French fries (I found myself rethinking my order), we made our way to McDonald's upper level, where there were empty seats. The lower level was packed with people, mostly Black and Latino, moms with young children, a few groups of teenagers, and a handful of elderly men and women. Once upstairs, we divided ourselves and sat at two adjacent tables. I was seated closest to Dionne, Joanna, and Amanda. As the girls hurriedly unwrapped their meals and dug in, I gingerly removed the plastic lid from my chicken Caesar salad. Prodding the chicken with a plastic fork, I silently considered that the grill marks appeared to be painted on rather than actually *grilled* in, and, as the smell of processed meat wafted to my nostrils, my stomach churned and I resealed the lid. I found myself in an odd anthropological field moment, recalling lessons I had learned in graduate school to the effect of "when in Rome . . ." and classic ethnographic texts involving food, such as Laura Bohannon's 1966 article "Shakespeare in the Bush," in which, in order to please the Tiv of West Africa, she reluctantly drank endless gourds of warm beer even though she "lacked their capacity for the thick native beer" (Bohannon 1966: 45). I was acutely conscious that my job was to eat what my "informants" ate and not to insult them by rejecting a meal they all appeared to be savoring. Still, it struck me as humorous that, in all of my training, the idea of the anthropologist stomaching unpalatable food was situated within dichotomies between East and West, between European or American fare and African or Asian "exotic cuisine." Moreover, my reluctance to eat the food seemed just as egregious as outdated judgments on "primitive" cuisines because mine undoubtedly had to do with two positionalities I had yet to fully claim: being "too old" and perhaps "too middle class" to enjoy McDonald's. I was confounded by my own reluctance because this was only one of dozens of meals I had shared with these girls. In the past, however, we had always either eaten at West Indian take-out joints in Crown Heights or ordered pizza at the museum. On other occasions, such as the time I accompanied the Museum Team program to Chinatown, I was the one coaxing the teens into eating food they found unpalatable or suspect. So it was certainly amusing that here, at McDonald's, the tables had turned.

James L. Watson has written with equal amusement and far greater insight on the cultural disorientation eating at McDonald's presents for the anthropologist. After close to thirty years conducting fieldwork in Hong Kong, Watson returned in 1989 to the host family into which he had gained membership. Expecting to treat the family to dim sum, he was told, "Let's go to the new place" (Watson 1997: v). The new place was, of course, McDonald's. As a student of Watson's, I had heard this story firsthand in graduate school. And, although he initially thought, "I didn't fly all the way from Boston to eat at McDonald's!," Watson did so on that occasion and continued to eat at McDonald's whenever he traveled to the New Territories (Watson 1997: v–vi). Unlike Watson's hosts, the girls with whom I sat had been eating at McDonald's throughout most of their lives. Even those of them who were born in the Caribbean had experienced American fast-food restaurants like McDonald's and Burger King back home. Just as Watson had argued, McDonald's had been *localized* to become their home cuisine.

All of these thoughts transpired in seconds, and, looking up at the girls, I realized that they neither noticed nor cared about whether I ate my meal. They were busy chatting about how Dionne was enlisting in a beauty pageant. When I asked if anyone wanted my salad, Dionne quickly blurted out, "Ooh! Me!," adding, "I have to lose some weight for this pageant." She had already polished off most of her ten-piece Chicken McNuggets. As we finished lunch and took our trays to the trash, I noticed that each of the girls had eaten almost everything she ordered. They were, of course, no different from most teenagers, whose enormous appetites tend to stun parents and other adults. The girls were behaving like typical teenagers, both in the American and in the West Indian sense, since the globalization of McDonald's, accompanied by the localization of its cuisine into Caribbean societies, meant that the lines between American and Caribbean fast food were blurred. Still, eating patterns among Black "inner-city youth," especially the consumption of highly caloric fast food, has come under scrutiny by health officials and public policymakers. In this way, even enjoying the pleasures associated with one of the hallmarks of Americana—the hamburger—has come to signify "at-risk" behavior for urban minority youth. We will return to issues of diet, body image, and obesity in chapter 4.

Movie Houses in Context

The girls planned our afternoon on this particular stretch of Court Street mainly because it housed a large twelve-screen multiplex. The adjacent Barnes and Noble and McDonald's made the strip a popular hangout for minority teens from the near and far reaches of Brooklyn. Living in Crown Heights, Flatbush, and East Flatbush, the young women accompanying me that afternoon often traveled to other Brooklyn neighborhoods to attend public, predominantly minority schools. They also traveled beyond their neighborhoods to frequent movie theaters such as the Court Street cinemas in the upscale brownstone neighborhood of Brooklyn Heights.

Perhaps the best way to illustrate the spatialized racial, ethnic, and class dynamics only hinted at in our observations at Barnes and Noble and McDonald's and within which Brooklyn's West Indian youth negotiate their subjectivities is by looking at public reactions when they crossed neighborhood boundaries. Consumer culture represents a revealing looking glass through which we can analyze such boundary crossings and the time span of my observations encompasses a period of "urban development" and global economic restructuring in which new consumer-oriented spaces were built in Flatbush, Crown Heights, and adjacent neighborhoods. In the late 1990s, when I asked teens at the Flatbush YMCA and BCM what movies they had recently seen and about their outings to movie theaters, most teens told me that they had not actually been to a cinema in years because there were no movie theaters in their neighborhoods. The example of the Albemarle Theater at 973 Flatbush Avenue, which originally opened in 1920, is indicative of what had happened to many of the neighborhood's movie houses. Throughout the 1970s and early 1980s, when I was a child living in Flatbush, the Albemarle had been a vibrant place to see films. However, in 1984, the theater closed after a fire. Ironically, the last film it showed was *Friday the 13th IV: The Final Chapter*.[2] Subsequently, the theater was purchased by Jehovah's Witnesses and converted into a Kingdom Hall.

For teens living in the neighborhood and its surrounding areas in the 1990s, such theater closings, coupled with the fact that many of their families could not afford cable television, meant that, unless they purchased bootleg films at sidewalk sales, many of them did not experience a leisure culture that involved seeing current feature films. In 1998, however, that was about to change when plans to build a twelve-screen multiplex and Barnes and Noble bookstore in the adjacent neighborhood of Brooklyn Heights were announced. The cinema was set to be built on Court Street, on a block that had once housed a pornographic theater and that was generally known as a blight on the affluent, mostly White community of Brooklyn Heights. However, plans for building the multiplex were met with disapproval from many Brooklyn Heights residents who voiced numerous concerns, reported in the *New York Times* in 1998:

> Opponents are concerned that the 200-foot-tall multiplex will dwarf the rows of brownstones on State and Schermerhorn Streets. They predict that nightly crowds will overwhelm the quiet neighborhood with traffic and

noise. They fret that parking, already a problem, will become impossible. And some people have another worry—that the multiplex will show first-run Hollywood action movies (Yardley 1998: n.p.).

The *New York Times* article directly linked one concern, worries about screening first-run Hollywood action films, as having "nothing to do with taste but everything to do with the teen-age audiences the action movies attract" (Yardley 1998: n.p.). Brooklyn Heights residents feared that if such films were screened, the new cinema would attract teens from throughout Brooklyn and patrons "from poorer neighborhoods, including nearby housing projects" (Yardley 1998: n.p.). The racialized elements of such fears were explicit, with one neighborhood leader remarking, "A lot of people have been very uncomfortable about the presence of a lot of teenagers—maybe black teenagers, maybe Hispanic teenagers, maybe poor teenagers—I've heard that expressed by my neighbors" (Yardley 1998: n.p.).

Plans for the Court Street multiplex came on the heels of the demise of one-screen neighborhood cinemas, such as the Albemarle, that catered to minority neighborhoods. The early-twenty-first-century multiplex boom in New York City was an attempt to capitalize on the fact that New York City had fewer movie houses per capita than any other large city in the United States, yet it had an extremely large movie going population (Yardley 1998: n.p.). The new Court Street cinemas proposal, although the theater would be located in upscale Brooklyn Heights, was part of a new trend toward movie chains constructing multiplexes, even in previously neglected minority neighborhoods. The many proponents of the United Artists Court Street cinema won out, and the giant multiplex opened for business in July 2000.[3]

When I asked a longtime Brooklyn Heights business owner and neighborhood resident to reflect on the controversies surrounding the new movie theater, he remarked that, leading up to the theater's opening, there was considerable discussion at his daughter's private high school in Brooklyn Heights, in the local press, over dinner tables, and in his store "about the perception that the opening of the multiplex would bring 'those people' into the hallowed precincts of Brooklyn Heights." A White man in his fifties, himself a keen observer of local culture, the business owner went on to share the following account with me:

Most people in the [traditionally liberal] Heights repudiated such fears as racist and were focused on the bulk and surface treatment of the building; their concerns were aesthetic and landmark district-oriented.

I do think, however, that when the project was announced, some people used preservationist arguments in absolute opposition to it as a veiled expression of their fears that black teenagers were going to be hanging out on their stoops before and after going to the movies, something which didn't really happen as far as I could tell. At least one brownstoner on State Street, a few doors west of the theater, put a rope across the bottom of the stoop to discourage sitting, but I think that actually predated the opening of the theater and was aimed at downtown office workers who would . . . and in warm weather still do . . . eat their lunches on the stoops of State and Schermerhorn, West of Court. The Brooklyn Heights Press had an on-going discussion about the architectural merits (or lack thereof) and zoning implications of the multiplex and about its "social implications" as well.[4]

The business owner's account is valuable for a number of reasons. It addresses the differences of opinion within the well-heeled but ostensibly liberal Brooklyn Heights community; many residents took their neighbors to task, interpreting the overt fears about the new theater as covertly motivated by discriminatory beliefs. The business owner's assessment reveals that racial and class-based prejudices that some White Brooklyn Heights residents held were not shared by all local residents. Some residents had legitimate concerns about the area's landmark architecture, and others used such concerns to hide racist sentiments. This particular man was perhaps well positioned to share such a thoughtful analysis because, although his store did not cater to adolescents, he had for many years employed youth of varying ethnicities and class backgrounds. Over the course of twenty-five years, he had come to be known as a mentor and surrogate father to many of these teens. Therefore, it is from an informed position that he observed that the suspicions that minority youth would overrun the neighborhood went unfulfilled.

The arguments against opening the Court Street multiplex have as much to do with architectural concerns as they have to do with a contemporary racial ideology that Eduardo Bonilla-Silva has termed "color-blind racism" (Bonilla-Silva 2010). Bonilla-Silva argues:

> whites have developed powerful explanations—which have ultimately become justifications—for contemporary racial inequality that exculpate them from any responsibility for the status of people of color. . . . Whereas Jim Crow racism explained blacks' social standing as the result of their biological and moral inferiority, color-blind racism avoids such facile

arguments. Instead, whites rationalize minorities' contemporary status as the product of market dynamics, naturally occurring phenomena, and blacks' imputed cultural limitations (Bonilla-Silva 2010: 2).

Bonilla-Silva includes impolite treatment in stores, restaurants, and other commercial sites among the discriminatory acts that accompany color-blind racism. Bonilla-Silva's framing of this contemporary racial ideology is especially applicable to the teens in this study and to the discourses surrounding the Court Street cinemas. Even after the cinemas opened, public commentary denounced what could be seen as examples of "blacks' imputed cultural limitations" for ruining the movie-going experience at Court Street. Comments posted to the "Brooklyn Heights Blog" website in 2008 illustrate that the veiled racism that had marked early concerns about the multiplex remained a salient part of the theater's life.[5] On the blog, Brooklyn Heights residents lamented that the theater was "nasty," with "yappy teenaged girls" and "an obnoxious crowd of people." Bloggers complained about the large numbers of crying babies (which one commentator attributed to special discounts for young children) and the presence of children at late-night screenings of R-rated films (albeit accompanied by parents). One blogger referred to Court Street as "the ghetto theater," sparking an online debate about whether or not those who complained about the theater's "rowdy" crowd were racist. Those who fulminated at the "dirty," "rowdy," "nightmarish," and "ghetto" theater far outnumbered those who suggested that poor urban teenagers deserve a place to see movies as much as anyone else and that the theater's problems with maintaining cleanliness and crowd spillover into the streets had to do with its being understaffed and having a lobby that was too small to accommodate its patrons. The nightmares that befell the cinema included two separate fires in the popcorn machines within the span of one year, which resulted in the activation of automatic sprinkler systems and full evacuations of the smoke-filled theater. Understaffing and poor design, discernable reasons for overcrowding, and trash and safety hazards at the theater received less attention than the minority teenage moviegoers. Even online commentaries that mentioned the popcorn fires quickly reverted to blaming minority audience members for disruptive viewing experiences, with one blogger lamenting, "The during the movie commentary is 'BS.' 'She didn't just do that,' or 'You go girl,' all during [the movie]."[6] The outbursts this blogger references hearing during the movie, including "She didn't just do that" and "You go, girl," have come to be known as elements of African American vernacular.

At the Movies

So it was in the face of this ominous backstory that the girls and I entered the Court Street multiplex to watch the 2006 remake of the 1976 classic horror film *The Omen*. As we entered, the poorly designed lobby was packed, unable to accommodate the patrons of the theater's twelve screens. The girls and I forced our way to the automated ticket machines, where I retrieved our tickets. Passing the concession stand, I asked the girls if they wanted anything and they all shook their heads "no." Mariah bristled, saying that theater food was too expensive and that usually she brought in her own candy when she went to the movies.

Upstairs in the auditorium, China's will won out, and we sat way in the back. The film had been out for several weeks, and the auditorium was only half full, with small groups of other teens and a few young parents with children ranging in ages from toddlers to preadolescents. I also spotted a few teenage couples huddled in the dark recesses of the last rows behind us. Of the moviegoers, nearly all were Black or Latino, with the exception of a group of three White teenage boys and a White couple in their twenties or early thirties. Seated in the middle of the eight girls, with China on my left and Amanda on my right, for the next 110 minutes I was engulfed by screams and cries of, "Look out!," "Oh no!," and "He's going to kill her!" China screamed the loudest and clung to my arm or to Nadine's (Nadine was seated on her other side). China's screams invoked laughter and additional gasps and shrieks from the other girls. Our group was not the only one from which screams emanated, and I wondered, had any been present, how older, White Brooklyn Heights residents might have responded to this vocal crowd. Whether seated in traditionally Black live-music venues such as the world-famous Apollo Theater in Harlem or in neighborhood movie houses, Black audiences are known for vocal, call-and-response interactions with what is being performed in front of them. Interactive Black audiences, especially in relation to the horror genre, have been lampooned in popular representations, including *Scary Movie 2*, directed by Keenan Ivory Wayans, in which a Black girl talks incessantly on her cell phone while watching a movie and retorts, "I'm on the phone!" when other audience members shush her and the hilarious Eddie Murphy bit from *Delirious* in which the comedian contrasts White families who stick around haunted residences in films like *The Amityville Horror* with a hypothetical Black family that, at the first demonic whisper of "Get out," responds, "Too bad we can't stay!" Both spoofs suggest a different cultural code for movie watching. Still, the girls' reactions that day had as much to do with gendered and age-based social norms as they did with African American culture. Put simply, in the youths' minds, part of the fun of seeing a scary film with your girlfriends is screaming bloody murder and clinging to one another for dear life. As "respectable" West Indian girls, China and the others carefully negotiated their behavior in the Barnes and Noble and, to a lesser extent, at McDonald's, but they also understood the conventions of African American consumer culture, including talking back in the movies. In the darkness of the theater and gripped by the suspense of a horror movie, the girls gained pleasure from screaming a little too loud and talking back to the White actors who made foolhardy decisions that resulted in their untimely demise. And, although no one shushed us on that afternoon, juxtaposed with the comments at brooklynheightsblog.com, the BCM girls might easily be stereotyped as the kind of "yappy teenage girls" who yelled "You go, girl!" and ruined the movie for more polite and conscientious (read White) viewers.

After the movie, most of the girls went home to work on chores, and China and Joanna headed to their part-time jobs. Reflecting on the afternoon, I thought of how the girls seemed vulnerable at the Barnes and Noble, careful not to attract attention from the security guard. The tense moment with the guard fit with many accounts the girls and other BCM teens shared. McDonald's was a more welcoming atmosphere, but not one without concerns; had I not been paying for lunch, the girls' orders would have been far more modest. And, although they knew I was treating, no one took advantage of my offer to buy them refreshments at the theater. It was also noteworthy that, despite Brooklyn Heights' residents' fears that, because of the movie theater, minority youth would want to hang out in their neighborhood, none of the girls stuck around after the film ended. Like most Brooklyn teenagers with whom I talked, these girls understood the unwritten rules about neighborhood turfs and knew where they were not welcome. The events of the afternoon provide only a small snapshot of the racialized and gendered constructions of urban space in which the girls carefully negotiated their subjectivities on a regular basis. The confines of BCM served as a comforting antidote to the potential dangers, racial stereotypes, and exclusions the girls faced as they engaged in the consumer sphere in Brooklyn Heights.

Introducing the Museum

I sat in the library of the Brooklyn Children's Museum with the twelfth-grade interns, known at the museum as "Explainers," as they worked with a young White female artist and bookbinder. The museum's educators had hired the bookbinder to teach the teens how to construct and write a book about being

African American and West Indian in Brooklyn. While the teens feigned concentration at the task of gluing pages into book spines and cutting images out of magazines, their *real* attention was on something far more interesting to them. The air became charged with gossip as they discussed the recent dismissal of Kareem, a boy who, without permission, had opened the desk drawer of one of the educators and taken his (Kareem's) paycheck. Kareem had been absent on payday and arrived on a Saturday to claim his check. Upon finding that the educator who allotted checks was not in, Kareem took his check. This marked the last in a long line of transgressions on Kareem's part, and the result was his immediate dismissal from the program. When word of Kareem's firing reached the other teens, a dialogue ensued among China, Nadine, and Kevin, China's sixteen-year-old half brother, who had been born in Brooklyn. As previously mentioned, China emigrated from Barbados when she was ten, and Nadine moved to Brooklyn from Trinidad when she was just a few months old. Nadine, who had dated Kevin a few years prior, was now living with him and China. After Nadine's mother took a job in a southern city, Nadine had moved in with China's family. Kevin, who wore removable gold plates over his teeth and large rhinestone studs in each ear, like the other boys, was usually quiet. China, the most extroverted and popular of the BCM girls, effortlessly negotiated between the favor of her peers and the museum educators. The two discussed Kareem's dismissal, and Nadine chimed in:

KEVIN: See, that would never happen to you. All you girls act real goody-goody in here.
CHINA, rubbing her thumb against the fingers on one hand: Yeah, right. It's all about getting paper.
NADINE: Anyway, I can't wait to get online tonight! Kareem will be chatting, and I can't *wait* to hear his take on this!

"Getting paper" or one's paycheck, for China and other girls, was more important than acting out or questioning the authority of the female educators. By asserting that "girls act goody-goody *in here,*" Kevin suggested that the girls intentionally *performed* obedience while within the confines of BCM, where they were not portraying their authentic selves. Knowing the value China placed on "being for real," Kevin attempted to strike a nerve. But China's response suggests that she valued "getting paper" enough to present a "goody-goody" self. Both the girls and boys were keenly aware that, while girls tended to excel in the BCM internship program, boys were more frequently dismissed. And, as Nadine indicates, the adult-controlled territory of BCM was in contrast to the liberating space of online chatting, where Kareem would be free to tell his side of the story.

For Black youth, New York City is made up of few "safe" places. Rather, Black teens often experience discomfort at the very least and blatant discrimination and police harassment at the worst when they venture into areas like Brooklyn Heights. We can use an ethnographic "mapping" of BCM and the youngsters' journeys within and beyond its confines to illustrate how the activities and meanings that coincide with the construction and consumption of products and spaces in New York City have bearing in the teens' lives. Extracurricular activities in and around Brooklyn Children's Museum emerge as spatializing forces that help to construct West Indian and African American adolescents' racial and gender identities. We can conceptualize BCM as a space that takes on the ability to confirm identity. Following Setha Low, I define spatialize as "locat[ing], both physically and conceptually, social relations and social practices in social space" (Low 1996, 2005: 111). We'll see that BCM is a space that is racialized as Black and gendered as female. Within the larger urban context of New York City, this speaks to the ability of cultural institutions to subvert, albeit precariously, dominant geographic and social constructs.

As evidenced in the debates surrounding the Court Street cinemas, BCM teens' presence in New York City public spaces is contingent on the degree to which Black teenagers are seen as threats to civilizing forces. Black teenage boys who frequent BCM recount stories of being detained and searched by police as they hang out with friends on the stoops of their apartment buildings in the Crown Heights and Flatbush sections of Brooklyn. Girls, however, are not immune from discriminatory access to public space. Both boys and girls experience race-based discrimination as they attempt to enjoy the same privileges as more economically and socially privileged peers. For example, BCM teens related instances when they were served last in White-owned eateries, even though they had been waiting far longer than White teenagers. When girls shopped in large department stores in Manhattan, they were often closely watched, not only by store clerks but also by White shoppers. Therefore, the adolescents tenuously negotiated leisure and consumption as they found that the farther they traveled from the confines of BCM, the more susceptible they became to discrimination.

While the youths' presence on the city streets is precarious, there are moments during which they can claim the city as their own and imbue public spaces with West Indian cultural identity. Such moments include the Annual

West Indian Day Parade (New York City's largest parade) and, as we will soon see, the 2006 New York City transport workers' strike. Roger Toussaint, a West Indian, symbolically usurped the city streets when the Trinidadian immigrant and president of the Transport Workers' Union (TWU) led the workers to strike. Although adults initiated the transport strike, BCM teens allied themselves with Toussaint by naming a float in the museum's Mardi Gras celebration after the union leader. This political alliance was played out in a symbolic enactment within BCM that demonstrated the teens' engagement with the city beyond the museum and illustrated their concern for issues not often pegged as adolescent preoccupations. The teens' conceptualizations of their BCM Mardi Gras costumes, along with the meanings attached to the gendered space of the museum, reveal how West Indian and African American identities are mutually constructed within and beyond this cultural institution. I problematize the notion that BCM is a "safe" and "female-centered" space by exposing the ways in which male violence and public educational policies threaten the youths' abilities to enjoy the program. Consumer culture, especially the use of cell phones, looms large amid these mediations because, for teens, transnational, racialized, and gendered identities are often forged within the realms of leisure activities and consumer culture, arenas revealed here as geographic, temporal, political, and social youthscapes (Maira and Soep 2005).

For David Harvey, "the intersecting command of money, time and space forms a substantial nexus of social power" (Harvey 1990: 227). If we juxtapose this with the time it takes to travel from the center of world finances in lower Manhattan to Flatbush and Crown Heights and consider the high proportion of racial and ethnic minorities among the populations in these neighborhoods and the absence of symbols of capitalist and governmental power, we get a sense of the ways in which the teens' neighborhoods are marginalized spaces beyond New York City's power structures. As Gupta and Ferguson have noted, "the establishment of spatial meaning—the making of spaces into places—is always implicated in hegemonic configurations of power" (Gupta and Ferguson 1997: 8). Characterizations of Flatbush and Crown Heights, then, as "West Indian neighborhoods," as "ghettos," and as "remote from Manhattan" all speak to the lack of economic and social power these neighborhoods wield.

As an anthropologist who observed these neighborhoods for more than a decade while researching this book and having lived in Flatbush during my childhood and adolescence, I can also reflect on the ways in which both Flatbush and Crown Heights experienced gentrification and "urban renewal" between 1999 and 2009. While in the late 1990s mom-and-pop West Indian grocery stores, eateries, and music stores dominated the busy thoroughfare that Flatbush Avenue represents, by 2008 a large Target store opened at the junction of Flatbush and Nostrand Avenue. Hip, upscale organic restaurants catering to middle- and upper-middle-class White professionals appeared along prominent side streets like Cortelyou Road. In Crown Heights, population data reflect these changes. The most recent Public Use Microdata Area (PUMA) data reveals a 10 percent growth in non-Hispanic Whites, who now account for 18 percent of Crown Heights' population. The non-Hispanic Black population has declined from about 79 percent of the total to about 69 percent.

The Internship Program: Play-Labor, BCM Style

The Museum Team Internship Program at BCM includes youth in grades nine through twelve. Ninth graders involved in the program are called "Volunteers-in-Training," tenth graders are "Volunteers," and eleventh graders are "Peer Mentors." These youth are not paid and learn skills they will need to gain admission as twelfth-grade "Explainers," paid interns who receive minimum wage and who work in BCM's early childhood, natural science, and education departments.[7] While these teenage interns are the central actors in this book, BCM also has programs for preschool and elementary school children. Some of the youth had been frequenting BCM since they were toddlers. For twelfth-grade Explainers, the BCM internship is a way to earn money after school (youth are paid to perform duties such as caring for plants and animals in the museum and assisting with the younger children), benefit from educational programs and field trips, and receive assistance with college applications. In order to be admitted into the Museum Team program, teens must have at least a C average and must pass an application interview. The program is immensely popular, and there is usually a long waiting list of students wishing to enroll. Participants typically come from Crown Heights and surrounding neighborhoods, and youth usually learn about the program through word of mouth. The BCM Youth Coordinator in 2002 reported that, in the previous year, 90 percent of the seniors in the internship program had gone on to college. BCM was successful in helping students get admitted to college not only because it provided tutoring for standardized tests and assistance with college applications but also because participating in the internship program gave college applicants a prestigious extracurricular activity that most likely made them appear more "well-rounded" in the eyes of college admissions officers.

In performing her duties at the museum, Joanna, the girl of Trinidadian (mother) and Jamaican (father) parentage who accompanied me to the Court Street cinema, exemplified play-labor, BCM style. Joanna's job included doing an animal show for "Kids Crew," an afterschool, weekend, and summer program for children ages seven to twelve. In "the Commons," a large stadium-style auditorium in the museum, I watched as Joanna, with help from another teenage intern, Naomi, brought out a group of the museum's live animals one by one for about forty squirming elementary-school-age children, the vast majority of whom were Black or Latino (I saw one Asian child). Joanna had carried out this demonstration countless times. With confidence and charisma, she demanded the children's attention, outlining the rules of conduct:

> Number one: Two fingers to touch the animals [demonstrating with her pointer and middle finger], head and tail. Number two: No talking, yelling, screaming, or jumping. Number three: No getting up from that spot where you're sitting.

Having laid down the laws of conduct, Joanna queried, "Are you ready to see the animals? You don't sound like you're ready! Are you ready for your first animal?!?!" The younger children clapped loudly as Joanna introduced a box turtle named R2D2, at fifty-three years old "the oldest animal in the museum." Joanna added expertly, "Box turtles are only supposed to live for forty years, so R2D2 has already exceeded his life span." After allowing each child to touch the turtle, Joanna brought out a lizard named Spike, who "eats crickets and blends in with rocks," followed by the show stopper, Isis, a ball python who wrapped herself around Joanna's waist while the observing youngsters gasped and let slip squeals and "ewwws."[8] Joanna, like most of the teenage interns (especially the girls), took her work at BCM very seriously; she memorized facts about each creature and, as she performed the animal show, seemed to channel flair and fearlessness reminiscent of wildlife experts invited to introduce exotic animals on late-night TV variety shows. Still, Joanna kept an element of playfulness about her, which mesmerized the younger children. All playing was set aside, however, when Joanna discussed her paycheck. As China noted, the girls were all about "getting paper." Joanna's average paycheck for two weeks of work at BCM amounted to $145. Lamenting her low wages, Joanna told me, "The biggest check I ever got was close to $400." While one BCM educator noted that some teens appeared the Monday after paydays with brand-new sneakers, most of the teens I interviewed and observed used their BCM earnings to buy afterschool snacks, music, and clothes. Seniors in high school typically utilized BCM wages to pay prom expenses and college application fees. Some of the adolescents also used their earnings to contribute to household expenses, helping their mother's pay for rent, utilities, and groceries. And, as we shall see throughout this book, a number of the BCM teens held other jobs in addition to their work at BCM.

Brooklyn Children's Museum in Context

The Brooklyn Children's Museum is located on the corner of Brooklyn Avenue and St. Mark's Avenue in Crown Heights.[9] The museum stands in census tract 341 and PUMA 4006, which is composed of the neighborhoods of Crown Heights, Prospect Heights, and Weeksville. This census tract is bordered on the north by Atlantic Avenue, on the south by Eastern Parkway, on the west by Flatbush Avenue, and on the east by New York Avenue. Established in 1899, the museum was originally located in Adams Building, a Victorian mansion in Bedford Park (now known as Brower Park). In 1929, it took over a second house, the Smith Mansion. These two original locations closed in 1967 (due to disrepair), and the museum moved to a temporary location at Bedford Avenue and Lincoln Place (also in Crown Heights). BCM's next edifice was built between 1972 and 1975, adjacent to Brower Park. The unusual museum structure included a 1900s-era trolley kiosk and an enormous remodeled sewer pipe through which visitors entered as they proceeded to the four exhibit floors. Between 2003 and 2008, the museum underwent another multimillion-dollar expansion from which it emerged, having doubled its size, as the city's first "green" or environmentally conscious museum. The *New York Sun*, describing BCM's postrenovation appearance, observed that it looked like a "shimmery spaceship that has just touched down among the brick and brownstone buildings of Crown Heights," a reference to the eight million banana-yellow tiles that now adorn the building (Taylor 2008). The *New York Sun* also reported that "the city provided $46 million dollars in capital funding," with the museum raising "an additional $28 million—from corporations, foundations, and individuals, as well as state and federal sources—for the endowment and for new programming" (Taylor 2008). Later in this chapter, we will explore these recent renovations in relation to the teen interns, and we will revisit the renovations and the museum's sources of funding in chapter 5.

Brooklyn Children's Museum exterior after renovations. Photo by the author.

Brower Park divides the block on which BCM sits. Public School 289, the George V. Brower elementary school, is located on the opposite side of the park, on the same side of St. Mark's Avenue as BCM. Rows of stately limestone townhouses stand opposite BCM and P.S. 289. Many of these houses were owned or occupied by Blacks in the 1990s, when I began my fieldwork, but by 2008 "for sale" signs signaled the arrival of gentrification. Leaving the museum's immediate vicinity and walking from Brooklyn Avenue to nearby Nostrand Avenue, one finds a busy shopping area. Although less bustling than Flatbush Avenue (one of Brooklyn's main thoroughfares, Flatbush Avenue leads from downtown Brooklyn to the neighborhood called Flatbush), Nostrand Avenue is home to West Indian American restaurants, Black hair salons, and Caribbean grocery stores. The street also reflects the neighborhood's ethnic diversity with African hair-braiding salons, Dominican beauty shops, Yemeni delis, and Chinese restaurants alongside businesses catering to West Indians.

Because it is located near Brower Park and P.S. 289, the blocks surrounding BCM are constantly filled with school-age children. According to Deborah Matthews, my original liaison to BCM in 1997, BCM became a home away from home, with many children attending throughout their childhoods. This practice spanned my years of fieldwork, during which I met girls like Amanda, whose older brother had attended workshops at BCM during his childhood, before Amanda started coming. With programs for children of all ages, including "Totally Tots," which caters to toddlers, BCM attracts children from the surrounding areas beginning at a young age; they come to BCM on a daily basis to view the exhibits, learn about plants and animals, and receive child care and help with their homework. Many of these young children continue attending the museum throughout their preteen and adolescent years (as both Amanda and her brother did). In addition to working in the capacities I have outlined, high school students receive prep courses for the SAT, go on trips throughout the city, and make overnight visits to college campuses. For children of all ages, time at BCM is extremely structured: They are doing homework, participating in workshops, listening to lectures, staging performances, or making crafts. And, as Joanna's behavioral cues to the "Kids Crew" members revealed, even for young children, play and labor converge, and play time is a learning experience for the children who participate in BCM's programs; it is characterized by the imparting of rules of conduct that teach children to sit quietly and follow instructions.

Offering an anthropological definition of museums in general and reflecting on the special relevancy museums like BCM hold for minorities, Richard Handler states:

> Considered anthropologically, the museum is first of all a social arena, not a repository of objects. . . . A museum is an institution in which social relationships are oriented in terms of a collection of objects which are made meaningful by those relationships—though these objects are often understood by museum natives to be meaningful independently of those social relationships (Handler 1993: 33).

Following Handler, in what follows I analyze BCM as a social space, focusing more on the social relations created and maintained within and beyond its boundaries than on the objects displayed. Still, the objects displayed in museums, where they come from, who owns them, and how they are framed warrant analysis. Handler summarizes the controversies surrounding museums in the 1990s, which included questions about who has the right to control cultural resources in the face of debates about "multiculturalism," "diversity," and "democracy" (Handler 1993: 34). Interestingly, Handler places museums within theories of "possessive individualism" ("an ideology which privileges not just individuals . . . but individuals defined in terms of the property they possess"), around which he sees modern culture revolving (Handler 1993: 35). Handler sees museums as embodying the values of possessive individualism in two primary ways:

First, museums create individuated identities—whether cultures, ethnic groups, historical periods, or even artists—by displaying objects that can be attributed to those identities, that is, by displaying cultural properties which are taken (tautologically) to prove the existence of the entities said to have created or possessed them. Second, museums are themselves individuated corporations whose existence or survival as independent entities depends upon a highly fetishized collection of properties (Handler 1993: 35).

Handler relates his second point to the museum's dependence on owning objects in the face of calls for repatriation. In light of Handler's insights about the saliency of possessive individualism for modern culture in general, and museums in particular, the Brooklyn Children's Museum becomes a critical site for analyzing young people's subjectivity formation vis-à-vis consumer culture. Moreover, as we will see, BCM "create[s] individuated identities," not just in the objects it displays but, more important, in the ways in which it works, especially with its teenage interns, to socially construct gendered, racialized, and ethnic identities.

Many of the questions Handler raises echo critiques offered by David Julian Hodges in a 1978 article titled "Museums, Anthropology, and Minorities: In Search of a New Relevance for Old Artifacts." Hodges situates minority children in relation to the traditional museum experience, arguing:

The term museum has come to conjure up images of a mausoleum-type building in the center of a city, adorned with ornate pillars and flanked by concrete lions. Inside, drafty halls echo the sharp clap of footsteps, causing many visitors to think what one Chicago third grader had the grit to say: "I'd sure hate to be left in here all by myself!" Priceless artifacts proclaim by their careful appointment in glass cases, what would otherwise be plainly written: Do Not Touch (Hodges 1978:148).

Owning boasting rights as the first museum created expressly for children and located in an overwhelmingly Black census tract, BCM resists such classification, purposely inviting children, most of whom are minorities, *to touch*. In opposition to traditional museums that disregard the interests of minorities in establishing collections and exhibits and in setting their programming priorities, Hodges introduces "the new museum concept" and makes specific mention of BCM:

The new museum can be seen in the "People's Center" at New York's American Museum of Natural History, where visitors observe and participate, where children touch and explore. It can be seen in the efforts of some Brooklyn community residents, who have formed the Society for the Preservation of Weeksville and Bedford-Stuyvesant History, and who are establishing a museum to preserve the artifacts of a nineteenth-century community of free blacks. The new museum can be seen also in the development of Heritage Museum, a children's museum established in an old vaudeville house balcony in the Bronx, New York; in the Anacostia Neighborhood Museum of the Smithsonian Institute in Washington, D.C.; in the Brooklyn Children's Museum; in the Children's Museum in Boston; in El Museo del Barrio in East Harlem, New York; and in many others throughout the country (Hodges 1978: 150).

Hodges's descriptions of "the new museum concept," including the roles of uplifting and raising pride in communities long disenfranchised, and the need to scale the study of humanity to a child's perspectives, to offer an alternative to school, gangs and street corners, and to design exhibits in which children literally drape themselves in African garb, apply to BCM (Hodges 1978: 151–152). In fact, like Hodges's example involving African garb, one of BCM's most popular and longest-running exhibits, "Global Shoes," encouraged children to literally step into the shoes of families living in disparate locales, from Mongolia to Uganda. Other past exhibits include "World Brooklyn," which brought the consumer sphere into the museum by re-creating stores such as a Mexican bakery, an international grocery store featuring Jamaican *ackee*, Indian *ghee*, and other global food products, a Chinese stationery store, and a West African import store, all scaled down to a child's size. The interactive exhibit, premised on the idea that Brooklyn represents the world's cultures, prompted children to practice cultural activities such as making paper lanterns in the stationery store and planning a Kwanzaa celebration or a kosher *Shabbat* with shopping lists at the international grocery store. And the museum's inventory of more than thirty thousand objects includes many African artifacts such as a wooden dog bell from the Democratic Republic of the Congo and a Liberian tortoise shell drum.

Much like the other "new museums" with which Hodges associates it, BCM, although it is funded principally by the New York City Department of Cultural Affairs, is seen primarily as a place for minorities in general, and Blacks in particular. This is not far from the museum's founding mission, which, according to former BCM president Carol Enseki, was to "serve the thousands of immigrant families" arriving in Brooklyn in the late 1800s (Taylor 2008).[10] While in 1899 the museum opened its doors to Eastern European immigrant families, the results of a museum survey posted on BCM's website in 2007 revealed that 60 percent of BCM's visitors were either African American or African Caribbean. The vast majority of the thirty or so teens who participated in the afterschool program were Black, with most of the participants coming from the West Indies. For these teens, BCM served as a surrogate home, a critical role for youth already removed from their native homelands in the Caribbean. Their journeys to and from the museum, their activities within its confines, and their negotiations of public social spaces in and around the museum speak to complex struggles over national, ethnic, racialized, and gendered notions of belonging. Amanda Lewis has argued that "schools play a role in the production of race as a social category both through implicit and explicit lessons and through school practices" (Lewis 2003: 188). According to Lewis, schools not only teach students to become racial subjects but also produce racial disparities in children's life outcomes (Lewis 2003: 188). Like schools, BCM constructs racial, ethnic, and gender categories, but the museum also hopes to subvert the racial disparities produced in schools.

Constructing Place, Race, and Gender at the Brooklyn Children's Museum

Following the sociologist and philosopher Henri Lefebvre, Dolores Hayden argues:

> For women, the body, the home, and the street have all been arenas of conflict. Examining them as political territories-bounded spaces with some form of enforcement of the boundaries-helps us to analyze the spatial dimensions of 'women's sphere' at any given time. And just as gender can be mapped as a struggle over social reproduction that occurs at various scales of space, the same is true of race, class, and many other social issues (Hayden 1995: 22–23; Lefebvre 1991).

Brooklyn's West Indian adolescent girls encounter an irresolute relationship between female identity and space. These girls draw upon both American and West Indian ideological constructions of space. Caribbean gender ideologies position women as linked to the "respectable" and stabilizing spaces of home and church; at the same time, West Indian matrifocal kinship structures have necessitated that women travel beyond the home to earn wages and provide financial support for their families (Smith 1987; Wilson 1973). In Brooklyn, West Indian girls have learned that they are "safer off the streets." Parents and educators see city streets as places where even "good" girls can fall victim to violent crime and teenage pregnancy. This is in contrast to the youths' characterizations of life "back home." When I asked girls about the differences between growing up in the West Indies and growing up in New York, they said, as one girl put it, "It's safer to go outside and play there [in the Caribbean]. All of the kids play outside all day and at night. Nobody worries." Mary Waters observes that West Indian immigrant boys in New York have more freedom to travel beyond the home than do West Indian immigrant girls (Waters 1999). My own research has revealed that West Indian girls feel they are bound to the home because they have more household chores than their male siblings or their female African American peers. One girl said, "I have to cook because in Jamaica the women stay home and cook" (quoted in LaBennett 2006). For this interviewee, and many others, feminine identity was constructed around "staying home" and doing "women's work."

This is not to say, however, that the girls' mothers' did not demand academic success. The girls' transnational subjectivities were partially predicated on their mothers' hopes that within the home they would be good, dutiful West Indian daughters and that outside the home their activities would ensure their upward mobility. Scholars focused on child rearing in the Anglophone Caribbean have noted the especially high expectations mothers hold for their daughters (MacCormack and Draper 1987; Sargent and Harris 1998: 207).[11] And conflicts between being the good, dutiful, respectable West Indian daughter and struggling for upward mobility and for one's autonomy within American society were beautifully dramatized in Paule Marshall's classic text, *Brown Girl, Brownstones,* about a West Indian household in post–World War II Brooklyn. I thought about Marshall's protagonist, a headstrong second-generation Bajan (or Barbadian) girl who defies her hardworking, protective mother as I listened to many of the BCM girls' stories. One girl's experience in particular revealed many of the complexities surrounding West Indian American femininity and mother-daughter conflicts, so richly described by Marshall. Amanda, the round-faced, second-generation Jamaican girl we met through the outing to Barnes and Noble, McDonald's, and the movies carefully negotiated between West Indian notions of respectable femininity and her own desires to pursue higher education and female autonomy. Amanda was a bookish girl who looked younger than her sixteen years and whose shy demeanor, chubby frame, and glasses resulted in her not receiving much attention from boys. Still, it was not her relationships (or lack thereof) with boys that preoccupied Amanda. She frequently shared her fears about pleasing her mother with me, on one occasion confiding that she was nervous about parent-teacher night because she had not performed well on a science test that day and was anxious about her mother's conversation with the science teacher. Amanda's mother kept a close watch on her, prohibiting Amanda from dating, wearing makeup, and hanging out except for her time spent at BCM. All of these prohibitions can certainly be seen as practical parenting. However, although Amanda typically excelled in school, she still could never seem to please her mother, who constantly drove the teen to "do better." It appeared that Amanda's mom's hopes for the girl were finally realized when Amanda was admitted into a special summer internship at an Ivy League college not far from New York City. However, the BCM educators and I were perplexed when Amanda arrived one day in tears, saying that her mother had prohibited her from attending the internship because it meant she "couldn't keep her eye on me." The BCM educators finally convinced Amanda's mother to let her attend the college program, where Amanda flourished. At the end of the summer, she was offered a chance to apply for early admission to the Ivy League school, but, once again, her mother intervened and forbade Amanda from even applying to the school. Her mother had already decided that Amanda would live at home while attending college in the city. For Amanda's mother, her daughter's safety hinged on the degree to which Amanda could be kept close to home. The mother's desire and her lifelong push for her daughter's success were undercut by her fears about letting the girl venture too far from home. And, although Amanda was, to everyone who knew her well, the last girl a mother should worry about getting involved in sexual relationships, this remained her mother's greatest fear. West Indian ethnic notions of respectable femininity seemed to govern Amanda's upbringing and limited her ability to take advantage of burgeoning educational opportunities.

Amanda's story reveals how, for first- and second-generation West Indian girls, respectable female identity is often contingent on the places into which they venture. Other than school, the Museum Team Internship Program was the only public space into which Amanda was freely permitted to go. It can be argued that the museum met with Amanda's mother's approval because it was an elite cultural institution that could be characterized as a "female" space. Here, I refer to the internship program as a "social space" unto itself, but since the entire museum is designated as a space for children, notions of traditional femininity that link women to child care would construct the museum in its entirety as a female space. Led by two female educators (one African American and one Southeast Asian) and under the management of a youth coordinator (a Jewish woman), the programs, excursions, and projects in which youth took part could almost all be characterized as "feminine" in that the educators engaged the adolescent female and male interns in activities that have been traditionally connected to women's work. These activities included the bookbinding project mentioned at the start of this chapter (facilitated by a young, White, female artist and bookbinder and involving the use of needle and threat to sew pages into book covers) and designing and sewing costumes for a Mardi Gras procession (overseen by a third-generation West Indian costume designer—a Black woman who creates costumes for the West Indian Day Parade). When I asked one of the educators at BCM if she thought that "feminine" activities such as these might be alienating the adolescent boys in the program, she said, "Well, we have a hard time inviting male guests to work with the boys. They are very confrontational with White men and are particularly turned off if they perceive a visiting teacher to be not masculine enough."

The result was the creation of a social space at BCM in which the teens were taught almost exclusively by women and engaged in many traditionally feminine activities. For female interviewees this meant that BCM was constructed as one of the few public spaces within New York City in general, and Brooklyn more specifically, that was female-centered. The educator's response also suggests that the Museum Team educational program is intentionally racialized as Black and *heterosexualized*. Acknowledging how BCM is heterosexualized assists us in exposing the ways in which patriarchy operates in an ostensibly female-centered space, much in the way that patriarchal power is operative even in the domestic sphere (Alexander 2005: 39). Thus, patriarchy seeps into the "safe" and "female-centered" space of BCM via the heteronormativity that we are presently considering and the male sexual violence that I will turn to shortly. Drawing on ethnographic data relating to Black teenage girls in North Carolina, Mary E. Thomas examines the "social-spatial practices that produce heterosexual space" (M. Thomas 2004: 774). Thomas argues that spatializing practices *produce* sexuality, rather than reflect inherent sexual identities (M. Thomas 2004: 778). In a similar way, the BCM educators' comment suggests that the female-centered, heterosexual space supported at BCM enables the production of heterosexual identities. Interestingly, the boys do not question the femininity of White guest teachers but, rather, are "turned off" by visiting males who are "not masculine enough." This hints at the ways in which Black heteromasculinity functions to define "real" Blackness. Perhaps more significant for our purposes, the heteronormative space created at BCM influences girls as well as boys. While the question I posed to the educator was focused on the effects of "traditionally feminine" activities on the boys, clearly such activities also enable girls' identity processes. Girls more effectively negotiated this female-centered space than did boys. I observed that girls were more successful in the internship program because they "behaved themselves" and got into the educators' good graces. The conversation among China, Nadine, and Kevin about Kareem's dismissal illustrates that the teens were conscious of these social dynamics and that they caused tensions between the two genders. In her study of West Indian, Haitian, and Dominican youth at a New York City public school, Nancy López explores the race and gender disparity in urban education and cites statistical data showing that minority women achieve higher levels of enrollment and matriculation than do minority men at the high school and college levels (López 2003). López reports, "In New York City public schools, home of over a million students, where the majority of the student population is also Black and Latino (86%), more women than men graduated from high school. In 2000, 44% of Latinas graduated compared with 35% of Latino men; for Blacks 49% of women graduated versus 39% of men" (López 2003: 2). In an attempt to ascertain why Caribbean immigrant girls tend to do better in schools than their male counter parts, López asks, "How do race-gender experiences differ in public spaces for men and women?" (López 2003: 5). Participant observation at BCM reveals that racialized and gendered experiences are also operative in teens' extracurricular activities, with girls outperforming boys in this arena, as well. While López is correct to call for more attention to the race-gender disparity in urban public schools, it is also critical to note that this disparity is at play in youths' family and leisure experiences outside school and that extracurricular activities are a vital component not only of the college application process but also of young people's socialization into the adult stage of the life cycle.

The observable gender disparity at BCM—girls outperformed boys and more commonly received praise for good behavior, while male interns were more frequently viewed as scofflaws—echoes findings by anthropologists who have identified a partiality for female children in the Caribbean (Bailey 1988; MacCormack 1988; Sargent and Harris 1998). Sargent and Harris's study of child-rearing practices among low-income families in Kingston, Jamaica, suggests that a Caribbean gender ideology associated with matrifocality is manifest in differing approaches to raising boy and girl children. Their research indicates that "higher mortality and morbidity among boys may be based on widespread cultural values favoring girls" (Sargent and Harris 1998: 204). Mothers in the study more frequently used adjectives such as "bad" and "rude" to describe boys, while ascribing terms such as "loving" and "reliable" to girls (Sargent and Harris 1998: 205). Interestingly for our purposes here, Sargent and Harris make a connection between the careful monitoring of girls' behavior and the greater freedoms granted to boys, and gender disparities on measures such as infant mortality rates and children's body weight and height. In brief, the authors found that preferential treatment of girls resulted in female children receiving better nourishment, being abandoned less frequently than males, and suffering lower infant mortality rates than boys (Sargent and Harris 203: 1998). While we cannot conclude that BCM educators are influenced by the same gender ideologies that shape child rearing in Jamaica, Jamaican immigrant youth were the majority among BCM teens. Moreover, Sargent and Harris's findings have implications for other Anglophone Caribbean nations that share similar gender ideologies and kinship frameworks. The implications here are twofold: (1) Following Sargent and Harris and López, we can glean that differential treatment of boys and girls home and at school also has implications for youngsters' socialization and achievement in nondomestic, extracurricular spheres; (2) West Indian girls, particularly Jamaicans (such as Amanda), enrolled in the program might arrive with advantages (in terms of both their cognitive and physical development and their "soft skills," or ability to communicate effectively with adults) because of preferential treatment by their mothers.

Girls' greater ease in negotiating the BCM internship program can also be attributed to the fact that the program was led by three female authority figures who employed overtly "feminine" pedagogical activities. For all of these reasons, I have characterized the space as provisionally "feminine." However, BCM was constructed not only as a female-centered space; it was also a "safe zone" for male and female youth. In his study of a youth community center in a midwestern American city, Greg Dimitriadis posits that, for Black male teenagers whose families had migrated from larger cities, the community center functioned as a place where boys could stay out of trouble and be "safe" from gang activity (Dimitriadis 2001). Urban, youth-oriented cultural institutions such as BCM, the Flatbush YMCA, and the community center where Dimitriadis worked are often built with the explicit intention of keeping "at-risk" teens off city streets. Although the vast majority of the youth who frequented BCM were characterized as "good kids," their very residence in "inner-city" neighborhoods positioned them as "at-risk" youth in the minds of urban policymakers. BCM and other institutions like it are meant to be safe spaces for youth. While I suggest that, to a limited extent, BCM was such a safe space, it also functioned as a controlling force in which teens like Kareem who exhibited disobedient behavior were dismissed if they did not succumb to the institution's discipline. Ironically, this practice of dismissing disobedient youngsters meant that the youth who perhaps needed the safety of the museum the most—teens who "got into trouble" because they refused to recognize adult authority—were the ones who were not permitted to stay.

BCM staff members remarked that the museum was also a space where teens were safe from having to appear "cool." The boys, however, often sought "coolness," more than the girls. The BCM youth coordinator explained:

> I think it's because they're [the boys] all new in the program. Kids who have grown up in the program know what we're about. We're not about "cool." BCM is a safe place for them where they don't have to act cool. They don't have to be embarrassed about wearing costumes. What happens in BCM stays in BCM.

The educator's comments suggest that girls remain in the program, while the politics of cool subvert BCM's efforts to retain male interns. I observed, on numerous occasions, teenage girls and, to a lesser extent, boys in the program engaged in activities such as wearing costumes, tutoring younger kids, and doing crafts—activities in which image-conscious teens might be less likely to engage in public school settings, where the politics of "cool" do not allow for such acts. Still, on the day of the Mardi Gras celebration, after donning her sequin-studded hat, China pulled the brim way down, obscuring much of her face. "Can you still see my face?" she asked me. Not understanding why she asked the question, I responded truthfully, saying, "Yes." China looked dejected and pulled her hat down even further. China's actions in this situation suggested that even for girls, "silly" and "child-like" activities such as wearing costumes were, at times, in conflict with adolescent desires to appear "cool."

"Our Museum": Space and Place within and beyond BCM

I witnessed the degree to which journeying beyond BCM took teens out of their comfort zones when I accompanied the youth on museum-organized trips around New York City. On a walking tour of Chinatown, the teens, who usually talked and laughed loudly while in the confines of BCM, were reserved and uncomfortable. Although the trip was intentionally planned in conjunction with a tasting festival sponsored by Chinatown restaurants, the teens were hesitant to eat Chinese food in Chinatown (although they frequently ate Chinese take-out in their own neighborhoods). Nadine remarked, "Well, who knows if chicken is really chicken here?" Of course, from the educators' perspective, the whole point of the trip to China-town was to combat such negative stereotypes and to broaden the youths' perceptions of Chinese culture in New York City. Nadine's stereotypical question suggested that she had missed the point of the trip, and it was tempered only by the fact that her physical posture within Chinatown suggested her extreme discomfort. Her comment reveals that the jour-ney from Crown Heights to Chinatown had magically transported Nadine and the others to a place where things were quite possibly not what they appeared to be.

On other occasions, the teens also seemed out of their element in sites such as the Jewish Museum on Manhattan's Upper East Side and, to a lesser extent, at an exhibit on slavery in New York at the New-York Historical Society. During the first trip, the usually quiet and reserved Odette, a four-teen-year-old African American girl, looked around at the exhibit with wide eyes and said, "This is much nicer than *our* museum." Odette was not the only teen to refer to BCM as "our museum." Yet, the way in which she contrasted the Jewish Museum with "*our* museum" alerted me to the teens' social practices of *place making* (Olwig 2007). As anthropologist Karen Fog Olwig reminds us, "A place comes into being, according to Marc Augé [1997 (1992): 43], when it is 'discovered by those who claim it as their own'" (Olwig 2007: 17). Odette and the others *claimed BCM as their own*. In this way, the teens engaged in a rather unexpected act of place making—they were black, predominantly West Indian teens that claimed a museum, of all places, as their comfort zone! This is in stark contrast to stereotypical pop-ular media images that often situate Black teenagers on street corners and basketball courts. Keeping in mind Gupta and Ferguson's insights invoked earlier, by establishing spatial meaning—that is, transforming the muse-um's *space* into *their place*—the BCM teens were taking part in a counter-hegemonic power struggle.

The educators' efforts to expose the teens to "high culture" and to make all of New York City accessible to them were limited by the relative geo-graphic isolation of BCM. BCM was marginalized not only geographically and in terms of its physical appearance but also in terms of the relatively lower status children's museums enjoy in relation to "high-culture" art museums such as the Metropolitan Museum of Art and the Museum of Modern Art.[12] BCM is an hour and a half's subway ride from Manhattan's Upper East Side and the affluent "Museum Mile," the mile-long stretch along Fifth Avenue where many of the city's top tourist-drawing museums are located. BCM's comparatively inaccessible location was viewed as a hindrance, explaining why non-Brooklynites visit the museum less frequently than Brooklynites. School groups routinely frequent the museum, but many of the parents and young children I saw utilizing it were residents of nearby Brooklyn neighborhoods. In this way, the museum functions much like a local community center.

By saying the Jewish Museum was "much nicer," Odette was referring to BCM's rather unsightly appearance as it was undergoing a multimillion-dollar, five-year renovation and expansion. Beginning in 2003, scaffolding, temporary walls, cranes, equipment, and construction workers surrounded the museum. Although the museum remained open during most of the renovation, the temporary walls obscured its entrance and made it difficult for visitors to enter. Therefore, in addition to the geographic barrier that the museum's location represented, there was also a literal physical and spatial barrier to entering the museum. While the staff lamented the unattractiveness of the construction, they looked forward to the time when the museum would re-emerge as a beautiful, state-of-the-art facility. In the meantime, teens complained that they would not be there to see the newer facility, since many of them would have graduated from the program before the renovations were complete.

For the teens, BCM remained a space that was designed explicitly for young children and not for adolescents, not only in terms of exhibits (most of which were geared toward preschool and elementary-school-age children) but also architecturally and in its appointments. The library, for example, where the aforementioned dialogue about Kareem's dismissal took place, housed a collection of books for much younger children and was furnished with chairs and desks designed for very small bodies. Lanky adolescents, both male and female, sat awkwardly in these seats, and boys seemed to feel especially uncomfortable as it was virtually impossible to "look cool" when sitting in a tiny, bright red, plastic chair. In this way, adolescent bodies were worked upon by the design of the institution, in a sense, rendering those bodies docile as the rules of conduct controlled and infantilized the teens (Foucault 1975). This meant that even within *their museum*, the teens had difficulty finding *their place*.

Finding Safety amid Violent Conflict:
Blacks and Hasidim in Crown Heights

It is also telling that Odette's proclamation that "This is much nicer than *our* museum" involved a comparison to the Jewish Museum in Manhattan. For the teens, frequenting BCM is also positioned against a recent history of animosity between Blacks and Hasidic Jews, of which some of the youth may only have an imaginary recollection but of which they are reminded through the museum's efforts to assuage the remnants of those tensions. In 1991, in Crown Heights, a Hasidic driver in the Lubavitch Grand Rabbi's motorcade struck and killed a seven-year-old second-generation Guyanese boy named Gavin Cato. While the driver, Yosef Lifsh, was swiftly evacuated by a Jewish ambulance service, Gavin Cato remained pinned under the car. The crowd of Cato's neighbors gathered at the scene felt that the Jewish driver had received prompt medical attention while the boy was left to die. Subsequently, Yankel Rosenbaum, an Australian Orthodox Jew, was stabbed to death by a group of Black residents. These two events and the riots that occurred from August 19 to August 22 are often referenced as defining moments in interethnic relations in Crown Heights. Significantly, much of the media coverage described Cato as a "Black boy" rather than as a West Indian immigrant and neglected to mention that one of the individuals convicted of stabbing Rosenbaum was sixteen years old at the time of the incident. These omissions gloss over the ways in which West Indian youth, in particular, are centrally connected to interethnic conflicts in the neighborhood. Moreover, during the riots, Black residents looted seven Crown Heights businesses, three owned by Korean Americans, one owned by an Arab American, and three owned by Jews (Shapiro 2006: xii). Such details suggest that, although framed as an anti-Semitic attack, the riots were arguably an attempt by Crown Heights Blacks to forcefully claim the public/consumer sphere (Shapiro 2006: xiii).[13]

The violence surrounding Cato's death was not, however, the first case of conflict between Crown Heights's Hasidim and its Black population. Thousands of Hasidim, many of whom were Lubavitchers, arrived in Crown Heights as Holocaust refugees (Goldschmidt 2002). They had chosen the neighborhood because of its high percentage of Jews; however, the Hasidim were visibly different from their secular neighbors, who did not wear black coats. In the 1940s and 1950s, the Crown Heights African American and West Indian populations quadrupled, concomitant with the arrival of the Hasidim. During the subsequent decades, the demographic shifts that created the

"Black inner city" saw most secular Jews leaving Crown Heights and its Black population, including a huge influx of Afro-Caribbean immigrants, rising to 70 percent by 1970 (Goldschmidt 2002). Researchers trace tensions between Crown Heights' Blacks and Hasidim to the late 1970s, when Hasidim beat a sixteen-year-old Black boy in the neighborhood (Goldschmidt 2002: 218). Black leaders attributed the attack to neighborhood patrols organized by the Hasidim (Goldschmidt 2002: 218). Thus, decades-old interethnic wounds were reopened with Cato's death and the subsequent violence.

Although the historian Edward Shapiro argues that there were no "additional serious incidents," conflicts continued to surface in recent times, with local news media reporting on numerous "hate crimes" between Blacks and Hasidim (Shapiro 2006: xiii). In 2008, for example, a number of violent crimes involved Blacks and Hasidim in the neighborhood. The year began with a sixteen-year-old yeshiva student and Lubavitch Hasid, Samuel Balkany, reporting that he had been brutally attacked by five Black teens who shouted, "Little Jew boy, you think you own this neighborhood."[14] Balkany's wounds included a gash in his head that required a medical staple. In April 2008, a Black community college student, twenty-year-old Andrew Charles, was reportedly assaulted by two Hasidic boys, one of whom pepper-sprayed Charles as he rode past him on a bike at the corner of Albany and President Streets.[15] According to a witness, Charles suffered another attack moments later when a Hasidic man in traditional dress emerged from an SUV driven by another Hasid and struck Charles with a nightstick. As with the 1978 incident, Black community leaders accused the Hasidic community patrol of the crime. Then, in May 2008, hundreds of Hasidim protested in the streets of Crown Heights when two Black men reportedly assaulted a sixteen-year-old Jewish boy and took the youth's bicycle, money, and cell phone.[16]

Media representations (local television, newspaper, and online sources) of each of these incidents usually left the ethnicity (African American, West Indian, or African) of Black individuals involved unspecified. However, the high percentage of West Indians in Crown Heights suggests that at least some of the Blacks involved were West Indian youth. Each incident involved male youths negotiating the public boundaries between Blacks and Hasidim in Crown Heights.[17] The 1991 conflicts provide an excellent starting point for parsing how West Indian identity was glossed as "Black" and for interrogating how contemporary West Indian and African American youth position their feelings about Hasidic Jews against notions of belonging and an imaginary "memory" of the early 1990s. These conflicts also speak to an additional spatial dilemma; BCM is precariously situated within Crown Heights, a community symbolically and literally divided by Eastern Parkway, a busy expressway, on one side of which resides the predominantly Hasidic Jewish community and on the other the Black West Indians. BCM educators negotiate this divide as they attempt to cultivate their young charges. BCM youth and educators offer insights that complicate the ways in which ethnic, racial, class and age-based identities continue to collide in Crown Heights.

After the teenage yeshiva student Samuel Balkany was attacked, a news conference with community and political leaders was held at the newly built Jewish Children's Museum, just a few blocks away from BCM, on the other side of Eastern Parkway. This conference was indicative of the ways in which the Jewish Children's Museum was seen as a "safe place" for Hasidim, as BCM was for Blacks on the West Indian side of Crown Heights. Tensions between BCM and the Jewish Children's Museum were evident in how BCM staff members talked about the new museum. In the summer of 2005, after a three-year absence, I remarked to a BCM educator that the modern, comparatively upscale Jewish Children's Museum (JCM) seemed to spring up quickly. The BCM educator responded, "We haven't been there [to JCM] yet. There's a bit of tension—it's too bad. But some of our staff are trying to collaborate with them." I learned that some staffers saw the very construction of JCM as an antagonistic act. One BCM educator asked, "Isn't the Brooklyn Children's Museum for *all* of Brooklyn's children?" The answer to this question appears to be "no" when we consider that the BCM afterschool program is overwhelmingly frequented by Black West Indian youth, along with a lesser number of African Americans and a few Latinos. Even in light of such efforts as the well-attended annual Sukkot festival (celebrating the Jewish holiday that takes place soon after Yom Kippur), which are designed to cater to Crown Heights's Jewish residents, BCM is seen as a place for Blacks. This meant that, although some BCM teens traversed several Hasidic residential streets as they traveled to and from the museum, they had no prolonged face-to-face encounters with their Hasidic neighbors. Kelly, the daughter of an African American woman and a Jamaican man, summed it up when I asked how she would characterize the relationship between West Indians and Hasidic Jews in Crown Heights:

I don't know. I've never really encountered it myself. But, you know, I walk my way, they walk theirs and we're all happy. I know they get really unhappy when the [West Indian] Labor Day Parade happens. That's what my mom says, anyway.

Kelly, like the other teens, was too young to remember the riots that ensued after Gavin Cato's death. The resurgent conflicts between Hasidic and Black young men did not directly touch any of the BCM youth with whom I worked. Like Kelly, many of the BCM boys avoided the neighborhood streets on which Hasidim resided, a strategy facilitated by the clustering of ethnic shops catering to West Indians and Hasidim in separate parts of the neighborhood. And, like Kelly, even if they were not directly connected to instances of violent conflict, many of the teens had learned from the news media and from their parents that there was tension between the West Indians and the Hasidim. The teens' most substantial exposure to Jewish identity, however, came from their interactions with BCM educators. All three of the BCM educators, including the Jewish American woman named Rebecca, were extremely well liked by the teens. Rebecca's African heritage (her father was from North Africa) and the fact that she was not an Orthodox Jew cast her in a light different from that in which the Hasidim living in Crown Heights were seen. And the BCM educators strove to expand the youths' worldviews in all respects, including their understanding of Jewish culture. To that end, the African American educator, Kiara, gave a special lecture on the Holocaust and chaperoned the teens on our trip to the Jewish Museum in Manhattan (not to be confused with the nearby Jewish Children's Museum in Crown Heights). I accompanied the youth on the Jewish Museum trip and, afterward, asked Nadine if visiting that museum had changed her impression of Jews:

> I was kind of more open when I heard about the situation [the Holocaust], but what really amazed me is that honestly, seeing people that are at that museum [the Jewish Museum] that are Jewish and you won't know that they're Jewish. The people [there] that are Jewish, they don't dress like the Jewish people I'm used to seeing [in Crown Heights]. Somebody really is Jewish—it's not really where it's just this group of people because they wear this, and they do this—that's why they're Jewish. It opened my mind to think that—I just found out that there was even Black Jewish people. It really opened my mind not really about the Jewish people here, but knowing other people and stop judging them. . . . I'd look at a Black person and usually if they don't have on something saying that they're Muslim or something, I'm like, hey, they're Christian or they just don't go to church before I think, you know what, they may be Jewish even. So I think that really, more—more so, more than the Jewish community here, I'm more— opened my mind about other people that may be Jewish. I still think about it, "Wow, what if that person I'm sitting next to on the train"—because

before I was like, [skinning her upper lip] "Jewish people?" And now I'm like, [with a pleased expression] "Oh." Really learning about their culture, learning about the things that they went through and everything really opened my mind about Jewish people. I like it a lot.

When Nadine ends her remarks by saying, "I like it a lot," she refers to enjoying having gained newfound knowledge about Jewish history and culture. It is telling that she uses a euphemism, "the situation," which distances her from the Holocaust. Interestingly, she indicates that her newly acquired knowledge did not really change her impression of Crown Heights Hasidim; she intimates that she still sees them as different because of their distinctive dress and customs. However, she now realizes that not all Jews dress the same. Nadine's comments also speak to the processes by which she and her peers have learned to distinguish between different Black ethnic groups. Here, because our conversation was focused on Jews, whom she sees as a religious group, she unpacks the social significance of distinctive dress to hypothesize that she could be in the company of a Black Jew without knowing it.[18] Interestingly, Nadine alludes to dress as an important ethnic marker. Especially for second-generation West Indian teens who do not speak in West Indian patois, fashion has become a key way of asserting West Indian identity, of distinguishing between African Americans and West Indians and of intra-West Indian differentiation (i.e., knowing an individual is Jamaican, rather than Trinidadian). Nadine and her peers rely on subtle identifiers such as national flag stickers on notebooks, flag key chains, and distinctively West Indian gold bangles to make quick assessments of who is African American and who is West Indian. In her comments about realizing that not all Jews wear distinctive dress, she interrogates her own ideas about religious difference among Blacks and realizes that, just as it is for Jews, religious identity is not observable if the individual does not "have something on saying they're Muslim," for example.

Halloween and 6/6/6: Real-Life Police and Gang Violence

Although calming West Indian/Hasidic relations loomed large among the goals of their educators, BCM teens worried most about confrontations with the police and with local gangs, not about violent conflicts with Hasidim. In the horror genre, both in movies and on television, the police cannot help you, adolescence proves to be the deadliest stage of the life cycle, and Black characters, in the rare instances when they are given screen time, are always killed first.[19] Unfortunately, such representational conventions also proved to be meaningful in the teens' real-life experiences and the girls' acts of talking back during our outing to *The Omen* can be read as a critical engagement with both filmic and actual scenarios in which violence is perpetrated. Police brutality against Black men characterizes Flatbush and Crown Heights as much as does the history of conflict between Hasidim and Blacks. Cases such as the nationally publicized brutal beating of a Haitian immigrant, Abner Louima, in 1997 by police officers who arrested him at a Caribbean nightclub on Flatbush Avenue still resonated with the boys. Boys frequently told stories of being harassed by neighborhood cops, and both genders distrusted the police.[20] Mothers and educators voiced constant worries about the museum's boys being racially profiled, and one mom asserted that she was more apprehensive about her daughter witnessing the violent treatment of Black men on the local nightly news than about the threat of school violence. In light of the constant risk of police violence, BCM served as a safe haven for these young men.

In addition to fear of the police, both boys and girls dreaded gang-related violence from turf wars between the Bloods and the Crips, who, according to the teens, were a regular presence when darkness fell on the streets surrounding BCM. Adolescent girls and boys told me that they stayed home from school and from BCM on Halloween because, in an example of life imitating horror, the Bloods and the Crips preyed on uninitiated teens on the holiday. On June 6, 2006, arriving at BCM at my usual time of about 3:15 p.m., I was surprised to find a number of the teens well entrenched in their duties, having been dismissed from school after only a half day. The group reported that their public high school (located not far from BCM) had dismissed the student body early because of rumors of "666" (6/06/06) violence between the Bloods and the Crips. Initially, the school sent out decoy flyers to students stating that classes would end at the usual time, 3:25 p.m., on June 6; then, when the date arrived, students were unexpectedly sent home after a half-day. In this way, the school administrators fooled gang organizers and avoided violence upon dismissal. When I asked a BCM educator about the threat of gang violence, she dismissed the teens as looking for excuses not to show up for work, noting that a girl had called her earlier that day to say that her grandmother would not let her out of the house because of the danger of a 6/06/06 attack. The rift I observed that day, with museum educators shrugging off the threat of gang violence as false and teens expressing legitimate terror, surfaced repeatedly around the issue of gangs. Years later, when I spoke with Amanda after she had graduated from high school, she voiced trepidation about her fifteen-year-old cousin, who now worked as a BCM intern. Amanda remarked, "All the BCM administrators live in the suburbs, and they clear out of there by 4 p.m. to beat rush-hour traffic. They're not leaving the museum at nine o'clock, when my little cousin is leaving after nighttime activities. She's only fifteen, and Crips *own* those streets at night." News reports support the teens' assessment of gang activity near BCM. A 2010 *New York Times* article, for example, reported that a twenty-one-year-old man was arrested in April in connection with shooting four teenage boys from the vantage point of a rooftop on Franklin Avenue in Crown Heights. The man was also held in connection with another Crown Heights shooting in October of that year in which a teenager was paralyzed. According to the *Times*, Police Commissioner Raymond Kelly said the suspect was a member of the Bloods and that the victims were Crips gang members (Rivera 2010).

Head Bitch in Charge: Confronting Sexual Violence

Thus, the safety both boys and girls enjoyed at BCM was in contrast to the dangers to which they were exposed outside the museum. As previously mentioned, for girls, city streets are often characterized as dangerous places. Of course, violent crimes against girls and women occur not only on city streets but also on public transportation and in homes, businesses, and schools within and beyond city limits. Still, parents who see urban spaces as especially menacing for girls react to the higher reports of violent crimes in cities. Streetwise and technology-savvy girls, however, do have the power to defend themselves, as one quick-thinking New York City seventeen-year-old girl did in October 2010 when an adult male sexually assaulted her on a Brooklyn subway. The girl took a picture of the man with her cell phone, and later, the police used the image to help apprehend the culprit. The incident, and others like it, were reported in the *New York Post*.[21] For girls in the program, the public spaces of the street and the subway represented constant threats such as the one experienced by this seventeen-year-old, while the museum served as a refuge.

BCM's ability to provide a safe space for West Indian and African American adolescents has been jeopardized, however, by sociostructural factors such as male sexual harassment and by public educational policies. A member of the BCM staff revealed that an adult male BCM employee who interacted with adolescents as they carried out their noneducational duties had been fired for sexually harassing a female adolescent intern. At first, I was not privy to the details of this incident—not surprisingly, since it was well known that I was writing a book about the BCM youth, and staffers were cautious about compromising the confidentiality of the individuals involved. After learning that the incident had taken place, I was forced to call into question the extent to which BCM could be accurately characterized as a "safe space" for girls. I also had to balance ethnical concerns against a desire to get to the bottom of things.

I had to tread very carefully, and my greatest concern was to avoid jeopardizing the privacy of the teenage girl involved. Over a year after the sexual harassment incident occurred, I asked some of the girls about it on a lunch outing with one intern and two alumni who were at that time enrolled in local colleges. The two alumni, Joanna and her cousin Maya, had returned to BCM for the summer to work as program assistants. The current intern, Naomi, had struck up a friendship with the two older girls and was eager to join us for lunch. We set out when the program took a break, with me offering to buy the girls lunch at Ali's, a popular Trinidadian-owned roti shop. It was a humid day at the end of August, and the four of us walked slowly along St. Marks Avenue, heading toward the busy thoroughfare that is Nostrand Avenue. We meandered along, both because of the heat and because Naomi had made the mistake of wearing ankle socks with her brand-new black leather high-top Nikes; her ankles were so badly bruised that she limped, forcing us to stop at a ninety-nine-cent store so that she could purchase thicker socks. After Naomi selected a pair of purple-and-white-striped shin-length sweat socks that perfectly matched her outfit, we continued on to the roti shop.

Joanna, a pretty girl with long, light brown hair, wore a bright pink tee shirt depicting a photograph of three women dressed in stilettos, lingerie, and thigh-high stockings with garter belts. The photograph pictured the women from the waist down, one woman bending provocatively with her rear end facing the camera. The caption read "Head bitch in charge." As we walked along Nostrand, a young man on the sidewalk nodded, eyeing Joanna from head to toe, and said, "Hey, Jo, what's up?" Joanna nodded back, responding, "Nothin' much." But, once we were no longer within earshot of the man, who appeared to be in his mid-twenties, Joanna revealed that she had "never seen him before in [her] life." Adding, "He's probably a friend of my ex." The coolness with which Joanna regarded the man (also displayed earlier when she introduced the "Kids Crew" members to Isis, the slithery python) suggested that, as her tee shirt asserted, she was "the head bitch in charge." Joanna walked slightly ahead of the three of us, and, with Naomi still limping from her bruised ankles, Jo became the head of a motley crew. Her coolness and self-assurance, coupled with her provocative shirt, brought my mind back to the sexual harassment incident several months prior, and I asked the three girls what had gone on. Joanna and Maya nodded know-

Joanna shows off her tee shirt. Photo by the author.

ingly. Joanna identified Kelly as the girl who had accused a staffer of sexually harassing her. When I asked for additional details, Joanna quickly and matter-of-factly blurted out, "It wasn't true! She lied!" Naomi, who had not been enrolled in the program at the time, interjected, "How do you know?" Joanna responded, "Because she said so! She lied about the whole thing! After she came out and accused him, she then took it all back. She admitted she did it for attention." According to Joanna, after Kelly recanted her story, the museum invited the accused employee back to work, but he declined. Joanna added that Kelly had flirted with the accused man and that he was a "nice guy who didn't bother nobody." Upon retelling the story, Joanna launched into an anecdote about a similar incident that had occurred at the Catholic high school she had attended:

> JOANNA: One of the teachers would talk to girls, and then he dated some of them after they graduated. Everybody knew he would talk to girls, but then they [the school administration] found out he was with this girl 'cause they found a text message he sent to her phone saying stuff like, "You're so sexy." They fired him and charged him with statutory rape, but I don't see that as rape. She consented.

NAOMI: But she wasn't old enough to say what was right. If she's under eighteen and he's over, it's statutory rape.

JOANNA: [Looking around] Then all these niggers on this street right now would have to be arrested for statutory rape because they all be with girls under eighteen!

NAOMI: [Glancing sideways] I'd be okay with that, if a lot of these men were arrested.

Joanna's reaction harkens back to some of Jody Miller's conclusions in her study of sexual violence against African American young women in a poverty-stricken section of St. Louis, Missouri (J. Miller 2008). In viewing Kelly's victimization as her own fault, Joanna suggests that it was the result of a flaw in Kelly's character. There is no indication from Joanna's reaction that an adult male staff member has greater authority than a fifteen-year-old female intern and that it was the responsibility of the staff member, as an adult, to deem any flirtatious interactions inappropriate. Still, unlike the unfortunate girls in Miller's study, Kelly had access to a group of professional adults who acted quickly and decisively to remove the male staff member. In this way, BCM made good on its goal of keeping girls and teens "safe." Still, the fact that Kelly subsequently recanted her accusation raises the question of whether peer disapproval influenced her to "take it all back" and whether BCM was correct in offering to rehire the accused man. The fact that peers like Joanna failed to understand why the male staff member had to be fired suggests that the museum missed an important "teaching moment," one in which educators might have worked to dispel the gendered stereotypes I heard from a number of teens who claimed that Kelly "asked for it" by dressing in tight-fitting clothing and enticing the male staffer. Miller rightfully notes that such "victim-blaming views have real consequences for how violence and its aftermath are handled, often including increased danger for girls" (Peterson in Miller 2008: xi).

For poised, self-possessed, and self-proclaimed "head bitches in charge," such as Joanna, sexual power could be successfully negotiated. Still, when Joanna asserted that "all these niggers . . . be with girls under eighteen," she spoke to the kinds of racialized and gendered victimization that Miller documents. This last remark, on the heels of a moment in which a stranger on the sidewalk had objectified her, revealed a contradictory vulnerability. On the one hand, Joanna had kept her cool when the young man checked her out; but, on the other hand, by saying, "then all these niggers on this street right now would be arrested," she highlighted the perils adolescent girls face as they confront advances from adult men. Here was another critical moment in which the street and the body became arenas of conflict. I encountered girls with varying abilities to manage these conflicts. A fearless, sophisticated, and experienced girl like Joanna, who went on to study criminal justice in college, seemed to masterfully negotiate sexual advances. And "brainy" girls like Naomi exhibited the knowledge to know what was and was not inappropriate behavior for adult authority figures. But I wondered how a self-conscious girl such Kelly, the one who made the accusation, faired in the face of gendered victimization. Before physically developing into a curvaceous adolescent, Kelly had been teased for being fat as a preteen. Having spent years at BCM she blended in and seemed to get along with the others at first glance. But the fact that Joanna said she "did it for attention" positioned Kelly as an outsider. How could the museum keep all of its girls safe even within its confines? What had really transpired between Kelly and the male staffer? Was BCM right or wrong if it offered to restore the fired employee to his former position? While I initially learned about the incident from a BCM staff member, when I subsequently asked an administrator whether BCM girls had experienced any sexual harassment from staff, the administrator said no. Since the administrator worked only indirectly with the teens (the teen educators reported to the administrator), it was possible that the administrator did not know about the incident. It is also possible that she was reluctant to discuss the incident with me for fear that it would jeopardize the Museum Team program. Yet, the incident provokes questions beyond the involvement of BCM, its youth, and its staff. Such examples of sexual harassment and the ways in which BCM teens blamed Kelly point to critical imperatives for schools, leisure institutions, places that employ adolescents, and parents to work in concert to offer training and counseling on the prevention of sexual harassment.

School Time Vs. Museum Time

Learning about the sexual harassment incident influenced me to carefully consider how BCM's role as a "safe space" was contingent and, at times, precarious. The museum's ability to maintain a safe haven for girls *and* boys was also jeopardized when the New York City Department of Education, in an effort to provide additional tutoring for standardized tests, lengthened the school day. Although the school day was extended by only thirty-seven minutes, if we keep in mind BCM's geographic location, coupled with the fact that the afterschool program runs from approximately 3:15 to 6:00 p.m., a thirty-seven minute delay of teens' arrival is significant, if not crippling to the program. This temporal barrier to attending BCM can be interpreted as one of the many ideological youthscapes that complicate the youngsters' lives. Moreover, extending the day by precisely thirty-seven minutes (as opposed to forty minutes) speaks to the notions of postmodern theorist David Harvey, for whom the construction and redefinition of time is a means of hegemonic control (Harvey 1990).[22] Although ostensibly presented as an aid to public school students with learning difficulties, the extended school day threatens afterschool programs such as BCM, which, arguably, are more beneficial to urban youth. Unlike the New York City Department of Education's extended school-day program, BCM provides college preparation and standardized test tutoring by individuals specially trained to administer these services.[23] Extending the school day for public school attendees and not for private school children allows private school students to enjoy extracurricular programs and actively denies these freedoms to largely minority public school pupils. Contextualizing the ways in which public schools police minority students' freedoms, especially as they relate to consumer culture and leisure time, reveals the complex ways in which the entrenched social inequalities of the public sphere make their way into the lessons learned at school. Attention to the New York City Department of Education's regulatory practices points to critical imperatives that govern the lives of urban youth of color.

The Alternet: Ringtones, Rhetoric and the Racialization of Youth Culture

In August 2008, on the last day of the Brooklyn Children's Museum summer program, the teens congregated during the informal snack time in an area of the museum where they could use computers and were free to use their cell phones for texting and playing music. Having ended their programs for the day, the eighth and ninth graders milled about, waiting for their turns on the computers (there were twelve teens but only six computers). I sat at a table with James, a second-generation Trinidadian, and two girls, Allison, whose parents were born in Jamaica, and Caroline, an African American whose family had relocated from New Orleans after Hurricane Katrina. James held up his cell phone and began taking pictures of Allison.

ALLISON: Delete that! I don't know where it will end up!
JAMES: I'll put it on the "Alternet"!
ALLISON: [laughing] The "Alternet"?!
JAMES: Yeah [laughing]. That's what my grandma calls the Internet!

The three teens and I cracked up. Later, though, as I reflected on their use of technological devices such as cell phones, iPods, and computers and on the ways in which the teens' access to such devices was limited and controlled both by their economic circumstances and their public schools' strict policing of students, I began to think of James's grandmother's misnomer, "the Alternet," as a fitting moniker for the alternative meanings attached to Black teenagers' use of cell phones and other technological devices. The museum became an alternative space, separate from the low-income realities of home and the militaristic control of school, where they relished limited access to these devices and to the freedom to play on the "Alternet."

Exploring the meanings attached to minority youths' cell phone usage in school sheds light on popular and public policy discourses that characterize urban teenagers of color as "problem youth." BCM teens' very residence in "inner-city" neighborhoods positions them as "at risk" in political and educational policy discourses. Public educational policies present minority youths' use of cell phones as "dangerous" threats to school safety and student achievement. While BCM educators allow limited use of mobile phones, the museum also attempts to keep its confines "safe" from the "corruption" of African American hip-hop music played on cell phones. In this section, we will analyze youth culture alongside prevalent rhetoric surrounding race, gender identity, and educational policies. Teens use phones to play American and West Indian music inside the confines of BCM, thereby resisting adult authority, fostering cross-cultural exchange between West Indians and African Americans, and claiming access to a consumer culture that more economically privileged teens take for granted. Cell phone usage serves as a springboard from which to critique broader Department of Education policies that threaten minority youths' abilities to enjoy extracurricular programs.

Off the Hook: Contextualizing the Ban on Cell Phones

New York City's ban on the use of cell phones in public schools is more than twenty years old, but in 2006, when the city tightened its laws to prohibit bringing cell phones onto school property, parents and civil rights groups mobilized to file lawsuits against the city (Gewertz 2006). The city's policies regarding cell phones on school property are among the strictest in the country, matched only by those in Detroit and Philadelphia. Most districts prohibit using phones at school but allow phones to be brought onto school premises. According to an *Education Week* article, when

Mayor Michael Bloomberg and New York City Department of Education (NYC DOE) chancellor Joel Klein cracked down on cell phones in schools and installed metal detectors for unannounced searches as part of a new school safety policy, within two weeks, the scanners detected "a dozen or so knives, some box cutters, a gun and more than 800 cell phones, which were confiscated" (Cooper and Lee 2006: 43). Considering that more than one million students attend New York City schools, the number of "illegal" items found is actually rather low.

As a teacher, I understand the learning distractions that cell phones can present. Yet, many of the city's principals and teachers disregarded the DOE's initial ban, choosing instead to implement their own practical solutions to the distracting presence of cell phones. In fact, in response to Bloomberg's and Chancellor Klein's ban, the United Federation of Teachers (UFT) voted in favor of *permitting* cell phones in schools. The UFT reportedly cited the usefulness of cell phones as "a parental lifeline" and agreed with the ban on the use of cell phones in schools but did not concur with barring them from school buildings (Cooper and Lee 2006: 44). Of the more than one million students in New York City public schools, 86 percent are Black or Latino (López 2003:2). As education scholars such as Jonathan Kozol have documented extensively, New York City's public schools are predominantly minority and poor, while the city's more affluent White children usually attend private schools (Kozol 2005). The ban on cell phones in public schools can therefore be seen as essentially a restriction on minority students' rights to personal property. It is useful to contextualize Bloomberg's draconian approach to mobile phones as it relates to more general policies affecting the city's largely minority public school population, which has been systematically criminalized and subject to strict policing. As evidenced by the UFT vote, Bloomberg's approach is in contrast to the views of educators most directly involved in students' daily learning.

The NYC DOE policy on cell phones and its implementation of scanning devices such as metal detectors can be seen as part and parcel of a general approach that criminalizes public school students, limiting their social freedoms and their access to the same consumer products and technological devices that more affluent, private school, and suburban teens take for granted. In her book *Hopeful Girls, Troubled Boys: Race and Gender Disparity in Urban Education*, Nancy López documents the damaging effects of aggressive policing in public schools on minority students' educational orientation. López writes:

In effect, overcrowding and the subsequent emphasis on social control by security personnel are turning urban public high schools, which are supposed to be institutions of learning, into spaces in which urban low-income second-generation Dominican youth, particularly young men, are humiliated and criminalized through searches and other demeaning encounters, as well as the eminent threat of physical violence (López 2003: 75).

López adds that these forms of control result in minority students being treated as "problem students" by school authorities. She details how public school students face daily airport-style security as they enter schools; there is strict policing of their personal property and appearance (many are required to wear uniforms and face penalties if they don't comply), and extra security measures are taken in overcrowded schools in which spillover classrooms are housed in trailers and security guards escort students between annexes and the main school building. Kozol paints a similar picture, uncovering how, rather than employing creative lesson plans, public school teachers "embraced a pedagogy of direct command and absolute control" (Kozol 2005: 64). This approach employs "scripted rote-and-drill curricula" and takes cues from disciplinary practices found in penal institutions and drug rehabilitation programs (Kozol 2005: 64–65). The vast majority of the youth with whom I worked at BCM attended public schools throughout New York City, and many recounted stories similar to those told by the students cited in López's and Kozol's studies.

The Digital Divide: Cell Phones "Back Home"

Contemporary adolescents living in disparate locals from New York City to Soweto are often characterized as "constantly plugged in" to technological devices such as cellular phones, iPods, and computers. Horst and Miller's anthropological study of low-income Jamaicans' uses of cell phones (part of a four-country study that also covered Ghana, India, and South Africa) offers valuable insights not only into the implications of new technologies for Caribbean youth but also for comprehending the significance of these technologies in relation to global development. These scholars alert us to the particularities of how cell phones are used globally, arguing that the notion of the "digital divide," or the "possible tendency of new technologies to exacerbate differences between the rich and the poor," should be problematized, especially from the perspective of the Caribbean region, where the cell phone is a ubiquitous device (Horst and Miller 2006: 2). By 2004, two million out of the total population of 2.7 million Jamaicans had subscriptions to cell phones (Horst and Miller 2006: 19). Writing about the broader global context, Horst and Miller compare the accessibility of the cell phone to the relative inaccessibility of the Internet:

> While most low-income populations (in effect the bulk of the world's population) still experience [the Internet] as a distant and curious phenomenon, the cell phone mushrooms up from inside mud-brick shacks and under corrugated iron sheet roofing to become an insistent and active presence that has us rushing to even acknowledge, let alone appreciate (Horst and Miller 2006: 11).

Horst and Miller's findings are crucial for understanding how Brooklyn's West Indian youth relate to the cell phone. For youth born in the West Indies, especially for Jamaican youngsters, the cell phone has long been a central part of daily life. While many rural Jamaicans do not have landlines, cell phones are available even to very poor people who often receive used phones as gifts when wealthier relatives get new phones (Horst and Miller 2006). And, once an individual has a cell phone, other devices such as watches and computers are often no longer necessary. Horst and Miller document how even poor Jamaican school children are able to afford cell phones by utilizing pay-as-you-go phone cards and by making sacrifices such as skipping lunch in order to afford the cards. Phones are commonplace in Jamaican schools; although a few schools have placed limits on cell phone usage, according to Miller and Horst, most schools permit phones on the premises and students and teachers alike utilize their phones throughout the day.

Moral Panics: Class-Based and Racialized Rhetoric

While there *are* cell phone related crimes in Jamaica, West Indian teens who enter the New York City school system encounter a very different attitude toward cell phones, where views on the devices are not framed around the "development" and "underdevelopment" discourses problematized by Horst and Miller. In the United States, the moral panics surrounding adolescents' use of cell phones employ dramatically distinct rhetoric when addressed to urban youth of color rather than privileged private school students and White suburban youth. Part of this discourse, as it relates to suburban youth, is centered on the dangers of texting. A 2009 Nielsen study on teens and media found a 56 percent increase in teen texting rates in the previous two years, with the "average teen" currently sending 2,899 texts per month or 97 texts daily (Burrell 2009: 25). The Pew Internet and American Life Project reports that wealthier teens are more likely to own cell phones and "nearly two-thirds (63%) of all teens from households earning more than $75,000 annually text every day, while 43% of teens from families that earn less than $30,000 text daily."[24] Clearly, privileged teens have greater access to cell phones than do the predominantly minority students enrolled in New York City public schools. However, the discourses surrounding the dangers of cell phones for suburban teens center not on the devices as threats to school safety and blights to educational success but rather on the issues of driving hazards and sleep deprivation. A November 2009 *Chicago Tribune* article, for example, argued that late-night texting results in sleeping problems for teenagers who text way into the night (Burrell 2009). An October 2009 CNN report titled "Crash Course in Texting Risks" portrayed White Oklahoma City teen drivers going through an obstacle course on a closed driving track to demonstrate the dangers of texting while driving.[25] Middle-class children are carrying cell phones at increasingly younger ages, and, while some of the rhetoric surrounding their use of cells centers on the potential health dangers of using these devices, for privileged youth cell phones are also seen as valuable safety tools, with parents purchasing phones explicitly designed to track younger children. These concerns are in sharp contrast to the rhetoric surrounding urban youth and cell phones, which centers primarily on the unauthorized use of phones in public schools.

While cell phones are seen as physical hazards to inexperienced suburban teen drivers and are feared to keep privileged teens from getting a good night's rest, the rhetoric rationalizing Mayor Bloomberg's and Chancellor Klein's ban includes an insistence that "cell phones are a distraction and are used to cheat, take inappropriate photos in bathrooms and organize gang rendezvous."[26] An article in *Education Week* also posited that students might use cell phones to videotape school staff acting inappropriately or to report perceived misconduct to parents during the school day, resulting in angry parents showing up to chastise staff or faculty before school officials had a chance to solve disputes (Cooper and Lee 2006: 44). This last rationale is especially troubling when we consider two factors: (1) The UFT actually voted against banning phones, demonstrating that the teachers did not perceive a threat to their authority; (2) New York City has a history of police brutality against minority men, and the strong police and security presence in schools has subjected male teens of color, in particular, to discrimination and harassment; a camera-equipped cell phone is one of few protections youth might have against racialized discrimination.

Rather than viewing them as potentially dangerous weapons, educators have seen cell phones in schools on the one hand as nuisances that should be turned off during class and on the other hand as possible pedagogical tools. Scholars in Great Britain, for example, conducted a study that tracked 331 teens in schools whose teachers incorporated cell phones with Internet access into lesson plans and found that students used phones to "create short movies, set homework reminders, record their teacher' readings of poems, time experiments via phone stopwatches, access relevant websites, and transfer electronic files between school and home" (Docksai 2009: 10). Canadian teachers cited similar positive usages (Docksai 2009: 10). And, in Jamaica, Horst and Miller cast the cell phone as an ambiguous device; although school children used it primarily to cultivate social relationships it also facilitated obtaining missed assignments and enabled teachers to communicate with parents (many of whom do not have landlines) about homework, school trips and disciplinary problems (Horst and Miller 2006: 147–150). In the hands of New York City's public school students, however, the devices have been overwhelmingly characterized as illegal contraband that must be confiscated along with guns, knives, and box cutters.

As recently as September 2009, the *New York Post's* online edition posted a story about Mayor Bloomberg's position on cell phones that was headlined "Mike's Message on School Cellphone 'Danger'" (Seifman 2009: n.p.). In the article, which summarized Bloomberg's weekly radio show, the mayor characterized cell phones as "a distraction that can harm a student's chances for advancing in life" (Seifman 2009: n.p.). The mayor is quoted as saying, "I suppose you could make the case that cell phones, you know, are hurting long term. . . . In the end, how well the child does in school is going to be a big factor in how well they do in the real world for the rest of their lives" (Seifman 2009, n.p.). Rather than focusing on the many disadvantages the city's low-income public school students face, including overcrowded classrooms, underpaid teachers, lack of access to computers and other learning tools, "teaching for the test" pedagogical approaches, and prison-style security measures, here Bloomberg argues that cell phones hinder students' chances for success. This reasoning is part of a broader discourse that pathologizes minority youths' consumption and racializes elements of popular culture as "corruptive." Bloomberg is severe enough in his position on cell phones in public schools to long for the ability to overturn students' civil rights and to jam their cell phone signals in schools, rendering the devices useless. He is quoted as saying: "Just put [a cell phone jamming technology] in every school, and even if the kid carried the cell phone in, they couldn't use it during the day. . . . And I'd love to do that . . . but I'm told that technology is illegal."[27]

Interpreting Racialization at BCM

I considered Bloomberg's rhetoric as I watched the BCM teens use their phones during the afterschool program. The analyses offered in this section demonstrate how the popular and educational policy discourses that portray minority students as "combat consumers"—which a decade ago centered around their being willing to kill each other for expensive sneakers and now entails their using cell phones as lethal weapons—has influenced West Indian and African American youth's perceptions of themselves (Chin 2001).

While it also employs security measures, the BCM program's approach to safety and cell phones is in marked contrast to that of the DOE. Like many of New York's public buildings in the post-9/11 era, BCM employs security guards to police its entrance. The guards stop parents who come to pick up children in the preschool programs, and all visitors' bags are searched upon entering. Museum Team interns are given identification cards or "key cards" that can be swiped to unlock office doors and other nonvisitor entryways. The museum is a public space within which private spaces are contained. In this way, BCM is quite literally a "safe zone." It is also a space that complicates traditional anthropological notions of the public-equals-male/female-equals-private dichotomy, as many of the educators and administrative staff are female and, as we have seen, girls experience greater success in the internship program than do boys. Teens enjoyed access to private office spaces normally reserved for adults and off limits to child and adult visitors to the museum; in this way, BCM situated the teens as "authorities" with access to spaces reserved for "experts." The museum is also a controlled space in which teens are "safe" from popular culture and are not permitted to speak on cell phones or listen to portable musical devices during learning programs. The educators were especially cautious about teens downloading ringtones featuring the latest hip-hop hit songs. Influenced by popular and academic discourses that tend to position hip-hop as an especially corruptive element, the educators strove to keep the teens "safe" from misogynist, homophobic, and violent lyrics while in the museum's confines. Yet, during the relatively informal "snack time," the period between approximately 3:15 p.m. and 4:00 p.m. when teens gather to await the official start of afterschool programs, educators were relatively lax about the use of cell phones. This approach seemed to serve both the students and the educators, because, by offering limited access to cell phones, the educators communicated that they trusted the teens to respect the rules and turn off their phones once the learning programs began.

During snack time, teens chatted informally and ate snacks provided by museum educators. Snack time was also characterized by the use of cell phones for various purposes other than actually talking. The majority of the Museum Team teens owned cell phones and used them to play popular songs that they had downloaded, to take photographs of each other, as James did of Allison, and to watch music videos. Teens downloaded the latest ringtones featuring popular songs as a way to negotiate the politics of cool and to assert West Indian and/or African American identities. Citing Carolyn Cooper's contention that "the politics of noise is a critical feature of Jamaican communication," Horst and Miller revealed that "obtrusive noise is central to the creation of community, often in resistance to the establishment" (Cooper 1995, 2004; Horst and Miller 2006: 16–17). The BCM teens' use of cell phones underscored Horst and Miller's findings regarding the central role music plays in expressive identity and the cell phone as an essential marker of style. For BCM teens "the affinity with the audio aspect of the phone as style [was] evident and [came] across not as obtrusive and artificial but in some ways as natural and welcome (Horst and Miller 2006: 64). The cell phones became fierce sites of competition between the majority West Indian teens and the minority African American teens. From time to time, arguments broke out over what genres of songs were played on the cell phones, with the West Indian teens usually favoring West Indian dancehall and the African Americans favoring hip-hop. Still, on one afternoon, the teens danced and sang boisterously and in unison to a frantic song called "Heart Attack" by the Jamaican dancehall artist Beenie Man. The unified enjoyment of "Heart Attack" speaks to how youth appropriate West Indian and African American musical genres to alternatively ally themselves with and distance themselves from African American and West Indian culture. Music functioned as both a site of contestation and a site of unification, since *everybody* could appreciate the pleasures of a "hot" hit song, and, with the lines between hip-hop and dancehall becoming increasingly blurred, enjoying music was not always seen as requiring a choice between disparate cultures.

The teens' use of cell phones to listen to music was both an act of resistance against the controlling/safe space of the museum and an indication of the degree to which these youth were able to enjoy the same access to consumer goods as more economically and socially privileged teens. This access was limited, however. It was only after saving her wages at BCM and from a second part-time job, as a cashier in a Manhattan department store, that

China was able to afford her own cell phone and calling plan. And, in order to qualify for her own cell phone plan, China had to mislead the cell phone sales representative into thinking that she was eighteen years old. The cell phone, a contemporary symbol of adolescent freedom and a given for most American middle-class teenagers, was, for these teens, a hard-earned consumer product.[28] And ironically, West Indian immigrant youth would likely have easier access and more freedom to use cell phones "back home" (Horst and Miller 2006).

Staging Blackness: "You Guys Have to Act!"

During workshops, BCM's educators routinely engaged the youth in role-playing exercises designed to expand the youngsters' ability to identify and think critically about racial and ethnic stereotyping. I observed one such role-playing exercise involving the Volunteers and Volunteers-in-Training. Led by Rebecca, five boys and five girls were asked to break up into two groups. Rebecca whispered a racial identity to one group of teens and asked them to create and act out a stereotypical scenario that would illustrate the group's race without any members of the group explicitly stating who they were supposed to be. The other group was told to observe the role-play exercise and guess the race of the group. In the acting group, composed of four youth (one African American girl, an African American boy, and two West Indian girls), an African American girl named Christina quickly emerged as the leader. Christina is a fourteen-year-old whose father is a corrections officer and whose mother works as a dental hygienist. Popular and extroverted, Christina is a tall, thin, and extremely fashion-conscious girl who told me that she wanted to be a fashion model but also intended to go to college and major in psychology.

Christina took charge of the small group after the members huddled in a corner, going over the racial identity assigned to them and planning how best to convey this group's identity in a scenario. As the actors prepared to perform their scene, Christina yelled, "I am Steven Spielberg, and you guys have to *act!*" The scene they performed took place in Popeye's, a fast-food restaurant that specializes in fried chicken. Christina played the Popeye's order-taker/cashier, speaking loudly into her cell phone as the three other teens, assuming the role of Popeye's customers, approached the counter. The "customers" waited for several seconds as Christina continued, loudly chatting into her cell phone and ignoring them. Then, finally appearing to notice her customers, feigning annoyance, Christina rolled her eyes and said, "Hello, welcome to Popeye's. May I take your order?" One of the three Popeye's customers, Anita, turned to the other two youth and said, "All right, I ain't got all day. What y'all two wanna' eat? Make up your minds, and don't be taking all day." The others proceeded to engage in a rowdy dialogue about what to order. Soon the Popeye's scene erupted into pandemonium, as Christina, Anita, and the other two youth, arms flailing, yelled incomprehensibly. As the scene came to a close, their observing peers quickly guessed that Christina's group depicted a scene involving Blacks. Christina explained that Black people are always talking on their cell phones when they're supposed to be working and that they are stereotyped as eating a lot of fried chicken.[29] Anita offered that she played the role of a Black mother with loud, unruly children whom she couldn't control in a public setting. Their observers agreed, with one onlooking girl remarking, "Yes, they were definitely Black people. Y'all were real ghetto."

Christina's group played out a scene depicting African Americans, *not* West Indians. While the group used the term "Black" to describe who was depicted, the popular stereotypes utilized were definitively stereotypes held of African Americans, rather than of West Indian Blacks. Interestingly, both West Indian and African American youth at BCM were aware of and utilized these stereotypes in characterizing Blacks in the scene. For our purposes here, it is important to note that this depiction of Black identity took place in a site of consumption, a fast-food restaurant, and involved notions of Black children as vulgar consumers and of Black mothers (with the Black father absent) as incapable parents. Moreover, the pandemonium depicted in the Popeye's role play was in stark contrast to the girls' actual behavior when I took them to McDonald's. Significantly, in the role play, the youth called on stereotypes of African Americans, often portrayed as having a poor work ethic, as evidenced in their "talking on cell phones when they're supposed to be working," with Black children depicted as rowdy and uncontrollable in a public setting. The teens' scene borrowed heavily from popular and public policy discourses that pathologize Black families and demonize African American consumer culture.

The group's depiction of the Popeye's scene echoes the city's policies regarding cell phone use in schools by suggesting that Blacks abuse such devices to the detriment of their ability to perform in work or school settings. Christina's group presents a critique in which improper use of cell phones and an inability to parent children become markers of Blackness. This racialization can be analyzed in relation to the DOE's official "Regulations of the Chancellor" on security in schools, which states:

If the school confiscates a cell phone, ipod [*sic*], beeper or other communication device, the principal/designee must immediately contact the student's parent and arrange for the parent to appear in person to pick up the device. The cell phone . . . should be maintained and secured by the school until the parent appears. If the parent repeatedly fails to appear to pick it up, the school should dispose of the item (NYC DOE, Regulation of the Chancellor, Number A-412, p. 9, November 8, 2006).

The DOE's regulation makes vague provisions for parents who "repeatedly fail," rather than providing for hardworking parents with little free time during school hours who may benefit from school regulations that are mindful of their schedules and their children's rights to personal property. Since most of the parents of New York City public school students are Black and Latino, this discourse positions both minority parents and students as "repeated failures."

Attention to youth such as the BCM interns, teens who are economically and socially marginalized, reveals much that is relevant for public educational policy and for understanding how adolescents in general engage with leisure activities and popular culture. These teens have spent much of their educational careers under the Bush administration's "No Child Left Behind" program and under Bloomberg's reign, which has extended to three terms. Bloomberg hinged much of his campaign for reelection on the "improvements" he had made to the city's schools which included stricter control of student property, frequent searches, and the extension of the school day for students "at risk" of performing poorly on standardized reading and math tests.

Many BCM teens left their homes before dawn for long commutes to public schools located far away from their Crown Heights and Flatbush neighborhoods. As we have learned, the extended school day meant that, by the time the teens arrived at BCM, the afterschool program was almost over. This, coupled with the ban on phones, meant that students who complied with the school rules would be unable to reach their parents and guardians from the wee hours of the morning until late in the evening when they returned home. Yet, the problems surrounding the policing of students' property and the curtailing of their abilities to engage in extracurricular activities have larger significance than simply prohibiting teens from enjoying the safety and conveniences associated with cell phones. As the youth researchers Neeraj Kaushal and Lenna Nepomnyaschy have argued, "disparities in wealth by race/ethnicity are related to gaps in children's educational outcomes, and . . . family socio-demographic and parental resources account for a substantial proportion of black/white and Hispanic/white disparities in children's participation in gifted programs, extra-curricular activities and grade retention" (Kaushal and Nepomnyaschy 2009: 963). Scholarly research points to racialized disparities in wealth, rather than to the "dangers" of cell phones, as the primary causes for gaps in children's educational outcomes. And it is no surprise that Black children face higher risks of expulsion than White children when we consider that minority children are subject to stricter policing by school officials (Kaushal and Nepomnyaschy 2009; López 2003).

Can You Hear Me Now? Taking Teens and Cell Phones Seriously

The limits BCM educators place on cell phone usage are attempts to shield teens from the "corruptive" influences of consumer culture, in the form of the cell phone as both a communication device and a portable device for playing hip-hop and dancehall music. By taking teens' engagements with cell phones as a serious site of analysis, however, we have seen that the BCM teens' actual uses of cell phones are much more innocuous than both the BCM teachers and Mayor Bloomberg acknowledge. The rhetoric surrounding the DOE's policies on cell phones blames minority students and parents for hindering public school students' chances for success. Mayor Bloomberg's and Chancellor Klein's draconian policies contribute to converting schools into heavily policed zones where students' civil liberties are harshly curtailed. Ethnographic analysis demonstrates how a technological device that is often dismissed as corruptive can be used not only to resist adult authority but also to unify African American and West Indian teens around the appreciation of music. As evidenced in the role-play exercise, Black teens are influenced by racialized notions of cell phone usage and critically engage with popular discourses that pathologize Black families and African American consumer culture.

Much of the public resistance to the DOE's ban on cell phones has centered around parents who have written complaint letters and have threatened to sue the public school system. City Council members have introduced legislation on the behalf of these parents (Clark 2006).[30] These groups will have to stay vigilant, since Bloomberg and Klein have remained steadfast in their refusal to lift the ban and, instead, are exploring how to override legislation prohibiting the "jamming" of students' phone signals.

How can anthropologists who advocate for marginalized youth intervene in educational, popular, and political discourses that pathologize Black youth culture? My concern as an anthropologist is less with this particular legal battle (although I think it is important) than with finding ways to influence the rhetoric surrounding minority students' cultural practices. Popular attitudes toward minority students and educational policies for "at-risk" adolescents are influenced more by public interventions in the blogosphere than by scholarly articles published in academic journals. In gauging public sentiment on Black youths' consumer culture, I relied on online sources, because, increasingly, these sources are the "go-to" sites for framing public debates. While there is a vibrant body of scholarship that takes youth culture seriously, anthropological approaches remain peripheral to popular and public policy discourses. As I perused sources, I was disheartened by the lack of online material written by social scientists that address the very real and significant roles cell phones and related technological devices play in teens' lives. Youth researchers can intervene into the discourses that position minority students as "at risk" by more actively injecting their voices as cultural critics into prevalent and influential online debates.

Infiltrating the Museum with (West Indian) Politics

On the same afternoon that the teens sang along with Beenie Man's "Heart Attack" as it played on one of the boys' cell phones, Kiara, the African American educator, brought snack time to a close by introducing a new project. All tiers of the Museum Team program, including Explainers, Peer Mentors, Volunteers and Volunteers-in-Training, about thirty teenagers, were gathered in the stadium seating of the vast room known as "the Tank" (because it was constructed within a large metal container tank). Kiara stood at the front, while the other educator, the youth coordinator, and I sat in the back uppermost row. Kiara hushed the clamorous teens and announced that, in support of the Hurricane Katrina victims in New Orleans, BCM's Museum Team would present a Mardi Gras celebration in March. Kiara added that the New Orleans Mardi Gras traditionally took place in February, but, since it was already January, the museum interns would not be able to organize and execute their Mardi Gras until March.

Kiara then screened a fifty-minute documentary film on New Orleans and Mardi Gras titled *Travel the World: New Orleans.* The film appeared to be created as a promotional device for tourism and was apparently produced years before the August 2005 hurricane—it made no mention of the recent crisis in New Orleans. After the film ended, interestingly, Kiara did not explicitly connect the youths' Mardi Gras event with a political show of support for disenfranchised Blacks in New Orleans. The U.S. government's failure to act quickly in the aftermath of the hurricane, the extreme suffering endured by New Orleans' Black residents, and the fact that the poorest Black New Orleans dwellers were the last to receive assistance had been extensively publicized on New York news programs and in national and local newspapers. Furthermore, hip-hop star Kanye West had brought the controversy to the hip-hop generation when, on September 2, 2005, appearing on an NBC hurricane relief telethon, he ignored the scripted lines provided by the network and launched into an impassioned diatribe about how Blacks were portrayed in the media. West punctuated his torrent by saying, "George Bush doesn't care about Black people." West's comment was discussed on hundreds of Internet blogs and satirized when he subsequently appeared on *Saturday Night Live*. Still, in front of the teens, Kiara simply said, "In support for the people of New Orleans, we are going to put on a Mardi Gras celebration. Each of the tiers of the internship program will have a theme and create a float around that theme."

Kiara went on to tell the teens they would receive assistance with their costumes from the previously mentioned West Indian Labor Day Parade costume designer. At the close, she had each group draw a slip of paper from a hat; on each paper was one of the four themes she had created. The Explainers' theme was "music"; the Peer Mentors drew "food"; the Volunteers received "Brooklyn"; and the Volunteers-in-Training were assigned "transportation." Each of the tiers separated into groups, and the groups were instructed to come up with a title for their float. There was much debate, and, after quite some time, the titles emerged: The Volunteers-in-Training were "Toussaint," the Volunteers were "Eastern Parkway," the Peer Mentors chose "Foodtown" (the name of a local supermarket chain), and the Explainers selected "Best of Both Worlds." For our purposes here, we will focus on the Volunteers-in-Training and the Explainers' conceptualizations of their Mardi Gras themes.

As the groups huddled in separate corners of the Tank, I shuttled from group to group, first asking the Volunteers-in-Training why they named their float "Toussaint." Christina, the same girl who orchestrated the Popeye's role play scene, responded.

CHRISTINA: We're Toussaint because of the Transit Union Leader!
OL: Why Toussaint?
CHRISTINA: Cause he conducted himself real well during the strike. He stood his ground.

The choice of "Toussaint" might very well have been an imposition of Christina's will, demonstrating that the Trinidadian was a hero not only to Black West Indians but also to African American youth. Regardless of who initially suggested it, the Volunteers-in-Training symbolically allied themselves with the Trinidadian president of New York's Transport Workers Union. It was particularly significant that Christina, an African American teen, was allying herself with the West Indian leader and basing her choice on territorial notions: "He stood his ground." West Indian migration scholars have documented the ways in which West Indian children learn negative stereotypes of, and attempt to distance themselves from, African Americans (Hintzen 2001; Waters 1994, 1999). Reuel Rogers and Irma Watkins-Owens, for example, have emphasized the tenuous political alliances between African Americans and West Indians (Rogers 2001, Watkins-Owens 1996, 2001). Christina's alliance can therefore be seen as noteworthy and spatially oriented, if not politically fraught. We will return to the contradictions inherent in Christina and the other teens' alliance with Toussaint after considering the Transport Workers' strike in context.

During the week of December 20, 2005, the Transport Workers Union had crippled mass transit in the city when New York's bus and subway workers went on strike for sixty hours in protest against a contract dispute between the union's leaders and the Metropolitan Transportation Authority (MTA).[31] For three days during the city's cold and busy holiday shopping season, New Yorkers were forced to walk, bike, and share cabs. The city was divided over the strike, with many seeing the transit workers as selfish and others sympathizing with the workers and viewing the MTA as a wealthy, oppressive employer. A class-based and racialized polarization occurred as the working-class, mainly minority, transit workers' grievances were seen as motivated in part by the belief that the largely White MTA officials and higher ups did not respect the workers. The public debate over the strike became explicitly racialized when, in a press conference, Mayor Michael Bloomberg used the word "thuggish" to describe the union leader. Toussaint later responded, "I can't imagine he would use that choice of words . . . if he was describing a White labor leader" (quoted in Fishman 2006: n.p.).

Roger Toussaint was omnipresent on local news programs during the strike, and, with his heavy Trinidadian accent, he brought West Indian New York to the forefront of public discourses. The strike can therefore be interpreted as a symbolic Black/West Indian takeover of New York City streets and media representations. Although the strike ended with an unresolved contract, a $2.5 million fine for the union, and a ten-day jail sentence for Toussaint,[32] the issue of whether or not the Transport Workers Union was successful is less significant for our purposes than the symbolic allegiance between the teens and the union leader. David Harvey characterizes strikes as attempts at commanding space and notes that capitalist states locate power in bourgeois space as they disempower oppositional spaces (Harvey 1990: 236–237). For Harvey, battles over space and class are, of course, wars over money. The youth's alliance with Toussaint and the transit workers can therefore also be seen as a race- and class-based allegiance.

From the standpoint of West Indian migration studies, Christina and the other teens' alliance with Toussaint is fascinating but not unprecedented. While scholars have extensively documented the rifts and tensions between African Americans and West Indians, they have also noted how West Indians and African Americans have banded together in the face of race-based discrimination. Arguably, Crown Heights' Black communities, including African Americans and West Indians, reacted to Gavin Cato's death in a unified front. A similar argument can be made for the massive protests when New York City police brutally beat Haitian immigrant Abner Louima in 1997. However, as evidenced in our earlier consideration of how conflicts between Crown Heights Hasidim and Blacks are represented, media discourses tend to ignore the ways in which "different, youthful subjectivities" play central roles in such conflicts (McRobbie 1994). Black adolescents have typically been left out of these discourses, more often being framed in the media as "predatory consumers" obsessed with "corruptive" rap music and rampant consumerism, rather than as political agents. West Indian and Caribbean subjectivities have been more often than not glossed as "Black." The BCM teens' symbolic alliance with Toussaint demonstrates that these teens are invested in the politics of social inequality that shape their lives beyond the museum. The fact that Christina, an African American, rather than a West Indian teen, initiated the "Toussaint" theme speaks to the bidirectional nature of identity development between African Americans and first- and second-generation West Indians. As Sherri-Ann Butterfield has suggested, instead of simply looking at West Indian youth as being *influenced by African Americans*, we should also be mindful of how African American identity formation *is shaped by West Indians*.

Simultaneously, on the other side of "the Tank," the Explainers were busy formulating the specifics of their theme: music. They were in a heated debate over whether the inspiration for their costumes should be hip-hop or reggae, and their title, "Best of Both Worlds," was meant to bridge the two genres. Still, the compromised title "Best of Both Worlds" did not solve all of the group's problems; members argued over which specific genres of those two worlds would be emphasized:

CHERIE: How about hip-hop and reggae?

CHINA: No! I don't like reggae! If it's two types of music one has to be calypso!

NADINE: Well, we can't only choose Caribbean music because the whole group isn't from the Caribbean.

DONNA: How about hip-hop and R&B? Everyone likes that.

NADINE, pointing to China: No. She won't like that.

In this dialogue, Cherie, an African-American girl, and a second-generation Guyanese girl named Donna, along with the best friends China and Nadine, attempted to conceptualize the musical focus of the Mardi Gras float, while keeping the national/musical interests of each member in mind. The boys in this group sat silently as the girls took charge. As I observed these negotiations, it occurred to me that, while in individual interviews West Indian teens often articulated strong preferences for West Indian artists over African American ones as a means of claiming West Indian authenticity, usually, within the context of their groups at BCM, nationalism and claims to West Indian genres were enacted in the vein of good-natured ribbing. Staking such claims became an issue only when, as in this instance, one genre had to be chosen over the other. Although the group had already negotiated a compromise by selecting "Best of Both Worlds" as its theme, the group members demonstrated that *actually having* the best of both worlds was not such an easy endeavor.

After weeks of preparation—cutting, sewing, and gluing on sequins—the day of the Mardi Gras celebration finally arrived. The Volunteers-in-Training, the group that had selected "Toussaint" as its float name, literally embodied the transit system in their costumes by pasting hundreds of discarded subway Metro cards (painstakingly collected over the past few weeks by Kiara) to hats and jumpsuits. In a surprising twist, however, at the last minute, the group members subverted the educators' will entirely by deciding that, because they had not completed their costumes on time, they would not participate in the Mardi Gras event. While the Toussaint float followed the defiant Transport Workers Union in all respects and fittingly boycotted the event, things went much more smoothly for the Explainers. This group crafted attractive aprons onto which the words "reggae," "hip-hop," "dancehall," and "R&B" were emblazoned in glitter letters. And, with the exception of China's previously mentioned attempt to cover her face under her hat, the Explainers participated freely, if not eagerly, in the Mardi Gras event.

West Indian culture and American consumption are juxtaposed in Crown Heights: Charlie's Calypso City is adjacent to McDonald's on Fulton Street near Nostrand Avenue. Photo by the author.

If we consider the four float themes selected by the teens—"Foodtown"(a local supermarket chain), "Eastern Parkway" (the major thoroughfare that crosses Crown Heights), "Toussaint," and "Best of Both Worlds," we see that the teens situated their Mardi Gras celebration within Brooklyn and the Caribbean. They conceptualized and, to a degree, executed a Mardi Gras event that was transnational and spanned their own youthscapes. Interestingly, their Mardi Gras floats made no overt nods to New Orleans' traditional Mardi Gras celebration. The teens' Mardi Gras did not even take place on "Fat Tuesday." On the one hand, it can be argued that the teens' Mardi Gras event had little or nothing to do with the "real" Mardi Gras in New Orleans. And, because their event was confined to the museum, it did not "take over the streets" the way Mardi Gras and West Indian carnivals such as *Junkunoo* have co-opted public spaces. Still, the ideologies of resisting colonial hegemony that are so dramatically played out in Mardi Gras, in the West Indian Day Parade, in *Junkunoo*, and in carnivals throughout the Caribbean are palpable in the teens' alliance with Roger Toussaint. The Toussaint group conceptualized its "transportation" float as the embodiment of Toussaint and the transit workers' strike.

Conclusion

The ethnographic descriptions provided in this chapter have important implications for how Black teenagers are understood in popular, public, and educational discourses. The popular media overwhelmingly represent Black teenagers either as "combat consumers" or "predatory consumers," that is, as willing to kill for the consumer goods they want or as threats to civilized notions of public decorum (Chin 2001). In actuality, Brooklyn's working-class and poor African American and West Indian teenagers must earn their own money in order to have limited access to the same consumer and leisure pleasures to which their White and middle-class peers have nearly unlimited access. BCM's teens earn wages not only from their work at the museum but also from additional afterschool jobs as babysitters, cashiers, salespersons, and stock clerks. In addition to working at BCM, Naomi made hand-knit hats and scarves, selling these crafts to earn extra money. A skilled photographer, she also had business cards printed, hoping to launch a free-lance photography business. Discussing her second job as a cashier in a large department store in Manhattan, China added, "But that job doesn't offer me health insurance, so I'm looking for another job where I can get that." China and the other teens strove to participate freely in the cultures of leisure and labor, while they pursued the privileges afforded to more economically well-off teens. Still, stereotypical racializations dog these teens' access to public spaces, while socioeconomic inequalities limit their access to consumer goods and force them to seek comfort, refuge, support, and wages in the unlikely setting of a museum.

While BCM's attempts to be a "safe space" and its identity as a female arena are both remarkable in light of the few public spaces which New York City's Black teenagers can call their own, we have seen that this safety is tenuous and that the female-centeredness is often won at the expense of boys' ability to achieve success in the internship program. We have literally "placed" West Indian teens by mapping how their journeys within and beyond BCM are spatializing forces that enable the production of gendered, racialized, age-based, and classed identities. The spatial, architectural, and educational policy barriers that these teens must traverse in order to attend BCM are exposed as geographic, temporal, and political youthscapes. The teens' negotiations between West Indian and African American musical genres reveal the contradictory and dynamic affiliations surrounding transnational identity formations. Their efforts to ally themselves with the president of the Transport Workers Union symbolically connects them to the strikers' class- and race-based usurpation of New York City and reveals that Brooklyn's Black teenagers are politically engaged in surprising ways.

Attention to youth such as these, teens who are economically and socially marginalized, reveals much that is relevant for public educational policy and for understanding how adolescents in general engage with leisure activities and popular culture. The public educational policy of lengthening the school day to provide tutoring for "at-risk" students threatens minority youths' abilities to enjoy extracurricular programs such as BCM. The educators' limitations on cell phones are an attempt to shield teens from the "corruptive" influences of consumer culture, in the form of the cell phone as both a communication device and a portable device for playing hip-hop and dancehall music. When we take teenage consumer use of cell phones as a serious site of analysis, we begin to understand how a technological device that is often dismissed as corruptive can be used not only to resist adult authority but also to unify African American and West Indian teens around the appreciation of music.

In assigning spatial meaning—labeling BCM "our museum"—these youth have demonstrated their agency amid social constructions that attempt to curtail their access to public space. Caitlin Cahill's ethnographic investigation of young women of color on New York's Lower East Side illustrates that global economic restructuring affects these young women and often turns the city against them, as gentrification erodes the public spaces to which they have safe access (Cahill 2007b). In light of studies such as Cahill's, and within the larger urban context of New York City, BCM's identity as a place for Black youth, albeit peripheral to sources of economic power, speaks to the ability of cultural institutions to subvert dominant geographic and social constructions. The museum's "safety" is tenuously positioned against the enforcement of its boundaries. And, as we noted earlier in this chapter, PUMA data indicates that gentrification has hit their neighborhood, with Crown Heights' White population increasing significantly in the first decade of the twenty-first century. In the conclusion to this book, we will return to the ways in which gentrification threatens BCM's identity as a "place for Blacks." Amid the challenges confronting these teens as they traverse the intersecting processes of racial, gender, and national identity production, they struggle to claim a "real" sense of self. In the next chapter, we turn to these authenticating subjectivity formations, especially as they relate to the consumption of hip-hop music and culture.

Dual Citizenship in
the Hip-Hop Nation

Gender and Authenticity in
Black Youth Culture

At a Hip-Hop Concert

On a frigid Friday night in January 2006, I accompanied the Museum Team interns and two BCM educators to a performance at the Brooklyn Academy of Music (BAM), in downtown Brooklyn. The performers were Urban Word NYC, a young spoken-word poetry troupe; M-1, a member of the hip-hop group Dead Prez, known for its political lyrics; and the 1990s crossover hip-hop sensation Arrested Development.

The trip was organized and chaperoned by Kiara and Neru, two BCM Museum Team educators. There were about fifteen teens, mostly West Indian, in attendance, with more girls than boys present. The girls included several whom I had gotten to know well: China, Hope, Christina, Amanda, Princess, Shante, and Odette. I was less familiar with the four boys there, but Tyrone, who until then had been shy around me, emerged as a class clown.

I had planned in advance to meet Kiara, Neru, and the teens in front of the venue, and I arrived to find fourteen-year-old Christina, the African American girl who took charge of the Popeye's role-play scene described in chapter 2, standing there, alone. I waved her over and suggested that we go inside and wait, escaping the bitter cold. Once inside, I invited Christina to the concession stand for a hot cup of tea. Although she declined the tea, she still followed me to the concession. I was surprised that she seemed to be treating me like an adult whom she would follow around and listen to in the absence of the educators. Since my role at BCM was that of a participant observer, I refrained from disciplining the teens. I took part in all of their duties and activities and had instructed the educators to treat me like one of the youth. The fact that Christina was treating me like an adult shattered my fantasy that I was positioned closer to the teens than to the grown-ups. I was also perplexed by her behavior because Christina was very confident and self-possessed. An extremely tall and thin girl, she was always dressed in the latest trends and routinely took the lead in group situations. I found myself feeling as if I were an adolescent—flattered that Christina wanted to stand with me; she could have just stood off on her own to wait for the others.

Soon, Kiara, Neru, and the other teens arrived, greeting me cheerfully, especially Amanda, the smart, chubby, and sensitive second-generation Jamaican fifteen-year-old with whom I had bonded over our common trait of bookishness. There was an air of adventure emanating from the group, with it being a Friday night and us meeting outside the museum. We went into the auditorium and took our seats, thrilled to find that Kiara had managed to reserve the first two rows.

Earlier, Kiara, Neru, and I had surmised that the teens probably had never heard of Arrested Development. Asking a few of them if they had only confirmed our suspicions. I explained that the band was a very popular hip-hop group (their first album sold more than five million copies, and they won two Grammys, for best rap song and best rap artist) in the early 1990s, when I was in college.[1] Here, in the theater, Kiara, who was also in her thirties, joined me in lamenting this obvious sign that we were getting old. Neru, who was twenty-four years old, remarked that she was ten years old when Arrested Development's songs were big hits—Kiara and I were juniors in college. In light of our age differences and the time that had passed since Arrested Development's heyday, coupled with the group's reputation for delivering "life music" and "African values for African American survival" (J. Morgan 1992: 64), I was concerned that the teens might not like this "soft," "college crowd" hip-hop.

Arrested Development and M-1 (who hosted the show and commented that he was happy to be here "because I live just down the block")[2] interspersed performances with the youth performers of Urban Word. The teens bobbed their heads to Arrested Development and M-1, but the night belonged to Urban Word. All of the spoken-word poets were in their teens and extremely talented, delivering eloquent and moving poems. Urban Word's poems were overtly liberal and steeped in political criticism. While most of the performers were Black, the group included a few Latinos and one Muslim young woman of Middle Eastern descent who wore a head scarf. The BCM youth cheered when the poets demonstrated verbal dexterity (one young male poet "put it into rewind" and recited his lyrics backwards!) and when the rhymes were especially "tight" or clever. The girls also visibly swooned for one boyishly handsome poet with high cheekbones and for another very attractive young man with full lips and long, flowing dreadlocks. When the dreadlocked poet, who was talented in addition to being good-looking, delivered an especially thrilling line, the girls shot out of their seats and gave standing ovations.

The poems were left-wing, antiwar, and critical of American racial politics. Many lyrics criticized the Bush administration's foreign policy in the Middle East and the war in Iraq. One poet delivered a line condoning gay marriage, to which Neru gave me a look that said "thank goodness." She was pleased at this tolerant influence, especially for the BCM boys, who had demonstrated homophobic sentiments, using the word "gay" to mean lame, or uncool and then substituting "fruit" for "gay" when Neru admonished them. The poets, male and female, also stressed the importance of not calling women "bitches" and demanded a more feminist agenda in hip-hop. This, when delivered by the young dreadlocked performer, had a special resonance with the girls, who jumped out of their seats once more and cheered loudly.

The boys rooted for a female performer who appeared to be about fifteen years old and who recited a poem about why Black youth should not call each other "niggers." The poem was narrated in the voice of a visiting male ghost from generations past—a slave who knew all too well the origins of the term. "Nigger wash my clothes, nigger make my food, nigger lie down so I can have sex with you, nigger get a rope so we can lynch that other nigger"—and so on. This young woman's poem was poignant and effective. She was also very pretty—petite with long hair, styled in ringlets. The boys leapt to their feet and pumped their fists at the end of her performance.

Arrested Development took the stage immediately afterward and edited out the word "nigger" twice in the song they performed. Kiara and I gave each other knowing glances; as "conscious" and as "down" as Arrested Development had purported to be in their heyday, it seemed that in the ensuing years the group had censored its original lyrics to disassociate itself from the controversies surrounding Blacks who use the "N" word.

Throughout the performances by Arrested Development, the audience rose to their feet, dancing and singing along. Older audience members like Kiara and me sang along with the group's big hits, including "Tennessee," "Mr. Windle," and "Everyday People." But the group also got the younger audience singing along with some call-and-response prompts. The BCM boys and girls participated enthusiastically. The lead singer broke the crowd up by gender with rousing calls of "Ladies Scream!," "Ladies in the house sing 'la la la,'" and "I want to hear the men sing 'mmm-yeah, mmm-yeah.'" The youth, male and female, dutifully responded. Neru and I noticed that Christina had a beautiful singing voice. The high point of the evening, however, was when Tyrone, a slight BCM intern, burst into a raucous, impromptu dance right there in the front row facing the stage. This was during the encore, with all of the performers on stage. Tyrone's moves were grounded in the dance phenomenon known as *krumping*, a style of hip-hop dance that borrows from break dancing.[3] Usually performed to heavy beat-focused music, *krumping* employs sporadic, convulsive movements with chest thrusts and concentrated, deadpan facial expressions—part clown, part virtuoso, Tyrone had everyone—the youth, the educators, and me—in stitches!

The scene I have just described can serve as a springboard for discussing a variety of issues in relation to Black youth culture; we can employ it toward interrogating the use of the word "nigger," it can serve as an illustration of how call and response is manifest in Black popular culture, it reveals how gender is articulated in hip-hop performances, it illuminates generational appreciation of music, and it speaks to homophobia among Black youth and to politically situated evolutions in hip-hop music and culture. However, the girls' enthusiastic support for Urban Word's critical stance on mainstream hip-hop's misogyny is perhaps most significant for our purposes here. This scene depicting Black urban youth having "good clean fun" at a hip-hop concert and of hip-hop performers using the genre to launch meaningful social critiques stands in stark contrast to how hip-hop is conceptualized in most popular, social, and even academic discourses.[4] While, clearly, both Urban Word and Arrested Development are peripheral to the mainstream, mass-marketed hip-hop targeted at contemporary consumers, the teens' unabashed enjoyment of the concert demonstrated their appreciation for politically conscious, alternative hip-hop of the sort popularized by artists such as Talib Kweli, Nas, India.Arie, and Mos Def, who have achieved varying degrees of mainstream success. Moreover, the performance at BAM can be situated within a vibrant alternative hip-hop scene that thrives throughout New York City, in which unsigned, young local artists with popular mix-tape CDs, such as Rebel Diaz, Patty Dukes, and La Bruja, utilize hip-hop music as "an educational tool, as a mechanism for political activism and as a springboard for articulating feminist ideologies" (LaBennett 2009: 109).

In relation to contemporary mainstream hip-hop, the politics of consumption is often perceived to be staged on misogynous, violent, and materialistic terms. In her book *Pimps Up, Ho's Down: Hip-hop's Hold on Young Black Women*, T. Denean Sharpley-Whiting argues that hypersexualized images of Black women are a critical component of contemporary hip-hop music and culture (Sharpley-Whiting 2007). Like academics such as Sharpley-Whiting, teenage girls recognize that the basic formula for most hip-hop videos consists of numerous scantily clad young Black and Latina women whose rear ends and breasts fill almost every frame and who appear to have no other desire than to give sexual pleasure to the male rap star. A host of scholars and cultural critics have interrogated hip-hop's misogyny and have sought to examine women's place in and to expose their cultural contributions to the production of hip-hop (George 1998; Guevara 1996; Kelley 1997; Keyes 2004; J. Morgan 1999; M. Morgan 2009; I. Perry 2004; Pough 2004; Rose 1994, 2004; Sharpley-Whiting 2007). Yet, as I have argued elsewhere, the experiences of marginalized people, especially adolescent girls and young women, are glaringly absent from much of this critical discourse (LaBennett 2009).

While Sharpley-Whiting purports to offer "the voices of young black women themselves," she, like many of the academics who tackle the sexual politics of hip-hop, neglects to place the actual voices, experiences, and interpretations of black *teenage girls* at the center of her analysis (Sharpley-Whiting 2007: 20). Sharpley-Whiting's chief subjects are college women, but it is young, Black, preadolescent and adolescent girls who are thought of as being the most vulnerable in terms of the potentially negative effects of hip-hop culture. Therefore, as an anthropologist, I must address not what adults, academics, feminist scholars, or moral guardians make of misogyny in hip-hop but, rather, how young girls themselves negotiate the cultural politics surrounding hip-hop. As we'll see, Brooklyn's West Indian and African American girls are surprisingly adept at recognizing sexism in the broader American society and at critiquing hip-hop's disturbing representations of women. A comparison between these teens and Sharpley-Whiting's subjects suggests, perhaps, that younger Black urban girls are more skilled in questioning antifeminine lyrics and videos than their older, more affluent peers (if we are to take Sharpley-Whiting's findings at face value). At the end of this chapter, we will expand this comparison to affluent White girls, and I will share what I learned in January 2008 when I spoke on the subject of "popular feminism" at a prestigious, predominantly White private high school in Manhattan. There, an educator told me that the school's extremely wealthy female students routinely fell passive victims to sexist taunts from boys. This educator made a connection between the boys' objectifying behavior and the girls' passivity and the images both genders see of women in popular culture. If this educator's assessment was accurate, the West Indian and African American girls I studied were bolder in the face of explicit sexism than some of Manhattan's most privileged daughters. The young women with whom I worked were nobody's victims and showed considerable creativity and agency in negotiating the racial, ethnic, and gender constructions they faced directly through leisure activities and indirectly through popular culture. Was this private school educator unduly influenced by the moral panic surrounding how popular culture affects female adolescents, or could Brooklyn's minority girls really teach more well-off young women a thing or two about standing up for themselves? And, perhaps most important, did BCM's girls' boldness enhance their chances of achieving the educational and social successes virtually guaranteed for the prep school cohort?

Consumption in Context and the Power of Resistance

These polemic questions, which we will revisit at the end of this chapter, are of course influenced by biased assumptions that routinely position minority girls as "victims" of hip-hop. These queries also engage long-standing arguments in consumer theory surrounding the degree to which people (women in particular) on the ground level are able to question and resist dominant ideology. From the early foundations of consumer theory—Frankfurt School scholars positioned consumer society as one in which hegemonic ideology is disseminated in a "top-down" manner, and Birmingham School scholars countered by perhaps overemphasizing the resistant possibilities of consumer culture—theorists have been bifurcated with regard to the relationship between individuals and consumer society. Harvey Molotch reiterates a critique of the Frankfurt School and subsequent postmodern theorists who see consumer goods as "texts" that can be "read" to reveal deeper understandings of society as a whole (Molotch 2003: 14). Molotch notes that, all too often, these textual readings of surfaces lead to interpretations of consumers as victims of the "shallowness of urban life" (Molotch 2003: 14). This "reading"-of-"texts" approach, rather than ethnographic fieldwork and analysis, has all too often been the chosen method of researchers exploring young people's consumer culture. Greg Dimitriadis points out, that particularly in relation to rap music, the interpretation of lyrics (as in the work of Tricia Rose) has been the primary method of analysis (Dimitriadis 2001; Rose 1994). Dimitriadis follows anthropologist Arjun Appadurai and champions ethnography combined with textual analysis as a more effective avenue for understanding the place of cultural products in youths' lives (Dimitriadis 2001). This approach represents the intervention I wish to make in the discourse surrounding the portrayal of women in popular culture and, more specifically, the ways in which West Indian and African American girls critique hip-hop's objectifying representations of females.

In his study of the origins and uses of objects, Harvey Molotch asserts that classical anthropology has much to teach us about material culture (Molotch 2003: 7). Molotch cites Mary Douglas and Baron Isherwood's analysis of the place of goods in society, in which they argue, "Consumption is the very arena in which culture is fought over and licked into shape" (Douglas and Isherwood in Molotch 2003: 7). Molotch goes on to posit, "The 'identity work' of goods does not occur in a single instance of consumption, nor even at particularly important rites of passage. . . . Instead, identities and consumption constitute one another through routines of daily acquisition and continuous use" (Molotch 2003: 8). Molotch follows Daniel Miller in arguing that "objects are social relations made durable"(Miller 1998; Molotch 2003: 10). Molotch's emphasis on the 'identity work' of goods is particularly useful for our purposes, in terms of how commodities such as hip-hop songs and the packaged personae of musical artists are "fought over and licked into shape" by adolescent girls.

Theorizing on Youth Culture and Consumption

Educators, psychologists, parents, and moral guardians have argued that mass-mediated culture presents a threat to youth, with girls seen as particularly "at risk"(Gilligan 1993; Pipher 1994). Within this discourse, adolescent girls fall prey to a "girl poisoning" culture that promotes unhealthy and unattainable definitions of femininity (Pipher 1994). Black girls have been largely ignored in this literature. Recently, however, scholars who have previously neglected minority girls have endeavored to correct this omission.[5] While these researchers have largely maintained their characterization of girls as victims of the culture industries, others, who have placed minority youth at the center of their analyses, see marginalized girls (and boys) as social agents with the ability to contest hegemonic forces (Best 2000; Cahill 2007b; Chin 2001; McRobbie 1994; Soep and Maira 2005). This latter group of scholars has directly and indirectly critiqued feminist scholarship that interprets girls' sexuality as problematic. As Mary E. Thomas has pointed out, feminist inquiry, particularly in the context of popular culture, has "relegat[ed] girls to an uncertain present and fix[ed] them with 'immature' subjectivities" (M. Thomas 2004: 775). Within this analytic strain, social scientists such as Mary Pipher are revealed as neglecting to present adolescent subjectivities from the girls' perspectives (LaBennett 2006; M. Thomas 2004: 776).

When Black youth are included in the discourse on adolescent identity formation and popular culture, they are often criminalized as "predatory consumers," and seen as in constant need of supervision; their informal use of public space and uncensored access to popular culture are deemed pathological (Chin 2001). Urban youth have been presented as "social problems," with, as we considered in the Introduction to this book, "inner-city" boys characterized as violent drug users and girls viewed as unable to control their bodies, and therefore susceptible to teen pregnancy (Nathanson 1991). Both urban girls and boys have been demonized as "high school dropouts" within a rhetoric that blames youth, rather than placing accountability on public schools and government policies (HoSang 2006). Such policies, including the ban on cell phones and lengthened school day, fail to provide minority youth with the same access to education and leisure as suburban, more economically privileged youngsters. Within this scheme, which frames urban youth in particular as savages, rap music is perceived as symbolic of a generation of "out-of-control" Black youth (Dimitriadis 2001: 48–49).

Yet, ethnographic analysis demonstrates that, although, in relation to contemporary hip-hop, consumer culture is seen as almost entirely corruptive, Black youth utilize hip-hop in unpredictable ways to resist class, racial, and gender inequality (Dimitriadis 2001; LaBennett 2002, 2009; M. Morgan 2009; D. Thomas 2004). These findings suggest that the meanings attached to hip-hop are not readily discernable by mere textual analysis and that hip-hop's significance must be studied within its cultural contexts. Context is key for a minority of migration theorists who have addressed the often neglected popular terrain. For these researchers, Blacks "negotiat[e] several sources of diasporic culture," including England, the Caribbean, Africa and the United States, and "these cultural influences are increasingly disseminated through forms of popular culture such as rap music and the wider hip-hop culture" (Codrington 2006: 300). Drawing on Angela McRobbie's notion of "different, youthful subjectivities," which is predicated on Stuart Hall's notion of "new ethnicities" and which emphasizes questions of ethnicity and sexuality, we can reveal the centrality and significance of consumer culture for forging adolescent transnational identities (McRobbie 1994: 178).

As Stuart Hall has asserted, Black diasporic identity is largely constituted within cultural representations that are hybrid in nature (Hall 1990). Following Hall, we can use consumer culture and popular representations as a lens for understanding how youthful female West Indian identities are dynamically fashioned. Some scholars have come to see consumption and media "as an alternative 'lived' curriculum" for youth (Dimitriadis 2001: 29; Giroux 1996). However, often even within this literature, popular culture is regarded, again, as a "text" to be read, and youth are interpreted as falling victim to its evil effects (Dimitriadis 2001). The ethnographic research I am presenting hopes to take a step toward correcting this bias.

Youth have been undertheorized as central players in the mediations surrounding globalization and the nation (Maira and Soep 2005: xix). Yet, as Sunaina Maira and Elizabeth Soep posit,

> Youth is, after all, often the ideological battleground in contests of immigration and citizenship as well as the prime consumer target for the leisure industry. Even when young people are not themselves traveling across national borders, or leaving their bedrooms, they find themselves implicated within transnational networks (Maira and Soep 2005: xix).

For Maira and Soep, such transnational implications include being the children of mothers who traverse continents to care for other people's children and being the consumers/producers/retailers of the beauty and entertainment industries (Maira and Soep 2005: xix). If as Molotch asserts, classical anthropology has much to teach us about material culture, then youth culture studies offers lessons about globalization. And while, as we have seen, scholars of West Indian migration have neglected material culture, youth culture analysis has a strong tradition of exploring consumer culture, "crystallized most clearly—if not unproblematically—in the analyses of the Birmingham school theorists of youth subcultures" (Maira and Soep 2005: xix). In other words, youth culture theorists have recognized young people's relevance to analyzing global consumer culture. In volumes such as *Cool Places* and *Global Youth?*, researchers have attempted to wed transnational approaches to youth-based analyses (Nilan and Feixa 2006; Skelton and Valentine 1998). Following these scholars, I am calling for a transnational, youth culture–oriented approach to West Indian migration, not only because, as Maira and Soep assert, youth are on the front lines of global processes but also because Black diasporic identity is largely constituted within popular representation.

Hip-Hop Nation/Hip-Hop Planet

> This is my nightmare: My daughter comes home with a guy and says, 'Dad, we're getting married.' And he's a rapper, with a mouthful of gold teeth and a do-rag on his head, muscles popping out his arms, and a thug attitude.... I realize to my horror that rap—music seemingly without melody, sensibility, instruments, verse, or harmony, music with no beginning, end or middle, music that doesn't even seem to be music—rules the world. It is not my world. It is his world. And I live in it. I live on a hip-hop planet (McBride 2007, n.p.).

The consumption of hip-hop is particularly significant for understanding transnationalism and West Indian youth identity formation because ideas about gender and nationhood are often played out within hip-hop music and culture. In her study of hip-hop artists in the Los Angeles musical underground, Marcyliena Morgan situates the production of hip-hop squarely within the struggle for citizenship: "The right to talk and represent oneself and one's community is a fundamental aspect of citizenship" (M. Morgan 2009: 146). The very terms "hip-hop generation" and "hip-hop nation" as ways of designating the graffiti art, fashion, dance, and music that unite young hip-hop producers and consumers speak to nationalist implications (Farley 1999). From its inception, hip-hop has been a transnational musical genre, borrowing from African, Caribbean, and African American musical traditions. Clive Campbell, a Jamaican immigrant popularly known as DJ Kool Herc, is widely credited with pioneering hip-hop when he migrated to the South Bronx in the early 1970s and began spinning records at house parties. While we are focusing here on transnational ties between American hip-hop and the Anglophone Caribbean, as the James McBride *National Geographic* article quoted earlier reported, the concept "hip-hop planet" has started to eclipse the notion of a "hip-hop nation," with hip-hop's popularity encompassing the far reaches of the globe. Youth in disparate geographic locals such as Brazil, Senegal, France, and Germany use hip-hop as the soundtrack for their daily lives. In fact, France is the world's second-largest consumer of hip-hop, behind the United States.[6] Although, for West Indian youth, cultural products such as hip-hop and West Indian dancehall music are utilized to stake claims on "authentic Blackness," the hybrid nature of both musical traditions renders separating "West Indian" and "African American" musical forms and cultures a slippery exercise. For Brooklyn's West Indian teens, then, being members of the "hip-hop nation" necessitates a complex, symbolic dual citizenship, since they are also members of the global "hip-hop planet."

Writing about the challenges Black women face as they pursue citizenship in America and in hip-hop culture, Morgan notes:

> Black women in particular have talked their way into visibility and worked to reframe family, womanhood, relationship, and sexuality to guarantee their right to represent women within American life. Yet no matter what image or ideology a hiphop woman represents, she operates within a male-dominated adolescent world where identities, roles, and status are constantly being explored and where participants are convinced that everything is at stake and everything is about them (M. Morgan 2009: 146).

The metaphor of dual citizenship takes on pernicious connotations for West Indian girls, because, for them, as females, pursuing dual citizenship in the hip-hop nation results, at best, in being second-class citizens in "a male-dominated adolescent world." Although, as immigrants, legal citizenship is a significant issue for some of these girls, here I refer to cultural citizenship. In this respect, my thinking is informed by Aihwa Ong, who, following a Foucauldian approach, defines cultural citizenship as "a dual process of self-making and being-made within webs of power linked to the nation-state and civil society" (Ong 1999: 738, quoted in Maira and Soep 2005: 67). Just as cultural citizenship in the United States as a whole is a complex process of negotiating one's self amid structural inequalities that are deeply entrenched in power relations, pursuing dual cultural citizenship as West Indian females and as members of the hip-hop nation is a contradictory process. Yet, in privileging girls' interpretations over my own more academic reading of the cultural politics of hip-hop, I have found that girls are savvy consumers who negotiate their gendered, racialized, and transnational identities in ways that affirm female artists who champion Black women's independence and celebrate their natural beauty.

In chapter 2 we considered the dangers city streets present for Black teenagers, both male and female, and addressed the particular spatial challenges at play for West Indian adolescent girls as they negotiate between American and West Indian notions of "where girls belong." We saw that BCM educators attempted to construct a "safe space" for girls and strove to protect both genders from the "corruptive" influences of popular youth culture in general and hip-hop music in particular. Kiara and Neru's outing to the "conscious" hip-hop concert at BAM was one such effort. BCM educators strive not only to protect girls and boys from the threats of police violence and racial discrimination but also to shield girls from the sexual violence that characterizes much of contemporary rap music and hip-hop culture. Recalling Dolores Hayden's assertion regarding the intersecting, conflict-ridden arenas that the body, the home, and the street represent for women (Hayden 1995:22) positions us to begin interrogating the social implications surrounding hip-hop's often degrading portrayals of women, because hip-hop lyrics, music videos, and fashions are all channeled through both public and private realms. These portrayals confront girls on television screens and in the pages of popular magazines and blast from car stereos along Flatbush Avenue; they formed the soundtrack for cheerleading practices at the Flatbush YMCA and were even heard as downloaded beats played on cell phones within the confines of BCM. Therefore, although strict parenting, especially of adolescent females, means that West Indian girls' freedom to travel beyond the home is limited in comparison to that enjoyed by their male peers, and even though BCM educators tried to shield all of the teens from hip-hop, hip-hop and its West Indian cousin, dancehall, infiltrated the girls' home and leisure arenas in meaning-laden ways.

Authentic Femininities

When I asked China, the Barbados native we met earlier, whose mother works as a ticket agent at Greyhound and whose stepfather is a contractor, to name her favorite singers, she said, "Definitely Mary J. Blige," placing the African American R&B artist and "queen of hip-hop soul" at the top of her list and constantly referring to Blige as "mad real." Although China's Blige-inspired gold-hued hair gave her an air of maturity, she consistently sucked her thumb, a habit she hoped to break by periodically donning false nails. When China used the term "real" to describe Mary J. Blige, she was not referring to the singer's artificial hair color (or her own, for that matter) but, rather, allying herself with the class, gender, and racial struggle she sees Blige as having over-come. For China, Blige embodied "realness"—an unapologetic representa-tion of Black femininity that does not "front" or make false gestures. Raised in Yonkers, New York, and the Bronx, Blige has built her persona on a "street credibility" image; it is widely known that she escaped a life of drugs, violence, and poverty, and many of her songs center on her identity as a strong, inde-pendent woman. China asserts that Blige, despite all her success, remains "real"—true to her background—and that this is evidenced in her style:

> She dresses . . . like the normal—for like me, I live where I live and I don't have all that money, so for me, jeans and sneakers and a nice top. But Mary and Alicia Keys is basic, just like regular people, so she [Alicia Keys] does the jeans and sneakers and when she goes out she'll put some boots on and—but Mary J. Blige, she'll flip it and she just throws on this with that and it just looks nice; I like her style.

Here, China compares Blige with another R&B/hip-hop singer, Alicia Keys, appreciating both their styles but favoring Blige's. China explicitly *places* her fashion choices and alludes to her economic limitations, saying, "I live where I live and I don't have all that money." China used the term "real" to describe Blige and again when I asked her about one of the most popular television programs among her peers, a reality show and modeling competition titled

America's Next Top Model and hosted by the supermodel Tyra Banks (we consider this program at length in chapter 4). When, in the middle of the show's fifth season, I asked China to identify her favorite contestant on the show, she answered, "Now? I guess I like Bre the best. I mean, she's the only *real* Black person left on the show." While the dark-skinned Bre qualified as a "real" Black person, interestingly enough, China did not include Nik, a very light-skinned, light haired, and light-eyed contestant who appears to be of Black/mixed racial ancestry, as a "real" Black person. When China selects Bre, the "only real Black" contestant on *America's Next Top Model,* as her favorite, she is negotiating between ideologically loaded youthscapes and affirming a Black beauty aesthetic that still remains at the margins of mainstream definitions of femininity. Yet, critical race scholars have problematized the pursuit of "real" Blackness. In addition to voicing fears that many Black youth may champion ultimately self-destructive behavior in the name of "keeping it real," Nicole Fleetwood follows Paul Gilroy in arguing:

> Realness operates in relationship to representations of racialized youth on multiple levels: as a concept alluding to that which is the essence of reality; as an aesthetic style in black popular cultural production, namely hip-hop music and film; as a set of visual tropes that constitute a particular racialized and gendered subject position (Fleetwood 2005: 163; Gilroy 1995).

China's assertion that only dark-skinned individuals are "real Black people" can be interpreted as serving to essentialize Blackness. Fleetwood argues that the fetish of "the real" in Black popular culture is ultimately co-opted by White America, whereby "keeping it real" means working outside the mainstream of White American culture and, as Fleetwood puts it, "White adult value systems" (Fleetwood 2005: 164). Yet, China's application of "real" complicates scholarly interpretations and popular appropriations. While, for example, rappers may see calling women "hos" and "skeezers" as "keeping it real," China's brand of realness has to do with what she sees as the positive attributes personified by Mary J. Blige. Therefore, for her, being "mad real" is grounded in self-reliance and the production of independent and empowered femininity. And Blige is interpreted as "real" not only because she embodies these characteristics but also because she is a brown-skinned Black woman with full lips and with a prominent facial scar that she proudly displays in portraits on the covers of her 1999 album, *Mary,* and her 2006 album, *Reflections: A Retrospective.* In this way, China is celebrating an unconventional and marginalized image of beauty.[7]

The girls routinely used the term "real" in this manner and in reference to musical artists. As Fleetwood and Gilroy posit, many of them utilized the term "real" to differentiate between "inauthentic" and "authentic Blackness"; in addition, and perhaps more important for our purposes here, they also used it to support definitions of beauty that challenged mainstream norms. When I asked Amanda, the second-generation Jamaican fifteen-year-old who greeted me cheerfully at the hip-hop concert and whose mother strove to "keep an eye on her," if she liked the extremely popular R&B singer and actress Beyoncé Knowles, she said no. Instead, Amanda named Beyoncé's darker-skinned and less popular former bandmate Kelly Rowland. Amanda explained: "Kelly Rowland—she is really for real. Beyoncé is fantasy." Amanda's statement is particularly interesting from a Lacanian psychoanalytic perspective. Ellie Ragland-Sullivan writes that Lacan's idea of the Real "has led to the description of the impossible" (Ragland-Sullivan 1986: 188). Ragland-Sullivan quotes Lacan from a 1974 television interview: "Reality is only the fantasy on which a thought is sustained, 'reality' doubtlessly, but to be understood as a grimace of the Real" (Lacan in Ragland-Sullivan 1986: 188). For Lacanian theorists such as Fleetwood, then, Amanda's distinction between Beyoncé Knowles as "fantasy" and Kelly Rowland as "really for real" is fraught with contradiction. Lacanian thought argues that both Kelly Rowland and Beyoncé Knowles are symbolic representations of "realness" and that "reality has little to do with the Real" (Ragland-Sullivan 1986: 188). While I acknowledge Lacan's applicability here, I am reluctant to employ Lacanian theory as wholeheartedly as Fleetwood does in her study of racialized youth's authenticating practices in the San Francisco Bay Area (Fleetwood 2005). China, Amanda and the many other girls who invoked an idea of "the real" are doing more than relying on essentialized notions of "authentic Blackness." Both China and Amanda are designating what constitutes authentic Blackness while also *staking a claim to authentic femininity*. In the girls' framework, authentic Blackness or "being for real" was constituted in looking "normal" and "really Black" (certainly problematic notions of Blackness), in displaying as little artificiality as possible, and in being a strong, independent woman. Black feminist scholars have interpreted this definition of Black beauty as culled "from the scraps of everyday life" and as offering "powerful alternatives[s] to Eurocentric aesthetics" (Collins 1991). In delineating a framework for Black feminist thought, Patricia Hill Collins writes,

An interviewee smiles for the camera in Brower Park, a popular hangout spot for Crown Heights youth. Photo by the author.

"From an Afrocentric perspective, women's beauty is not based solely on physical criteria because mind, spirit, and body are not conceptualized as separate, oppositional spheres. Instead all are central in aesthetic assessments of individuals and their creations" (Collins 1991: 89). The girls viewed performers like Blige as constructing their feminine styles from everyday materials that they "flipped," or creatively refashioned. This view of authentic femininity was also framed around the absence of artificiality, although the girls utilized a sliding scale in terms of curbing artificiality in their own self-fashionings; false nails were perfectly acceptable, but, save for lip gloss, none of the girls wore makeup (a factor also attributable to strict West Indian parenting). Girls like Amanda and China proclaim their preferences for feminine personae that do not fit hegemonic definitions of femininity and base Black authenticity within femininity that is not constructed in a hypersexualized fashion. These are particularly critical assertions when we consider that, in relation to hip-hop, authentic Blackness is often necessarily masculine and decidedly sexist.

West Indian Youth, Identity, and Transnational Racial Ideologies

Notions of authentic Blackness are particularly nettlesome for West Indian youth, as they have learned that they can assert or circumvent American racial ideologies through their strategic consumption of goods. They have also become versed in the identity politics at play in an American culture of consumption that has social inequality at its core. Throughout their history in this country, beginning when they themselves were sold as products, continuing when their access to goods was limited by segregation, and perhaps most visibly during the civil rights movement, African Americans have consumed certain products and boycotted others to demonstrate pride and to protest discrimination in the consumer realm (LaBennett 2006: 283). Civil-rights-era Black youth were at the forefront of effecting social change as groups such as the Student Nonviolent Coordinating Committee (SNCC) protested at lunch counter sit-ins, public performances, and bus station rest stops, demanding the same access to consumer goods and services that their White peers enjoyed. This era helped establish the current notion of identity politics—the idea that how one constructs her identity vis-à-vis consumption is a political act.[8] Central to what can be called an African American women's culture of consumption, ideas about Black femininity as alternatives to Eurocentric notions of beauty, along with historical knowledge of Black women's struggles, find their way to today's young Black girls through community arts programs (like those offered at BCM), in neighborhood church teachings, and via popular music (M. Morgan 2009: 138). Morgan interprets this as socialization into an "ideology of self-reliance and self-respect" (M. Morgan 2009: 138). For Black girls, ways of engaging with popular culture, especially music, are also passed on through less tangible routes via what ethnomusicologist Kyra D. Gaunt has termed *oral-kinetic lessons* (Gaunt 2006: 4). Musical styles and the gendered Black musical body, or "girls' kinetic orality," are significant elements of Black social memory; powerful responses that "assert 'somebodiness' [and] have remained a critical mode of expressing our inalienable rights to freedom . . . even when freedom and democracy was being denied African American citizens in other realms" (Gaunt 2004: 4–5).

Yet, in contemporary American society, African Americans' consumption habits and leisure activities continue to be demonized as uncivilized, violent, and unhealthy. These negative connotations surfaced in chapter 2 as the girls negotiated the outing to Barnes and Noble, McDonald's, and the Court Street cinemas. All too often, Black youth are the explicit focus of negative readings of African American consumer culture. West Indian teens negotiate their consumption habits not only with a keen understanding of the African American politics of consumption but also in relation to these negative stereotypes of African American youth. West Indian girls are not the only ones who situate immigrant identity formation in relation to African Americans. As we saw in the Introduction, overwhelmingly, comparisons between West Indians and African Americans have also been a preoccupation in the scholarship on West Indians in New York, and West Indian awareness of the negative connotations attached to African American cultural practices emerges as a common thread in many works (Basch 2001; Kasinitz 1992; Model 1991; Rogers 2001; Waters 1999, 2001).

Notions of West Indian ethnicity, as distinct from the ethnicity of African Americans, then, are wrapped up in conceptualizations about identity as (re)produced through consumer culture. But, these perceived differences and culturally rooted expectations, which position African Americans as "lazy spendthrifts" and West Indians as "diligent penny-pinchers," are also steeped in gendered distinctions between West Indians and African Americans. Percy Hintzen has illustrated how the negative stereotypes West Indians hold about African Americans are embedded in and contrasted against West Indian notions of "success" and gender propriety. Discussing a Guyanese man who was experiencing marital problems with his African American wife, Hintzen writes:

> Bryan saw his wife's welfare-dependent background as confirming his own understanding of African Americans as lazy and immoral. He also saw African American immorality in his wife's sense of independence and her refusal to submit to his will. He complained to his family that he had little control over her behavior. Her impertinence conflicted with his notions of male authority and female subservience. . . . Bryan increasingly turned to his mother and sisters back home for emotional support. . . . They began to insist that he take measures to ensure that [his wife's] behavior comported with the expectations of "reputation" and "respectability" imposed on black lower-class wives throughout the West Indies (Hintzen 2001: 94–95).

According to Hintzen, these conflicts apply "particularly to the social, economic, and cultural contexts of gender relations in black inner-city neighborhoods" in which African American behavior is interpreted as deviant and immoral and is linked to excessive drinking and partying (Hintzen 2001: 95). Again, this is contrasted with West Indian femininity, which is predicated on maintaining household duties and mothering daughters (Hinzten 2001: 95).

Hinzten notes that his respondent, Bryan, interpreted his wife's welfare dependency, low income, and "failure" to take advantage of her high school diploma as detrimental to his aspirations to gain legal status and to send for his family back home in Guyana. Notions of West Indian success, then, are partially dependent upon immigrants' associations with African Americans. Mary Waters suggests that West Indian youth who claim an African American identity run the risk of limiting their chances for success (Waters 1999). Moreover, Waters alerts us to the fact that West Indian children learn negative stereotypes about African Americans from popular culture and from their parents. Therefore, some children who identify as "ethnic" and "immigrant" might try to distance themselves from African Americans in order to avoid being stigmatized in a similar fashion.

While my work confirms many of Waters's and Hintzen's conclusions, I found that teens demonstrated a great deal of fluidity; they moved quite frequently from identifying as "ethnically West Indian" to identifying as "Black American," often asserting a number of identities simultaneously. More often than not, when asked how they identified, girls said, as one respondent put it, "I'm both. I can't call myself West Indian or American, I'm both." Still, speaking about which box she checks when asked to designate her racial identity on a form, China said, "If I see just 'African-American' [as a choice] I put 'Other.' If I see 'Black,' I check that." Here China makes the assertion that she is Black but explicitly *not* African American. Yet, in China's daily life, her identity assertions are more often forged in the realm of leisure activities and consumer culture than they are in designating her race on surveys. In other moments, China and other girls like her *do* ally themselves with African Americans. Her contention that the African American singer Mary J. Blige is "mad real" allies China with African American notions of beauty, female independence, and situated power.

Transnational Negotiations and Alliances

Considering music, television, and fashion, we find that these realms are principal arenas through which youth witness racial, ethnic, and gender representations as they assert particular identities. Take, for example, Tracy, a fifteen-year-old who was born in Trinidad but who moved to Brooklyn when she was just eleven months old. Tracy, whose mother is a social worker and whose father is a hospital cook, says her Trindadian family teasingly calls her a "Yankee" because they perceive her to be very American. Yet, Tracy prides herself on her vast knowledge of West Indian musical artists who are not well known in the United States. Her favorites include, to name a few, Sizzla, Spragga Benz, Vybz Kartel, Marshall Montana, Bernard Collins, and my personal favorite, the Trinidadian Soca singer Oneka. Surprisingly, Tracy said, "You'll only catch me listening to reggae or old R&B. I don't like rap at all. Everything [in rap] is mad cursing." Here, Tracy is being critical of the musical genre dominant not only among Black youth but also arguably among all youth in America (a 2000 article in the *New York Times* titled "Guarding the Borders of the Hip-Hop Nation" reported that 70 percent of all hip-hop CDs are purchased by White youth). In a fascinating contradiction that we will address shortly, Tracy criticizes profanity in rap music but turns the other cheek to the violent masculinity promoted by dancehall artists such as Vybz Kartel.[9] Tracy, like other teens, allied herself with West Indian artists and musical genres when she wished to assert a West Indian identity. Here, not wishing to confirm her family's "Yankee" label, Tracy disassociated herself from American music.

Whether girls allied themselves with West Indian or African American musicians also had to do with factors such as seeking parental approval; parents often saw American hip-hop as a corruptive influence because of its violent and sexually explicit lyrics. Girls' identity assertions and consumption choices were also motivated by looking to distance themselves from the negative stereotypes I mentioned earlier. Still, youth who privately professed their preferences for West Indian artists and claimed West Indian authenticity by downloading obscure artists or getting relatives to bring back the latest West Indian CDs contradicted such assertions when they were among African American peers. Often, such youth sang along with *and knew all of the words* when their African American counterparts played the latest chart-topping hip-hop song. Therefore, West Indian youths' choices and identifications were contradictory and contingent on a whole host of factors.

Unlike BCM, where children and youth engaged in play-labor, the Flatbush YMCA was strictly a site of play. Music could always be heard at the YMCA, and the television in the lounge was often on. The cheerleaders' use of music in their practice sessions enabled me to contextualize songs within the ethnographic space of the YMCA. The YMCA girls negotiated contradictory gender politics in relation to popular female hip-hop artists such as Lil' Kim and Foxy Brown. On the one hand, they admonished Kim and Brown as "only looking to get the interests of men" and as not being "positive role models for girls." On the other hand, these same girls, in different moments, enthusiastically sang along with and enjoyed Kim's and Brown's then current hit songs.

In the late 1990s, when I initially conducted fieldwork at the Flatbush YMCA, sexist and degrading lyrics and videos by male artists such as the Notorious B.I.G. and female artists such as Lil' Kim and Foxy Brown were tempered by the arguably more conscious and unconventional work of artists such as Lauryn Hill and Missy Elliot. Elsewhere, I have argued that teenage girls are critical consumers who see through the veneer of image management artists use to sell records (LaBennett 2006). For example, when I asked a YMCA cheerleader her opinion of Lil' Kim and Foxy Brown, she responded curtly, "They're hookers." For these girls, Lauryn Hill's and Missy Elliot's more "positive" images were derived in part from Hill's middle-class respectability and her successful appropriation of West Indianness and from Elliot's androgyny, creative artistry, and independence. Ironically, the American-born Lauryn Hill, in drawing so heavily on West Indian musical traditions and in maintaining a persona as an empowered female, might be seen as the artist most successful at negotiating dual citizenship in the hip-hop nation. Although she hails from New Jersey, by frequently wearing her hair in dreadlocks, by taking one of Bob Marley's sons as her romantic partner, and by overtly borrowing from West Indian musical traditions while critiquing lower-class African American definitions of femininity, Hill came to embody West Indian female respectability in the YMCA cheerleader's eyes. In fact, Hill's appropriation of West Indianness even sparked confusion online, where bloggers chatted about whether she was in fact, African American or West Indian. On her immensely popular 1998 album, *The Miseducation of Lauryn Hill*, Hill raps, "It's silly when girls sell their soul because it's in, look where you be with hair weaves like Europeans, fake nails done by Koreans." Here, Hill critiques markers of working-class Black femininity embodied in "fake nails done by Koreans" and in hair weaves that mimic "Europeans." This is clearly a disparagement of working-class Black femininity and a call for a more "authentic Blackness."

Interestingly, although a number of the girls with whom I worked wore hair weaves and some donned false nails, they did not see such self-fashionings as inauthentically Black. The following exchange, which took place one afternoon during snack time at BCM, illustrates how girls defended their self-fashionings even in the face of critiques of inauthenticity. A casual time to "hang out," snack time was also an opportunity for good-natured ribbing. On one afternoon, an African American boy nodded toward Donna, a second-generation Guyanese girl. Looking to get a rise out of Donna, the boy asked, "Why you gotta' wear that hair weave?" There was a loud round of "Ooooh!" from the other teens—the whole group recognized this as a blatant dis. Donna, a short, dark-skinned girl, wore long, thinly breaded synthetic hair woven into her own, real hair, which was much shorter. Although Donna was small in stature, her two gold teeth, numerous gold necklaces (including a nameplate necklace spelling out "DONNA" in gold), and tomboy attire projected toughness. She did not miss a beat and responded, "I look *good* in this weave!" Only somewhat defeated, the same boy quickly turned his attention to Nadine. He asked, "Why is your face so Black?" Nadine also responded immediately: "Keep telling me I'm Black!" She said, " I know I'm Black. That's a compliment!" This exchange illustrates many of the contradictions and essentializing notions of Blackness with which these young people grappled. On the one hand, the boy was launching a critique of artificiality similar to Lauryn Hill's. On the other, he was using dark skin, one of the traits on which the girls based "real Blackness," to challenge whether Nadine's skin was legitimately attractive. Both Donna and Nadine were quick to defend themselves, and neither one apologized for or was shamed by her Black femininity—both in its "authentic" form of dark skin and in its "inauthentic" form of wearing a hair weave.

The contradictory alliances and identity assertions that come into play for West Indian girls disclose valuable insights about American and West Indian racial and gender ideologies. The girls sometimes applied a double standard, by judging African American hip-hop as a corruptive influence and privileging West Indian musicians and genres (even though *both* musical traditions rely on explicit and profane lyrical content). At other times teens allied themselves with African American personae and supported the identity politics paramount to African American consumer culture. Significantly, at the Flatbush YMCA, cheerleaders' mothers, who kept careful watch over practices, felt that one of their primary duties was policing their daughters' access both to actual sex and to sexually explicit lyrics in hip-hop music. The proximity of the all-boys basketball team, coupled with the rap music played at cheerleading sessions, resulted in a social space at the YMCA that the mothers saw as inherently corruptive. One mother, Shirley, explained her concerns when I asked her why she had reservations about her daughter, Aiesha, listening to hip-hop:

She listens to this song by Jay-Z [an American rapper], and I was in a cab going home, I had gone grocery shopping. And the guy in the cab was playing a tape. You know, the uncut version of the song. I was like, 'we're going to have to discuss this song.' Because I want to know, does she really know what the words in the song are? Listen . . . I'm funny about what she listens to. . . . The stuff is sexual . . . some people think I'm obsessed with it, but I'm really scared about it because. . . . When I got pregnant with her, that was like the worse thing that could have happened is me becoming pregnant. Now, the worse thing is you can get AIDS. My aunt works with people who have AIDS and my aunt has clients who are twelve years old with full-blown AIDS. So it's no joke. I watch my daughter.[10]

Shirley, who became pregnant when she herself was a teenager, makes a conceptual leap from her daughter's listening to explicit hip-hop to her becoming sexually active and then contracting AIDS. Interestingly, Shirley, an African American single mom, contradicts the stereotype of African American parents failing to police Black youths' access to "corruptive" consumer culture. This characterization of the breakdown of the Black family because of parents who are more concerned with buying expensive sneakers than with investing in their children's educations attracted public scrutiny when it was voiced by actor and African American icon Bill Cosby.[11] The four West Indian mothers who routinely watched their daughters' YMCA cheerleading practice sessions also discouraged their daughters' enjoyment of American hip-hop. Yet, these Caribbean mothers did not admonish the girls for allying themselves with West Indian dancehall artists such as Beenie Man, Vybz Kartel, Spragga Benz, and Lady Saw. However, even a cursory glance at these artists' works reveals many of the same sexually explicit portrayals found so distasteful in American hip-hop. For example, in a duet titled "Healing," on the album *Passion*, Lady Saw sings the following lyrics to her collaborator, Beenie Man:

> Beenie Man with yuh nine millimeter yuh would get any gal
> Nuff waan fi war but mi know mi official
> Mi nah watch nuh face
> Mi a wife material
> The rest a them a just scandal
> When yuh gi mi wah yuh have say mi nah blow yuh job
> Yuh a outlaw and mi hot gal
> Want it real raw
> Beenie Man yuh nah stall
> Give mi the loving make mi bawl

In these lyrics Lady Saw presents a conflicting definition of femininity. On the one hand, she presents herself as "wife material," while on the other she is an eager sex partner for Beenie Man, who is not her husband: "Give me the loving, make me bawl." Lady Saw's self-presentation in "Healing" is in direct opposition to the notion of female respectability discussed in chapter 2. This female dancehall artist's brash "sex talk" (e.g., in the first line she equates Beenie Man's penis with a gun) goes against the "drive to . . . religiosity [and] familial forms sanctioned by the church" that characterizes the "respectable" Caribbean female (Miller 1992: 171). The dancehall music theorist Donna Hope has asserted that "While female Deejays, like Lady Saw and Tanya Stephens, can ascend to high positions of status and legitimacy via the throne of 'slackness' or sexually explicit lyrics," ultimately, female artists fall short of the role of lyrical "Don" that is manifest in the overtly violent performances of male artists (Hope 2006: 127). Within the cultural space of West Indian dancehall, then, women can embody "slackness," but hypermasculinity reigns supreme, reflecting larger gender ideologies and gendering processes in Caribbean society.

Women's Studies scholar M. Jacqui Alexander argues that, for Caribbean women, defiant sexuality and erotic autonomy have been interpreted as signaling "danger to the heterosexual family and to the nation" (Alexander 2005). Discussing Bahamian governmental attempts to define law-abiding female sexuality, Alexander contends:

> And because loyalty to the nation as citizen is perennially colonized within reproduction of heterosexuality, erotic autonomy brings with it the potential of undoing the nation entirely, a possible charge of irresponsible citizenship, or no responsibility at all. Given the putative impulse that eroticism is corrupt, it signals danger to respectability—not only to respectable black middle-class families, but most significantly to black middle-class womanhood (Alexander 2005: 23).

Alexander astutely exposes the ways in which ideas about respectable sexuality are inextricably connected to heterosexuality and to notions of citizenship in the Caribbean context. The dialectic relationship between hip-hop's misogyny/hypermasculinity and its homophobia is also apparent in dancehall, hip-hop's West Indian close kin. Scholars have documented the ways in which African Americans espouse homophobia in the name of religious faith (Hawkswood 1996), and gay, lesbian, and bisexual teens have denounced American hip-hop artists such as Lil' Wayne for injecting the phrase "no homo" into songs in order to distance themselves from gay communities. In the Caribbean milieu, researchers have analyzed violent homophobia in Jamaican dancehall, with Deborah Thomas arguing that dancehall lyrics such as "raise your hand if you think gay men should be shot" "reflect values generally held throughout the population" (Thomas 2006: 114). Donna Hope suggests that violent and homophobic dancehall lyrics are fraught sites of masculinity for marginalized young Jamaican men who reside sociospatially removed from dominant masculinity (Hope 2006). The filmmaker Isaac Julien has explored the controversy surrounding violent homophobic lyrics in dancehall artist Buju Banton's song "Boom Bye Bye" and has documented the protests launched by gay communities in England against Banton's music (Julien 1994; Skelton 1996). These findings underscore how conflicting dualities of citizenship predicated on women's marginality and on heteronormativity are simultaneously operative in the production and consumption of both hip-hop and dancehall. And, just as female dancehall artists are able to critique patriarchy and celebrate female sexuality with erotic lyrics, so, too, do female hip-hop producers and consumers resist the status quo while asserting less than respectable femininity. Yet, while the girls grappled with the problematic femininities presented by African American hip-hop artists such as Foxy Brown and Lil' Kim, neither my adolescent respondents nor their mothers saw the consumption of West Indian musical products as "negative."[12] Therefore, the perspectives of West Indian parents and West Indian girls themselves indicate that what is "negative" about the representations of women in hip-hop has less to do with differences between hip-hop and dancehall's portrayals of women than with American racial dynamics and the social space in which hip-hop music and culture are being consumed. And I hasten to reiterate that both hip-hop and dancehall are hybrid musical traditions that have long borrowed from mutual aspects of African diasporic cultures. West Indian and African American artists are increasingly drawing on one another's work and collaborating on tracks. Therefore, there are no hard and fast lines between what is hip-hop and what is dancehall. The operative issue here is not which musical tradition is "worse" for adolescents; rather, what is at stake is cultural critics' neglect in recognizing the critical agency that Black youth and their parents routinely display as they forge identities within the complex and contradictory realm of mass-mediated popular culture. We should therefore be identifying the ways in which Black girls creatively reframe the "primary conditions of citizenship" within a larger culture that marginalizes their sexuality and demonizes their consumer habits (Alexander 2005: 29).

Boys, Books, and Babies

In these mediations, as girls and mothers strive to define West Indian authenticity, music and the body emerge as critical sites of social production. In the example provided earlier, Shirley, an African American mother, makes a connection between her daughter's listening to a Jay-Z song and her getting pregnant and possibly contracting AIDS. For West Indian mothers, too, teen pregnancy loomed large but was seen as oppositional to West Indian respectability. None of my closest respondents became teen mothers. This, of course, does not mean that none of the girls got pregnant. Understanding that notions of propriety would influence girls to hide unplanned pregnancies, I asked a BCM educator with more than twenty-five years' experience at the museum to reflect on teen pregnancy at BCM:

> I'm not gonna tell you that we didn't have pregnant teens before. . . . A Trinidadian girl who did well in high school and was going on our college trips, she got pregnant. She was going into the eleventh grade. She lived with her dad and stepmom. The family spoke to me, and the girl had confided in us. The family decided to have an abortion. But then she disappeared, and we were calling her dad and asking what happened to her. They sent her back to Trinidad! I was like "No!" But both parents were remarried, I think they were in shock and didn't know what to do. She lived with her grandma in Trinidad. The young boy [who got her pregnant] was a neighbor. We never heard from her again. The whole idea of her coming here was to have her go to college, to finish high school and go to college. But those are the only instances I've experienced in about ten years. Have there been other girls who got pregnant who I didn't know about? I'm sure there have been.

The administrator compared this example with that of the only other instance she had experienced in the past ten years, which involved an African American girl:

> A while back, we had a child in the Museum Team who was obviously a child with special needs. She lived with her father, who was enrolled in a social service organization. And at that time in the program we had some emerging social workers who came to the museum to work with kids if they needed help. We refer people if we perceive that the kids need help. We are not a social service organization. The young lady had participated

before and then was no longer involved [in the Museum Team Program]. But she came back because she was pregnant and she felt comfortable at the museum. She was obviously a child with special needs. And I wanted to know what kind of grown man got her pregnant?!? At the time, Rebecca [a BCM educator] was working there, and Rebecca knew [the girl] very well, and she wanted to come back, so we let her in. She was fifteen or sixteen. Her water broke at the museum, when she was attending one of the workshops! And here's what I mean when I say she had special needs, learning needs. Here's where her brain was at: Her water broke, and Rebecca was saying we have to call 911, call her doctor and get her to the hospital. And the girl said, "Oh, but I got to got to school tomorrow!" I told Rebecca to call a doctor, and I was like, "You're not going to school tomorrow!" The girl didn't understand that her life had changed. She didn't comprehend what having a baby meant; her learning capacity was not there.

These two examples, the first involving a West Indian girl and the second an African American girl, came up when I asked the administrator, Shelly, a Trinidadian woman in her mid-forties, to reflect on whether the term "at risk" was useful for defining girls at BCM. We will contemplate the administrators' rejection of the "at-risk" label in the conclusion to this book. For the moment, however, the two examples can be situated within the policing of adolescent girls' sexuality and within West Indian notions of authenticity and respectability. Clearly, there are class issues here as well; already under the surveillance of social services, the African American girl who also had special learning needs had few options when she became pregnant. She had returned to the comfort of the museum but at that point evidently had not received adequate counseling to prepare her for the realities of motherhood. The Trinidadian girl, from an upwardly mobile background, confided in the museum educators and either decided or was persuaded by her parents to have an abortion. However, after the girl's abortion, her father and stepmother elected to send her back to Trinidad, a decision that was frowned upon by the BCM educators but that, for the parents, served as protection against future dangers (and perhaps a solution to the social stigma that might accompany their daughter's pregnancy). In the Trinidadian girl's example, the Caribbean homeland emerges as a transnational solution to the dangers threatening youth in New York City. Parents routinely sent girls (and boys) who got into trouble "back home" to be disciplined by West Indian grandmothers.

Therefore, Caribbean homelands figured into the girls' notions of themselves as "dual citizens" in conflicting ways. Shelly's alarmed reaction signaled that, for the educator, being sent home to the Caribbean represented a dangerous limitation of the girl's future opportunities. The Caribbean serves as a site of rehabilitation and as a "civilizing force" for a girl who had strayed from her parents' notions of respectability by getting pregnant. However, as suggested in the explicit lyrics voiced by Lady Saw, the Caribbean also represented a site of wanton sexuality and danger. And, as with the blurred lines between West Indian dancehall and American hip-hop, many teens routinely traveled between the West Indies and New York, growing up in both places simultaneously. China's story speaks to these complex journeys. China did not permanently migrate to the United States until she was ten years old. When she was an infant, her mother moved to New Jersey and then later to Brooklyn. China stayed, along with one of her siblings, in Barbados, being raised by their grandmother. But she spent summers and Christmas holidays throughout her childhood with her mother in Brooklyn. While China missed her mother during their long separations, she said, "That [holiday visits] was good enough," adding:

> I still had my friends, it's not like I was away from my family, my mother used to call every Sunday . . . my mother called every Sunday at the same time. So I would wait for her phone calls—it wasn't like I wasn't missing out on much, but then she said, "You know, China, I think you're at the age where we need to be together." I said okay and I moved up here, not willingly, but yes.

Interestingly, during China's preadolescence, China's mother decided she was "at the age" when they needed to be together, suggesting that the impending changes that accompany adolescence called for firsthand parenting. China also noted the increased opportunities in the United States to attend college as among her mother's reasons for relocating her daughter to New York. However, when asked about the similarities and differences between growing up in Barbados and in Brooklyn, China also pointed to the dangers that accompany childhood in the Caribbean:

> CHINA: Similarities is that the people that I—I live in a Black neighborhood and my friends are Black and I know this is common—Most Black houses, you get, you get beat. So you get whipped. So that's a similarity. Because most White families, you know, they don't beat their children,

they may get spanked. But differences, is that—I think—well for me, how do I say this? Up to what I see is like kids here are more sheltered, as in like, their parents baby them a lot, as to say, how I was brought up. Like we don't—okay, we don't have sidewalks [in Barbados]. It's more like this much of the road [gesturing with her hands to indicate a narrow space] and then it's the thing, the road where cars are coming. And so, from the time I was little, I was walking that by myself, going to school, going to the supermarket. And then I moved up here and I had friends who—like, like I'm older, but I have friends who are younger than me and their mothers are telling me that, "Oh I don't want my child to, to go around the corner because it's six o'clock at night." I said, "What?" That makes no sense. Like I'm walking on the—there's this much sidewalk and I'm young—I think it's just more sheltered up here.

OL: Okay, yes. I know what you're saying. I'm from Guyana, and it's like that, too, we don't have any sidewalks in the rural areas, and cars and cows and all sorts of things are going back and forth in the street, and there's a wide, deep gutter, you could fall right in the gutter and kids are just walking on the road, right?

CHINA: Yes! And the buses come around the corner just [makes screeching sound], and I just fall back because I get scared. You can get hit by cars and buses and you're a kid walking alone.

In this exchange, China sites corporal punishment as a mainstay of *both* West Indian and African American parenting and notes that in both Barbados and Brooklyn she lived in predominantly Black neighborhoods. However, China recalls some of the dangers experienced by young children in the Caribbean, which include poor infrastructure and unsupervised youngsters running errands and journeying to school on dangerous roads. As previously mentioned, scholars such as Cindi Katz have noted that children's social worlds vary greatly between economically privileged countries and poorer nations (Katz 2004). China's insights add complexity to the conundrums of citizenship and belonging that West Indian girls navigate. And she brings the conversation back to policing girls' sexuality when I ask if there are any differences between West Indian and African American parenting:

Yes. They [West Indians] don't let the girls have boyfriends. My grandmother, and my mother, and my aunt always said the three "Bs"—boys, books, and babies—don't mix.

Here, the three "Bs" speak both to West Indian mothers' yearnings for their daughters' success and to their "inherited discomfort with the emerging, restless sexuality of their own daughters, a sexuality that is often viewed as threatening or anxious to usurp" (Alexander 2005, 65). And, as we have seen, that "restless sexuality" is all too often played out in the lyrics and personae of female rappers and West Indian dancehall artists.

Conclusion

In this chapter, we have met girls who demonstrate strong preferences for female artists whose personae exist outside hypersexualized and derogatory definitions of Black femininity. To be clear, however, neither West Indian teenage girls nor their African American peers categorically reject *all* of the ways in which hip-hop and notions of authentic Blackness sexualize and objectify women. Just as teenagers have done since this lifestage first appeared in 1950s in conjunction with the mass marketing of products to adolescents, these teens took great pleasure in enjoying that which their parents feared or disapproved of the most. So even "good West Indian girls" who dutifully hung out at a museum after school and who aspired to attend college sometimes celebrated the blatant disregard for parental authority embodied in the most violent and sexually explicit rap lyrics. Part of these girls' boldness rested in their appropriation of the empowered and aggressive female sexuality represented in the "bad girls" of rap. Still, to borrow John Jackson's term, in their most sincere moments, when I asked them what they *really* thought, the girls used critical eyes and voiced preferences for musical artists who, by their terms, were "really for real."[13] Their notions of realness were often predicated on dark-skinned Blackness and on a definition of Black female beauty that counters hegemonic definitions of femininity. In this way, West Indian girls negotiate a slippery and symbolic dual citizenship in the hip-hop nation; on the one hand they took pleasure in the often objectified "bad girls" of rap, while on the other they remained loyal to performers whose personae championed counter hegemonic femininities.

These negotiations can inform questions surrounding how girls in general perceive of and are influenced by popular culture. At the beginning of this chapter, I related my experience visiting an affluent private school in Manhattan. I was invited to lecture there as an intervention by an educator who voiced her extreme concern for the ways in which young women at the school were, to her mind, uncritical of popular culture's and, in turn, their male peers' debasement of females. The educator related instances of boys taunting girls and calling them "sluts" as they passed in the halls. The girls, she lamented, did nothing to protest this treatment. Interestingly enough, one of her other examples of the school's problems involved rap music. An upper-class White boy was reprimanded for composing a rap song about a female peer in which he used profane and derogatory language in describing the girl. When confronted by school administrators, the boy said that it "was obviously a joke," that he was just writing a song like the ones that were popular at the time and that it "was no big deal." After my lecture, in which I discussed the ways in which my Brooklyn interviewees were critical of popular culture and analyzed examples of how third-wave feminism is often positioned along the lines of young women's entitlement to sexual freedom, as embodied in television programs like *Sex and the City*, several teachers approached me and thanked me for what they saw as a much-needed intervention. This led me to see that the educator who invited me was not alone in her concerns. Still, to be just to the two hundred or so adolescents I addressed that day, the prep school girls convinced me during the question and answer period that they were just as able to decipher the codes of popular culture as the BCM and YMCA girls.

I am therefore reluctant to unabashedly champion the Brooklyn girls as better equipped to defend themselves against sexism than their more well-off peers. Visiting the Manhattan school did, however, reaffirm the salience of place in my understanding of Brooklyn girls' critical engagements with popular music. Class, race, ethnicity, and age intersect at specific junctures for Caribbean and African American girls in Flatbush and in Crown Heights. These girls' quotidian interactions with consumer culture and leisure activities presented particular challenges, but the youngsters also drew on resilient Black diasporic practices in the form of African American women's culture of consumption and West Indian women's notions of respect. Black girls are the most glaring targets of hip-hop's misogyny. We see the faces of young Black models and struggling actresses in hip-hop videos on BET and MTV and in the pages of hip-hop magazines like *The Source*. Young Black women are a primary subject of hip-hop songs and mandatory accessories for the industry's most successful male artists. By allying themselves with artists such as Mary J. Blige, Alicia Keys, Lauryn Hill, and Missy Elliot, the girls rejected definitions of femininity that undermined their identities. The complex ways in which they make sense of popular culture in general, and hip-hop more specifically, have important implications not just for the discourse surrounding hip-hop but also for our broader understandings of how adolescents across the board engage with consumer society. While they may be second-class citizens in the hip-hop nation, West Indian and African American girls excelled at BCM, and, as we saw in chapter 2, they out-performed their male peers in the internship program, just as Black and Latino girls outnumber their male counterparts among high school graduates and college attendees (López 2003). I would hardly describe these girls as "victimized by hip-hop"; rather, they are fierce contenders who willfully claimed positive definitions of femininity.

China, Amanda, Tracy, and Donna illustrate how West Indian girls alternatively ally themselves with and distance themselves from African American popular culture. Listening to these girls' voices complicates the scholarly work on West Indian migration and transnationalism. Female adolescents of West Indian and African American descent negotiate complex, "different, youthful subjectivities" as they parse out what constitutes "real" and respectable femininity. Their subject formations speak to larger inquiries surrounding what constitutes Blackness in the twenty-first century, and their mediations shed light on how female adolescents can critically interact with consumer society. In this chapter, we placed these mediations within the meanings attached to music, Caribbean homelands and the female adolescent body. Notions of the body continue to emerge in chapter 4, as the teens reflect on a popular television program.

"I Think They're Looking for a Skinny Chick!"

Girls and Boys Consuming Racialized Beauty

The twelfth graders' mood switched from the cool resignation they often displayed when a museum educator introduced a new project to one marked by rambunctious, animated chatter when they realized that the "project" I was introducing involved eating pizza and watching an episode of *America's Next Top Model*. Their critiques of my pizza topping selections not withstanding—"Vegetable?!?!"—the teens showed real excitement, with the girls quickly weighing in on the show's previous seasons and its winning contestants. One or two boys chimed in, while the other male teens just appeared relieved that at least they weren't being asked to sew Mardi Gras costumes or bind books. I explained that we would be watching an episode from Cycle One of the program, and they proceeded to talk about the most recent season, Cycle Six.

CHINA: Season Six is the one that just finished?

NADINE: Yeah.

CHINA: Who was on it?

NEEMA: Danielle and Jade.

CHINA: Oh, I *hated* Jade! Oh my God! Danielle is my favorite though. I like her 'cause she's Black. I like Black people/ [laughter]

TYRONE: [Teasing] /You're racist=

NEEMA: =She's not Black though, she's mixed. She looks mixed.

CHINA: Who?

NEEMA: Jade.

CHINA: She is mixed. Mixed with everything=

NADINE: =What about Furonda? You like her? Furonda, the real skinny girl?

CHINA: No.

NADINE: Nnenna?

The girls continued to chat about Cycle Six's contestants (the show is demarcated in "cycles," rather than the more traditional "seasons" that typically demarcate television programs), including Jade, Danielle, Furonda, Nnenna, and Joanie. Out of the thirteen contestants on Cycle Six, they named all four black contestants and only one White contestant (Joanie). Thus began our focus group discussion of the extremely popular reality program *America's Next Top Model* (*Top Model*).[1] Over the course of two days in June 2007, I screened an episode from the first cycle of the program and conducted focus groups, first with the Brooklyn Children's Museum's Explainers (seniors in high school), then with the Peer Mentors (juniors).[2] I was interested in how the girls and boys would interpret the program and how they would voice their views in a mixed-gender setting. The girls talked constantly about *Top Model*, so it was not surprising that they selected it after I prompted them to choose a program for me to screen. I was curious as to whether the boys watched the program, too (or whether they would admit to watching it), and how both girls and boys would interpret the racial and gender identities portrayed on the program.

Our focus group discussion took many turns, with the youth quickly switching from topic to topic and sometimes talking over one another. After screening the episode and before embarking on our discussion, I handed out a questionnaire consisting of seven questions designed to facilitate an analysis of our conversation. This ensured that I had a written response with each teen's name, sex, country of birth, and parents' country of birth, in addition to written responses to each of my questions. The exercise also enabled me to observe the teens in a coed setting while they worked quietly on a "written assignment."

The focus group discussion revealed insights into the gendered dynamics of how BCM teens interact in a pseudo-classroom setting. The girls were much more talkative (naturally, perhaps since *Top Model* is a female-oriented program), but their gregariousness went beyond reacting to the program, also encompassing girls "policing" the boys. For example, while filling out the questionnaire, China reprimanded some of the boys for talking too much and looked over their shoulders, cajoling them to change their answers. Two boys used the discussion as a means to voice their criteria for attractive female partners. The exercise demonstrated the teens' capacity for critical thinking in relation to consumer culture. They hypothesized, "I don't want to be a model but, if I did, I wouldn't behave that way." It also revealed a heartbreaking moment when one boy, Mark, took the judges' rejection of a contestant as "telling somebody they can't do something" and related it to his own experiences in public high school. Perhaps surprisingly, Mark and some of the other boys identified with the female contestants on *Top Model*.

I was keen to hear what the boys had to say but found myself challenged by some of the same pedagogical difficulties that the BCM educators faced; while the girls tended to raise their hands and wait their turns, the boys often spoke without raising hands and stating their names. By obeying the rules of conduct, the girls ensured that their comments would be heard. Later, when I sat down to replay the conversation, I had difficulty identifying boys on the audio recording; not only did they often neglect to state their names, but they also tended to speak in softer tones. These gendered discourse styles are an integral part of the exchange and have bearing on the views expressed by the teens. In her study of the leisure activities of Bay Area boys of color, Elizabeth Soep has explored the "relationship between gender and communication" and the notion that "language contains stereotyped arrays of features and practices conventionally associated with gendered identities" (Soep 2005: 180). Soep summarizes some of the relevant literature, which argues that "so-called men's talk" is traditionally concerned with "toughness, hierarchy and control," while female speech displays "nurturance, emotional expressivity, connectedness and sensitivity to others" (Eckert and McConnell-Ginet 1998: 485, quoted in Soep 2005: 180). After transcribing the preceding exchange, which marked the start of the BCM teens discussion of *Top Model*, I noticed some of the discourse features Soep identified and used some of her indicators for patterns such as "latching" (marked in my transcript by the "=") , which indicates "no audible pause between conversational turns," and simultaneous speech, which is marked by the "/" in the transcript excerpt (Soep 2005: 181). Soep notes that linguistic scholars have hypothesized that youth tend to engage in interruptive speech more than adults, and this was certainly the case with the BCM teens. Although at the time of our conversation I had spent many months interacting with this group of teens on a daily basis, it was sometimes hard for me to keep up with their conversation. No surprise there. More notable, however, was that the unexpected gender speech practices that Soep uncovered with Bay Area boys of color were also present in my transcript of the BCM teens' conversation. Both Soep and I have noticed that minority boys convey intimacy, sensitivity, and solidarity in their discourse features even though these are supposed to be "feminine ways of talking." These findings, which counter general ideas about gendered speech, support anthropologist Marjorie Harness Goodwin's assertions regarding the role of speech in the social organization of Black children in a Southwest Philadelphia neighborhood:

Research on women's speech has argued that it is different from the talk of males, and indeed I found that when playing by themselves, the girls on Maple Street used talk to build types of social organization that systematically differed from those of the boys. However, in cross-sex interaction the girls not only used the same speech as the boys but frequently outperformed the boys in verbal contests. . . . Stereotypes about women's speech thus fall apart when talk in a range of activities is examined (Goodwin 1990: 9).

In a setting such as BCM, where the girls generally outnumbered and outperformed the boys, I argue that, in fact, the *boys* used what scholars have deemed "girls' speech." Therefore, although my research ostensibly focused on girls, issues surrounding gendered discourse, the education achievement gap between minority girls and boys, and minority boys' aspirations resurfaced again and again.

When I began researching West Indian teenagers in Brooklyn in 1997, I set out to study adolescent girls. However, combing over the anthropological data accumulated in more than a decade spent studying the topic of identity formation among West Indian and African American youth, including repeated periods of fieldwork, revealed a great deal about boys. This chapter places my findings within a particular social context. The geographic context is the Brooklyn Children's Museum in Crown Heights, Brooklyn, a context we have observed in previous chapters. The consumer context is the teens' interpretations of *Top Model*. However, we shall see that, although *Top Model* was used as our springboard, the discussion spanned issues and ideologies that strike at the core of what it means to be Black, West Indian, and adolescent in contemporary New York.

Intertextual Spaces: The Tyra Show and America's Next Top Model

Top Model is a reality competition, hosted by model-turned-television-host-and-producer Tyra Banks, in which female contestants live together while vying for the title "America's Next Top Model" and competing for prizes including representation by a prestigious modeling agency and a contract with CoverGirl cosmetics. Banks also hosts *The Tyra Banks Show* (later changed to *Tyra*).[3] On that program, typical episodes include titles such as "Ex-Factor: Should We Give it Another Try?," an episode that aired on March 31, 2009, about what to do if you are "still hooked on your ex." The same episode also featured a segment about the stars of the reality show *The Bad Girls Club* and the latest castoff from *Top Model*. In this way, *Tyra* is both a separate entity and an intertextual vehicle to promote *Top Model* and other programs.

   Top Model and *Tyra* are especially relevant to minority young women's ideas about beauty, femininity, and body image because, on both programs, Tyra Banks ostensibly aims to "redefine beauty" and present the perspectives of "real women," although critics have argued that *Top Model* is "undeniably in the service of beauty culture, which in general has been less accepting, if not hostile, to black women" (Sharpley-Whiting 2007: 29). As the focus group with the BCM teens revealed, however, audiences do not always uncritically accept Banks's attempts as legitimate endeavors to redefine modeling industry standards, since, arguably, the winning contestant of each cycle of *Top Model* has adhered to or has been molded to fit industry norms.

   As noted in my earlier treatment of West Indian girls' readings of the television program *Buffy the Vampire Slayer*, the TV shows teens watch are part of a "pervasive mass-mediated culture of consumption" reflected in what Baudrillard has called "'emancipated signs' which no longer have any fixed referent" (LaBennett 2006: 283; Baudrillard quoted in Campbell 1995: 98). These emancipated signs span various media from television to music to the Internet, and celebrities such as Tyra Banks become pervasive fixtures in teens' daily lives. When youth visit websites for *Tyra* and *Top Model*, they are invited to click on tabs for topics that range from celebrities to beauty and fashion to fitness and health. And, of course, they see advertisements for a dizzying array of products on these sites. Like these websites, while our focus group was framed around *Top Model*, it was really about much more. The screening and discussion shed light on a number of themes and issues that I did not anticipate, including religion, morals and ethics, speaking in a West Indian accent as opposed to Standard American English or African American vernacular, race-based alliances, standards of female beauty (for girls and for boys), and gendered interpretations of TV programming. Although the episode I screened, "The Girls Get Really Naked," was from Cycle One of *Top Model*, it remained current to the teens because it was running in syndication on VH1 around the time I conducted the focus groups. On the day I taped the episode, VH1 also aired episodes of *My Fair Brady*, a reality show featuring Adrianne Curry, the contestant who won Cycle One of *Top Model*. In this way, the episode I selected had the appeal of featuring contestants with whom girls regularly who watched the show would be familiar while also featuring Curry, a "star" who had branched out from the program.

Synopsis of Episode 7: "The Girls Get Really Naked"

Episode 7 of Cycle One takes place in Paris, France, and features four remaining contestants: Shannon, Robin, Adrianne, and Elyse. The four finalists have conquered all manner of challenges to make it this far, and personalities begin to clash, with the final cut and the title "America's Next Top Model" in sight. The episode opens with Shannon and Adrianne trying on dresses at a "go-see."[4] The final four women represent four distinctive "types"; Shannon Stewart is a blond, blued-eyed, thin eighteen-year-old from Franklin, Ohio, who describes herself as "blessed by the Lord in many ways";[5] Adrianne Curry is a twenty-year-old brunette from Joliet, Illinois, who chain smokes, flaunts a dark, edgy style, and favors TV shows like *Buffy the Vampire Slayer* and rock bands such as The Doors and Led Zeppelin; Elyse Sewell, like Adrianne, represents an "editorial" look, in model industry parlance. Also twenty years old when the show aired, Elyse is a clinical researcher from Albuquerque, New Mexico, and a self-professed "nerdy scholar." Robin, the only African American of the four women, is, at five feet nine inches tall and 160 pounds, also the one with the least model-like physique. A day-care assistant from Memphis, Tennessee, Robin is also the oldest at twenty-six years old, and, if Shannon can be described as "religious," Robin is defined by her religious convictions; she frequently quotes her grandmother and the Bible.

Scenes One and Two: At the start of the episode, after being photographed by Banks in what is presented as a spontaneous photo shoot, the women go to a Paris couture house to try on gowns. The next day, the contestants are given free time, and a previously blooming fissure becomes even more apparent as they fight over how to spend the day and eventually divide into two groups. Adrianne wants to visit Jim Morrison's grave, while Robin cannot see the allure of visiting a cemetery and would prefer to spend the day shopping. Adrianne says, "I didn't want to have to listen to what that bitch had to say. She's psychotic!" Elyse sides with Adrianne and begins "crying out of frustration" because she cannot understand why Robin will not accompany them to the gravesite. Shannon and Robin choose to spend the day together as Adrianne and Elyse team up. Elyse says, "I'm trying to keep it from becoming [Adrianne] and me versus the two of them," but that is exactly what appears to be happening.

Scene: Upon returning to hotel, the women are instructed to get ready for a spectacular night out. They next face the "Couture Challenge"—they are sent to don couture dresses to dine in a fancy restaurant with four "Paris society gentlemen." As the women are served French delicacies such as foie gras and escargot, they all appear hesitant at first. But, while Adrianne and Elyse manage to at least taste everything and Shannon appears perpetually smiley and bubbly, Robin sneers at the French cuisine, remarking later to the camera, "The food was nasty. It wasn't all it was cracked up to be." Robin remains solemn throughout the evening, describing the four men as "These cat-daddy lustful types of men . . . you could tell they weren't socialites." She adds, "That's why I just tuned them out."

Scene: The women are brought back to the palatial presidential suite at Le Meridien Hotel with flower petals in the luxurious bathtub and champagne, chocolate, and flowers throughout the room. The men, charged with deciding the winner of the challenge, deliberate among themselves. "I wouldn't vote for Robin," one man says. "She didn't live up to this social scene." They announce Adrianne as the winner, and she selects Elyse to join in her reward, which is a night in the presidential suite. Robin and Shannon return to the lesser hotel, while Elyse and Adrianne celebrate by taking a bath, jumping on the plush bed, and eating chocolate. Adrianne makes several tongue-in-cheek remarks about her and Elyse's "romantic night together," and the women decide to go to sleep topless.

Scene: The next morning, the contestants receive "Tyra Mail" indicating they will be doing advertisements for diamonds. Mr. Jay, a makeup artist who directs the program's photo shoots, announces that they'll be posing nude. Although he explains that their hair will cover their breasts and that in fact they will be creating "the illusion" of nudity rather than actually revealing their completely naked bodies, Robin is visibly shaken. Adrianne and Elyse are up for the challenge and are the first two to complete the photo shoot. Mr. Jay creates an intimate setting "so they won't be exposed" and stresses that the outcome of the shoot is the illusion of nudity. The contestants are permitted to wear underwear and can elect to use a cloth band around their breasts (although neither Elyse nor Adrianne chooses this option). Robin says that even the illusion of being nude bothers her. Shannon decides to try out the band that would conceal her breasts. Robin claims she wants to try it, too, but ultimately both she and Shannon decline to do the shoot. Meanwhile, Mr. Jay tells Elyse that previously Robin had opened her robe and exposed her breasts to him and that Tyra had witnessed this. Shannon remarks, "I was trying to imagine the [nude] picture in my head and it just would not be me," while Robin explains her refusal by saying, "Serving the Lord ain't easy, but in the end you'll always be on top." In her one-on-one interview to the camera, Robin goes on to say, "You're looking at a representative for not only

"I Think They're Looking for a Skinny Chick!" | 141

young women but America as a whole and a woman that has integrity." To Mr. Jay, Robin launches into a tearful soliloquy:

Last week it was bra and panties, I would probably never have done that. This week it's two strands of ribbon and a thong. What is it gonna be next week? My grandmother always used to tell me if you don't stand for something you'll fall for everything. [Crying] So this stand right here I'm taking might make me eliminated but if my time here is up then I'm okay with it. I'm okay with it.

Final Scenes: The camera opens on views of Paris as the contestants pack to return to New York City. Robin addresses the camera, saying France has left a bittersweet taste in her mouth. The show ends as all episodes do, with a final cut scene facing Tyra and a panel of judges, who in this episode include Janice Dickenson, one of "the first supermodels"; Beau Quillian, a fashion editor for *Marie Claire* magazine; Kimora Lee Simmons, president and creative director of Phat fashions (and former wife of hip-hop mogul Russell Simmons); and Derek Khan, the contestants' stylist throughout their journey to Paris. One final test awaits the contestants, Derek sends them upstairs to fashion themselves in couture garments in just ten minutes; they must demonstrate what they've learned in Paris. Elyse and Shannon are the first two to face the judges, with Elyse receiving praise both for her final couture look and for her nude photo shoot, while Shannon is admonished for not heeding the advice of Parisian designers who thought her look was not "edgy" enough. Each judge then chastises Shannon for not participating in the nude photo shoot. Offering a revealing glimpse into her own complex contortions of realness and contingent representations of sexuality, Tyra Banks remarks, "I don't pose nude. But I will simulate it, meaning a G-string and then later they'll retouch the G-String out on the side. For me that's not nudity." Adrianne appears next and receives accolades both for her final couture look and for her nude photograph. Robin follows, and, as she prepares to receive criticism from the judges, Tyra rehashes a contradiction that surfaced in the episode when Robin flashed her topless physique for Mr. Jay. Tyra adds, "I was very eager to talk to Robin about the simulated nude shoot because when the cameras weren't rolling I saw something that was very out of character for her. And it shocked the hell outta me."

Asked why she refused to pose nude, Robin tearfully responds, "I didn't want to feel uncomfortable. You know my body is mine. I just didn't think that is what I needed to do in order to get ahead." Tyra and Janice take Robin to task, with Janice asking, "Where was your Bible when you were shaking your boobs?" Last, Tyra explains that Robin should have seen the nude photo shoot as an opportunity to demonstrate the beauty of her larger figure: "If you had done that photo shoot and showed that a big *ga-dunk-a-dunk* can be beautiful and it can be sexy and I can stand right next to these other girls and serve and be fierce, I think that could have been a very strong platform." Following a deliberation scene in which the judges consider the outcome of the nude photo shoot for each contestant, the episode ends with Shannon and Robin placed in the bottom two positions and Robin being voted off the show.

The Teens Respond

During the screening, most of the teens were dutifully quiet; they had been instructed by their BCM educators to be "on their best behavior." Still, at pivotal moments during the episode, snickers and groans escaped from the girls, as well as from the boys. They groaned when Elyse cried because Robin refused to visit Jim Morrison's grave and laughed when Adrianne alluded to her "romantic night" with Elyse. They also bristled at Robin's chaste reasoning for refusing to pose in the nude. China sang along with the jingle to a Nair commercial. Throughout the discussion, I reminded the teens to state their names before speaking so that I could easily identify them later when I listened to the recording. This did not always happen; some teens spoke without identifying themselves, while others hammed it up by loudly calling out their names in the direction of my recorder.

Although I already knew the answer in respect to the girls, I asked the teens if they had watched *Top Model* before and, if so, how often. Of the seven Explainer girls in the first focus group, five said they watched the program often, while the other two responded that they watched it occasionally. Of the seven boys in the group, two said they never watched the program, three said they "hardly ever" watched, one said that he occasionally watched, and one did not respond. These responses did not surprise me. I was accustomed to hearing the girls talk about the program and reasoned that, even if some boys watched, they would be loath to admit it. The dialogue that proceeded was lively, to say the least. We began by discussing some of the commercials that had aired during the program in order to get a sense of whether or not the teens understood the marketing aspects of television programming. They raised their hands and called out the names of products we had seen advertised, including two Nair commercials, a cell phone ad, a Sprite commercial, a promo for the program *My Fair Brady*, and a FIFA soccer promotion. I then asked the teens if they thought these commercials were random or if they thought the ads were geared to specific viewers of the program. Joanna responded:

> I think they show the commercials cause they know what type of audience be watching the show, so how they picked the Nair one because they know women are going to be watching this show. Women have hairy legs and they need to shave.

The other teens erupted in laughter as Joanna said, "Women have hairy legs." Nadine added that the advertising people knew that women and young people would be watching the program and therefore aired Burger King commercials and commercials for cell phones. Kelly and a boy named Anton then engaged in a debate about whether or not the advertisers thought any men were watching and whether or not men in fact watched the program.

> KELLY: I think men would watch it cause they want to see the women on the show. So that's why they had the Amped ad [a cell phone company].
> ANTON: Nope!
> KELLY: You wouldn't watch it? You disagree with me? Well, all right. I think *some* men would wanna watch it so that's why, like the Amped mobile commercial. There was also a commercial for HD TV, like for High Definition TV, and a lot of guys are into that.

These exchanges revealed that, while they disagreed about which genders viewed the program, the teens were savvy enough to know that TV programming is a business. They ascertained that advertisers and programmers work together to plan which ads would air during which programs and that advertising slots revealed information about who watched any given program. The debate between Anton and Kelly addressed gendered consumer habits targeted in the commercials that accompanied the program. If Kelly was right, male consumers favored the Amped cell phone company and cared about high definition TV more than women. If she was right about that, it logically followed that some men must be watching *Top Model*; why else would advertisers air these commercials during the show?

Black Beauties: "I Think They're Looking for a Skinny Chick!"

Next, I asked the teens to name their favorite contestant (if they had one) from the current cycle or any previous season and to explain why they liked this contestant.

> KELLY: I liked Danielle because she's funny and she took good pictures. But my favorite one was Jade because she also took good pictures and her attitude, you know, was entertainment, [imitating Jade] "Oh, this is not *America's Next Best Friend*, this is a modeling contest."
>
> OL: Okay. Anybody else? Which one did you like, Nadine?
>
> NADINE: My favorite person was Danielle because I think her attitude—She always had a—I think she didn't get caught up in the mess that was going on. And I thought she was really, really pretty. But I did think that Jade brought a lot of ratings to the show because a lot people just look 'cause they know she's bringin' drama.
>
> OL: Okay, anybody else? Yes, say your name.
>
> JARLEN: [Dramatically into the tape recorder] Jarlen! All right [dramatic pause]. My favorite contestant [dramatic pause] is Eva, Season Four. [Jade and the other girls giggle, mumbling that he's got the wrong season.] The reason she's my favorite contestant is because she's beautiful [dramatic pause] naturally beautiful [rubbing his hands together]. Her eyes are just hazel and light, her hair—[the others cut him off by erupting in loud laughter].

Jarlen, a shameless flirt, was the only boy who named a favorite contestant on the program. While he and Tyrone participated enthusiastically in the discussion, their comments were more in the class-clown vein than like those of an actual viewer of the program. It is significant that Jarlen named Eva Pigford, a contestant who, after winning *Top Model*, went on to have a moderately successful acting career on TV commercials, on a short-lived series, *Kevin Hill*, starring the actor Taye Diggs, and as a regular on the daytime soap opera *The Young and the Restless*. Eva had appeal beyond *Top Model*, and Jarlen mentioned having seen her on *Kevin Hill*, a show about an African American attorney raising an infant on his own. During the cycle in which Eva competed, viewer controversy stirred over her hair and skin color and those of the other finalist, Yaya DaCosta, with the lighter-skinned, lighter-eyed Eva defeating Yaya, whose unprocessed hair and darker tone were deemed "Afrocentric."[6] Significantly, Jarlen used my prompt to name his favorite contestant not only to elicit some laughs but also to describe the kind of woman he found attractive, "naturally beautiful" with "light hazel" eyes. The girls undermined Jarlen's preference for the light-skinned Eva by interrupting him and calling his bluff because he had incorrectly stated which cycle Eva starred in (she was the winner of Cycle Three). In this way, the girls not only rejected Jarlen's choice of Eva but also positioned themselves as "experts" regarding the show and exposed Jarlen and the other boys as casual, uncommitted observers. The three contestants the teens named— Danielle, Jade and Eva—are all either African American or of mixed racial identities including African American. While Jade and Eva can both be described as light-skinned with light-colored eyes, Danielle is dark-skinned. Danielle's racial and ethnic identity came into play later on in the teens' conversation. I next asked what qualities they thought the judges were looking for in the contestants.

> NATASHA: Confidence, enthusiasm, and beauty.
> JOANNA: I think beauty, the attitude, their emotional stability. Like how far they're willing to go . . . if they want to pose nude or next to a naked man.
> OL: Okay, attitude and sort of their beliefs about certain things?
> TYRONE: Morals.
> OL: Morals, yes.
> NADINE: Beauty, style, diversity, personality, courage, and determination.
> AMANDA: Stability, passion, spirit, and someone who would take risks at any time.
> CHINA: [In a matter-of-fact tone] I think they're lookin' for a skinny chick!

China's characteristic "tell it like it is" attitude and her comment that the judges were simply looking for "a skinny chick" were an explicit critique of the answers her peers had been providing. She interjected the idea that, while the judges claimed to be looking for remarkable traits such as courage, determination, and beauty, what they really wanted above all else was a "skinny chick." I asked if anyone agreed or disagreed with her.

> MALIK: [very quietly] I disagree with her. I kinda disagree with her. I think they're also looking for someone who can walk.
> OL: A particular kinda model's walk?
> JOANNA: I disagree [with China]. Because you can see how [the judges] are like, "I wish you could stay because you could represent all the big girls." So they want skinny girls, but they want one or two big girls so they can mix it up too. So it won't be all straight up skinny girls.

Joanna alluded to the episode we had just viewed in which Tyra Banks and Beau Quillion, one of the other judges, explained that Robin could have made a strong stand for larger women. Often on the program, when women whose physiques do not conform to the typical "model look" are voted off, one or more judges laments her departure because of her potential to "redefine beauty standards." China continued in her usual style:

> CHINA: [To the audio recorder] This is China again! [laughter] But check, they be keeping the big girls, right? And they always [emphatic] *eliminate* them by the time it get to the end! So who's playin', son? [laughter]
> NATASHA: How big is big?
> CHINA: I mean they don't always—look at Toccara, she got the boot, she didn't get that far.
> NADINE: But it's not like they eliminated her because she was fat. It wasn't like, "Yo, you can't stay cause you fat" cause they actually was giving her a chance. If anything, they would have eliminated her from the *beginning* beginning. And there was another thick girl, too. I think it's just more a matter of not filling the niche at that time, that point in time, you know? I don't think it had nothing to do with size.

Nadine noted that no contestant is ostensibly voted off because she is "fat," and Natasha suggested that "big" is subjective. However, China's comment charged that the program presents false rationales for ejecting fat participants, noting that bigger contenders never get far and surmising that the weight factor is often the *real* reason for eliminating these contestants. Amanda entered the discussion, adding an alternative reason why larger models ultimately do not succeed in obtaining the title, and a wonderfully rich exchange followed.

> AMANDA: I agree with Nadine. I think that during the time when they have plus-sized women on it . . . they don't show their full potential sometimes . . . they might sometimes be insecure. And Toccara, on the other hand, she was totally secure . . . I think the episode where she got booted off she was acting you know—
> UNIDENTIFIED Girl: Kinda wild?
> AMANDA: —and they couldn't handle that, so they booted her off. I just think the only reason why they vote plus sizes off is because they don't live up to their full potential.

"I Think They're Looking for a Skinny Chick!" | 147

OL: Hmmm. Okay, so do you think the plus-size women have a particular attitude that gets them voted off? It's not necessarily the judges not selecting the plus-size women.

AMANDA: Yeah, that's what I think.

KELLY: It's not just that she was acting wild. It's that after a while she lost her spark because she sort of like had all the pressure of competing with all these skinny people against her. And they saw it in her pictures, and so they let her go.

OL: What was her name again?

SEVERAL girls in unison: Toccara.

CHINA: Not to get on, back on the big girls—

NATASHA: Oh God!

CHINA: But they put them in situations that make it hard for them. There was one episode where they had to go to one of these places and try on clothes and they had all these small clothes. She had to squeeze herself into these small clothes! So if they know a big girl comin' get big clothes!

NEEMA: Maybe they didn't know.

TYRONE: Ashley Stewart! [a plus-size store] Ashley Stewart! [laughter]

NADINE: The typical model is skinny. It's not like they did it to be against her. It was go-sees that they was going to for that episode. So it wasn't like, go-sees is gonna have clothes for skinny girls because skinny girls are usually models. It's just now that big girls are comin' out it's not that they were tryin' to get against her, it's not like that.

TYRONE: I like big girls, too! It's Tyrone!

Kelly was a very light-skinned girl who wore revealing, tight-fitting clothing and always had perfectly styled hair. She received a lot of attention from the opposite sex, including, as addressed in chapter 2, unwanted attention from one of the adult staff members. For Kelly, the pressures of competing with skinnier contestants caused the larger models to "lose their spark" and perform poorly in photo shoots. Ever critical, China reasoned that if the program seriously supported larger models, it would have provided larger clothing to fit bigger contestants. The jokester, Tyrone, interjected the name of a popular plus-size clothing chain, Ashley Stewart, as a solution to the larger models' clothing issues, and Nadine continued to defend the program, suggesting that the producers could do only so much when industry norms dictate skinny models. The harsh life experiences and stark social inequalities all of these teens have faced permeate this exchange. Nadine's separation from her mother taught her that life is not always fair. She missed her mother terribly but wanted to complete her senior year and knew that her mother could not afford to relocate Nadine to the southern city where she had been forced to take a job after experiencing chronic unemployment in New York. Still, Nadine's mind-set was usually hopeful, and she tended to "look for the best" in people. China, on the other hand, was often an acerbic social critic. Kelly, after accusing a staff member of sexual harassment and later recanting, knew all too well the pressures aimed at young women. A number of Kelly's female peers sided with the staffer, viewing Kelly's tight clothing and the fact that she had voluntarily engaged in text messaging with the man as signals that she had solicited his attention.

Body Image, Obesity, and Minority Girls

Meaningful themes surrounding self-esteem and body image also surface in the preceding exchange. And, because three of the six "big girls" or heavier contestants on *Top Model* have been Black (including the previously mentioned Robin and Toccara), the program and the teens' conversation about it have both been laden with intersecting ideas about Black body image. Of all the teenage girls I interviewed at BCM, perhaps only one or two had typical model body types. Nadine and Amanda, the two girls who initiated the idea that heavier contestants might suffer from lower self-esteem, can both be described as "plump" or overweight. Amanda, a round-faced girl with a short, rotund stature, continued to struggle with her weight after graduating from high school and enrolling in college. She later told me that her mother, who is also overweight, "does not like fat people" and kept Amanda on a strict weight-loss routine, waking her to exercise at 6 a.m. even when the family went on vacation. Amanda was a quiet, studious girl who wore glasses and had never had a boyfriend. While more confident and outgoing, Nadine, like many of the teenage girls with whom I worked, can be described as slightly overweight. Because she had a taller frame than Amanda and because she knew how to dress fashionably, Nadine did not appear to be "fat." And her ready smile, long, straightened hair, and mature, self-assured personality attracted a number of boys. Nadine had steady romantic relationships with two boys; one was China's half-brother (Nadine moved in with China's family after the two broke up), and the other was a first-generation immigrant from Grenada who attended Nadine's high school.

Although very different girls, both Amanda and Nadine were overweight by American medical standards and distinctively "plus size" by model-industry norms. Nadine and Amanda are not atypical. According to the American

Academy of Child and Adolescent Psychiatry, between 16 and 33 percent of American children and adolescents are obese.[7] The Centers for Disease Control (CDC) reports that childhood obesity rates have increased threefold since 1980. The notion that all Americans, and children in particular, are experiencing an "epidemic" of obesity is a hot-button topic both for the news media and for public policy concerns. In April 2009, a *New York Times* editorial titled "Selling Obesity at School" argued that the easy availability of unhealthy foods in school vending machines had fueled an "epidemic" of obesity and undermined any gestures school breakfast and lunch programs made toward healthier options.[8] Addressing the American Medical Association (AMA) on June 15, 2009, President Barack Obama also described childhood obesity as an "epidemic" and urged the country to take a preventive approach to health care. "It . . . means cutting down on all the junk food that's fueling an epidemic of obesity," he argued, "which puts far too many Americans, young and old, at greater risk of costly, chronic conditions." And, in February 2010, First Lady Michelle Obama officially launched a nationwide initiative, "Let's Move," aimed at eliminating childhood obesity in one generation.

While I am not qualified to make medical diagnoses of the teens with whom I worked, health authorities such as the CDC and the American Academy of Child and Adolescent Psychiatry use a body mass index (BMI) formula to classify individuals as obese. Within these standards, a child is considered obese when his or her weight is at least 10 percent higher than what is recommended for their height and body type. Such guidelines are, of course, based on culturally relative medical standards. Still, according to these guidelines, Amanda would undoubtedly be considered obese and Nadine would likely be considered overweight. Perhaps Nadine and Amanda's weight colored their interpretations of larger contestants on *Top Model*. Interestingly, however, while China admonished the program for wanting only "skinny chicks," Nadine and Amanda seemed to "blame the victims," suggesting that the larger models' poor self-esteem truncated their chances for success. Yet, the two girls were not far off the mark in suggesting that overweight young women might have lower self-esteem. The American Academy of Child and Adolescent Psychiatry also reports that child and adolescent obesity is associated with a higher propensity for emotional problems, including low self-esteem. The contestants on *Top Model* were themselves barely out of their teenage years, with an average age of about nineteen.

The concerns Nadine and Amanda raised were relevant beyond our discussion of *Top Model*. Their concerns exposed ironies and contradictions in American discourses surrounding female body image and consumer culture, spotlighting the marginalization of girls of color in such discourses. Popular and academic critiques often position consumer culture and modeling-industry norms as contributing factors in adolescent eating disorders such as anorexia. Unrealistic female body types portrayed on television and in fashion magazines are seen as unduly influencing young girls to starve themselves. Yet, Americans are experiencing an "epidemic" of obesity, and more youth suffer from obesity than from anorexia. Social critics argue that American popular culture encourages unhealthy overeating while promoting hyperthin models and actresses as normal. Certainly, this is a mixed message. However, Nadine, Amanda, China, and the other teens demonstrate that adolescent girls are critical social agents who do not unquestioningly accept what popular culture offers. Perhaps most troubling for these girls are the ways in which young women of color are either left out of or are sweepingly generalized in discourses about diet and body image.[9] The CDC reports that obesity rates have markedly increased among all Americans and tripled among children "irrespective of age, sex, race, ethnicity, socioeconomic status, education level, or geographic region."[10] Yet, when one delves more deeply into analyses relating obesity, race, ethnicity, and socioeconomic background, there are contradictory indications. The *New York Times* cites the CDC in an article about how prevalent obesity is among the urban poor:

> Obesity is a growing problem among all groups in the United States. But according to the Centers for Disease Control and Prevention, 27 percent of blacks and about 21 percent of Hispanics of all ages are considered obese, or about 30 percent overweight, compared with just 17 percent for whites. That means that 26 million blacks and Hispanics in the country are obese, and as a result, at risk for serious health problems. And lower income minorities are at even greater risk, according to federal statistics (Barboza 2000: 5).

The *New York Times* article points to lack of nutritional knowledge and the inaccessibility of stores with healthy foods as contributing factors. The issues we considered in chapter 2 regarding the racialization of social spaces in New York City and in Brooklyn have bearing on this matter because the teens did not have easy access to the health food supermarkets and grocery stores that are more readily available in affluent sections of the city. Cindi Katz has explored the ways in which global economic restructuring has reshaped children's lives in sites as disparate as New York City and a rural village in northern Sudan, where changes to traditional ways of life mean that tasks such as fetching drinking water monopolize youths' daily routines. Katz analyzes how global capitalist forces such as the increase in knowledge-based jobs and the inadequate educational opportunities offered to minority youth result in limited access to social and material wealth (Katz 2004). Along these same lines, the BCM teens' meager paychecks meant that shopping at supermarkets that sell healthy foods would be out of the question even if such markets were more accessible. These barriers to healthy eating options suggest that simply arguing that Black and Hispanic youth suffer from obesity at higher percentages is shortsighted if we neglect to take socioeconomic and sociospatial considerations into consideration.

Televisual Portrayals of "Plus-Size" Minority Women

More influential for BCM girls than statistics quoted in the *New York Times* or provided by the CDC are the pervasive mass-mediated stereotypes of Black girls and young women. And the episode of *Top Model* that we watched together can be interpreted as reinforcing many of those stereotypes. When the African American "plus-size" contestant, Robin, faces the judges in the final cut scene, Tyra Banks uses the African American slang "ga-dunk-a-dunk" to refer to Robin's butt. Banks suggests that had Robin posed nude, she could have countered the idea that larger female bodies are not beautiful. But, by using Black slang to refer to Robin's butt, Banks racializes Robin's body and reinforces the stereotype that Black women's rear ends are larger than White women's.

In each of its cycles, *Top Model* has had between ten and fifteen contestants, with an average of about thirteen contestants. Of the contestants who appear in each cycle, three or four, on average, have been Black. However, keeping in mind that race is socially constructed, it is difficult to say definitively how many contestants have been Black—as I tried to ascertain the racial identities of *Top Model* contestants I found that on each cycle about three contestants "appeared to be Black," while one or two additional contestants appeared to be interracial, with some African American ancestry. The prevalence of fair-skinned contestants of indeterminate ethnicity speaks to T. Denean Sharpley-Whiting's astute observations regarding the beauty industry and the hip-hop generation's preference for "'ascriptive mulattas'. . . whose physical beauty transcends characteristics such as darker hues, full lips, and the like, historically prefigured as less than ideal (non-European). . . . Yet the 'mulatta' has also been deemed in literary and film annals as the most ideal in the arena of feminine beauty, and the secretly longed for in the heterosexual marketplace of desire" (Sharpley-Whiting 2007: 27). Tallying the number of "plus-size" contestants is equally problematic. I used the BCM girls' interpretations of which contestants were "big," "big boned," or "heavier" to gauge how many "plus-size" contestants had appeared on the program. Retailers typically designate American women's clothing sizes 14–32 or 12–32 as "plus-size." Following the girls' interpretations, as well as how the contestants were portrayed on the program and on Internet blogs devoted to *Top Model*, I concluded that approximately 6 plus-size contestants appeared during the program's run (out of 141 contestants total through spring 2009). Therefore, plus-size contestants were certainly in the minority, and the number of larger women on the program does not accurately reflect American society. Of the six larger-size contestants, three have been Black, two have been White, and one has been Latina. Therefore, half of the program's plus-size contestants were Black or Latina.

Black Women's Bodies: The Hottentot Venus Lives On

The teens' readings of *Top Model* are an anthropologically rich mixed bag of accepting and denying racialized and gendered constructions, many of which are steeped in age-old stereotypes and pseudoscientific notions applied to the commodification of Black women's bodies. Joanna brought us back to the topic I had initially raised: representations of Black bodies on *Top Model*.

> JOANNA: We're still talking about Black people right? . . . I think that for the black people on the show they're trying to get them to show their bodies more.
> OL: More than the white contestants?
> JOANNA: Yeah. But they got more body to show!
> JARLEN: Not always. Not always.
> JOANNA: Well, most likely. They have more body/
> CHINA:/Well, I'm not talking about me cause this ain't me. But a lot of black people got booty and all this stuff right [laughter] and when Tyra be like showing them and showing what they can do, she be like "suck in your butt some" so they really in a depiction of how black people are, they're saying "you can't be as voluptuous as you really are, you gotta confirm to this flat behind, flat titty type thing you got to," you know what I'm saying? That's just me, that's how I think.
> OL: Okay, so Tyra sort of encourages them to portray themselves in a particular way or molds their bodies/
> JARLEN: /But she got them curves=

CHINA: /Cause she be like suckin' it in, she's sucking her butt in, moving like that [demonstrates], and then they retouch it even in the picture so she's saying "be smaller" so when they retouch it they don't have that much to retouch, 'cause retouching costs money.

JARLEN: She got a big butt.

Joanna's observation that *Top Model* objectifies Black bodies to a greater degree than White bodies initiated a conversation about whether Black bodies are truly different. Interestingly, two girls, Joanna and China, argued that Black women's bodies are indeed more voluptuous, while Jarlen disagreed, saying, "Not always." China seemed to allude to Banks's "Kiss my fat ass" soliloquy (discussed later in this chapter), offering that, while her own butt is not large, China saw large butts as a racialized Black trait and that Banks encouraged Black contestants to follow her lead and perform in ways that minimize the size of their body parts. A number of fascinating issues emerged here. Joanna's and China's comments represent a fertile contradiction: On one hand, the show exploited Black bodies and "shows them more"; on the other hand, Tyra Banks taught the contestants tricks of the trade aimed at minimizing voluptuous, perhaps even "grotesque" Black body parts. Banks walked a tightrope of opposing messages. Moreover, China suggested that Black bodies can cost the modeling industry more since retouching "costs money."

The teens' talk about how Black bodies, women's butts in particular, were represented on the program demonstrates how colonial-era racialized definitions of beauty remain salient in the present day. The notion that Black women have larger butts can be traced back to the 1800s and the exploitation of Saartjie "Sarah" Baartman.[11] Also known as the Hottentot Venus ("Hottentot" was a derogatory term used by Dutch explorers for Baartman's people, and "Venus" was added in cruel irony), Baartman was a young South African woman brought to England in 1810 and publicly displayed as a freak so that Europeans could ogle her "bizarrely large" buttocks and genitalia. Baartman has been written about and extensively documented in film, so I will not restate these valuable treatments here (duCille 1996; Ifekwunigwe 2006; Maseko 1998; Sharpley-Whiting 1999). However, we must briefly revisit Baartman's example in order to better understand the origins of present-day stereotypes of Black women's bodies. After preoccupying British popular culture as a freak shown in Piccadilly Circus and as a moral cause for abolitionists who tried to free her, Baartman was taken to France in 1814, where she became the focus of "scientific" and "medical" research, influencing European conceptions of Black female sexuality (Maseko 1998). Although contemporary anthropologists who have studied Baartman's remains find nothing remarkable about her physique, for the European observers of her time, Baartman embodied the wanton female sexuality that they strove to repress or suppress under multilayered garments. Scholars have linked the notion of larger butts as an attribute of Blackness to Social Darwinists' attempts to provide scientific justification for racial categories (duCille 1996; Chin 2001: 157).

> Georges Cuvier, one of several nineteenth-century scientists to dissect and to write about Bartmann, maintained that the black female "looks different;" her physiognomy, her skin color, and her genitalia mark her as "inherently different." Long since recognized as morbidly racist, the language of Cuvier's "diagnosis" nevertheless resembles the terms in which racial difference is still written today (duCille 1996: 56).

Ann duCille has applied the fascination with Baartman's posterior to her study of present-day ethnically correct dolls, and anthropologist Elizabeth Chin has engaged in a dialogue with duCille, teasing out the meanings attached to Black dolls such as Shani, who allegedly has a larger butt than Barbie. Although both are created by Mattel and appear to the naked eye to have been made from identical body molds, duCille's interviews revealed that Shani's designers claimed to have given the doll the "*illusion* of broader hips and an elevated buttocks [*sic*]" (duCille 1996: 53, emphasis in original). For Chin, "These ethnically correct dolls demonstrate one of the abiding aspects of racism; that a solid belief in racial difference can shape people's perceptions so profoundly that they will find difference and make something of it, no matter how imperceptible or irrelevant its physical manifestation might be" (Chin 2001: 158).

Tricia Rose has argued that the racialization of Baartman's allegedly large buttocks is echoed in twentieth-century rap songs, such as "I Like Big Butts" and "Poison" (featuring Bell Biv Devoe's famous refrain, "You can't trust a big butt and a smile"), that link Black women's bodies to a vulgar and dangerous sexuality (Rose 1994: 167). We can add the hit song by Destiny's Child, "Bootylicious," a more contemporary example. Although it can be argued that the latter song celebrates Black women's bodies (the trio sing, "I don't think you're ready for this jelly . . . 'cause my body's too bootylicious for you babe"), "Bootylicious," like its predecessors, channels in the (albeit tongue-in-cheek) belief that Black women's bodies are distinct and hypersexualized.

Interestingly, this ideology has diversified to include other racial and ethnic groups with the objectification of women such as Jennifer Lopez and Kim Kardashian. Arguably, Lopez, who is Puerto Rican, and Kardashian, who is of Armenian and European ancestry, have capitalized on the (largely male) consumption of their posteriors in Lopez's own music videos and in Kardashian's infamous sex tape and reality program. In the late 1990s, British and American tabloids reported that Lopez had insured her body parts for millions of dollars, with local papers such as the *New York Daily News* and the *New York Post* focusing on the alleged exact amount for which her famously large derrière was insured. Kardashian gained notoriety when a sex tape featuring her with Black rapper Ray J was leaked to an Internet pornography film company. After Internet gossip alleged that Kardashian achieved her large buttocks through plastic surgery, she reportedly credited her voluptuous rear end to her Armenian ancestry. Controversy surrounding the sex tape and the subsequent fascination with her derrière launched Kardashian's career, which included a reality show, *Keeping Up with the Kardashians*, that featured an episode in which Kim receives a spa treatment—administered in her underwear—to minimize cellulite on her behind, as well as a stint as a contestant on *Dancing with the Stars*.

Most meaningful for our purposes, one blog, BrownPride.us, featured a celebrity forum titled "Armenian vs. Puerto Rican, Jennifer Lopez vs. Kim Kardashian," which juxtaposed full-body profiles of the two women and encouraged bloggers to compare their butts.[12] These images are reminiscent of Sarah Baartman's "freak show" exposure in London's Piccadilly Circus when crowds gathered and paid to peer under her loincloth. When I taught a college course called "Constructing Race," many of my students, from diverse racial backgrounds, blistered when I suggested that Black women's butts are not actually any larger than those of other racial groups. My students had accepted the stereotype as fact. Overwhelmingly, social scientists argue that we add social significance to physical features that hold no real scientific difference (Omi and Winant 1994). In other words, there is no scientific basis or "proof" that Black women's behinds are any larger than those of women from any other ethnic group. Cultural factors such as diet and nutrition affect bodies, and social norms have influenced White women to cover up certain body parts that African American and Caribbean women have boldly displayed and celebrated. Considering the bustle dresses that were the rage at the time, it is arguable that nineteenth-century Europeans signaled their own obsession with larger behinds and projected their own sexual repression onto Baartman. However, as Chin has argued, in the present day, this translates into race as commodity: "The commodification of race and the introduction of racialized commodities have not erased the color line so much as they have replaced it with lines of color, an array of products intended for minority consumers" (Chin 2001: 154). Chin's assertion can certainly be applied to *Top Model*, as it markets Black contestants, with whom minority girls are expected to identify, even as it racializes these contestants' bodies as modeling-industry aberrations. China keenly highlighted the racialized commodification of *Top Model* contestants when she said that larger butts have to be digitally retouched out of pictures and "retouching costs money." A telling contradiction lies in the fact that, for women such as Lopez and Kardashian, larger butts *make* money.

As much as this chapter reveals the BCM teens are savvy consumers of popular culture, we would be remiss not to give due diligence to the ways in which they are influenced by music videos and reality programs such as *Keeping Up with the Kardashians*, which focus a male gaze on the physiques of young women of color. All of these images and ideologies surfaced as the teens continued their conversation about Black women's bodies on *Top Model*.

KELLY: But in the episode we saw they were actually complimenting Elyse [a White contestant] on how voluptuous her butt looked/—
CHINA: /Cause she don't got none!
JOANNA: Right cause she don't got no damn booty!
CHINA: They ain't saying "be a wall" but don't be stickin' out, like, you know?
KELLY: Well it depends on what kinda picture they're taking, like if they want a picture of a nice girl walking a dog in a park they're not gonna want to see like my butt instead of the dog, but if you're like taking a picture of like/—
JOANNA: /If you got a booty they're gonna see it anyways.

China's, Joanna's, and Kelly's remarks addressed the conflicting standards the modeling industry demands (models must not have "too large" a butt, though they should also not "be a wall") and suggested that, if indeed Black models have larger butts, they would not be suitable for demure shoots featuring "a picture of a nice girl walking a dog in the park." This harkens back to the idea that Black women's bodies represent indecent sexuality. Joanna's final comment, that there is no hiding a large butt, suggests that Black models' racialized bodies set limits on the kinds of modeling jobs for which they will be hired (a suggestion that Banks's transition into lingerie modeling seems to confirm). Furthermore, here the mere *perception* that Black women have larger butts is enough to limit the Black contestants' chances for mainstream or commercial success. And, although China tried to distance herself by saying "this ain't me," the teen girls' own sexual identities are implicated in the ways in which young minority women who are not too different from them are depicted on television.

In a passage reminiscent of the scrutiny directed at Sarah Baartman, Cornel West has written, "Americans are obsessed with sex and fearful of black sexuality. . . . The dominant myths draw black women and men either as threatening creatures who have the potential for sexual power over whites, or as harmless, desexed underlings of white culture" (West 2001: 83). What West terms "dominant myths" Patricia Hill Collins has described as "controlling images." For Black women, these controlling images include "the Mammy," "the Matriarch," "the Jezebel," and "the Welfare Mother," powerful stereotypes based on interconnected constructions of race, class, gender, and sex (Collins 1991). These controlling images surface not only on the teens' television sets but also on Internet blogs, in popular hip-hop and dancehall songs and music videos, and in the global flow of countless commodities. They cross national boundaries and have been applied to Caribbean women's bodies. In her study of sex workers in the Dominican Republic, anthropologist Denise Brennan has shown how, throughout the Caribbean's colonial history, the *mulatta* has represented illicit sex (Brennan 2004: 35). Just as Baartman's, Lopez's, and Kardashian's butts have been defined as sites of illicit, profitable sexuality, so, too, have the bodies of Dominican sex workers, whose sexuality has been largely defined within global "sexscapes" that traffic in powerful myths about "the exotic *mulata*" (Brennan 2004: 34–36). And we see these contradictory myths at play in the teens' attempts to make sense of how Black women's bodies are portrayed on *Top Model*. I hasten to emphasize that these images and myths about the sexuality of women of color are contradictory because, just as Lopez and Kardashian can be interpreted as gaining power and wealth through the commodification of their derrières, scholars have analyzed hypersexualized femininity in hip-hop and dancehall as potential sites of feminist power. "For these scholars, irreverent and sexually explicit rappers like Foxy Brown and Lil' Kim are not merely pawns of a sexist recording industry—indeed, a sexist culture—that can't get enough of brown-skinned T&A. Instead, they are independent, they demand respect, and they refuse to discount women's sexual desires and pleasures"

(D. Thomas 2004: 256). While throughout this text I acknowledge the ways in which, especially within the context of Black female hip-hop artists, irreverent sexuality represents the "ongoing struggle for control over black female sexuality" (D. Thomas 2004: 256), the BCM girls revealed that, in the context of *Top Model* and programs like it, Black women's bodies are often exploited sites, framed as aberrations to hegemonic definitions of beauty.

Religion, Morality, and Protecting/Presenting the Black Body

Questions of morality alongside ideas about presenting, protecting, and representing Black bodies came to fore when the teens turned their attention to the choice faced by the *Top Model* contestants. I asked if they thought Elyse and Adrianne had made the right decision to pose nude or if they felt Robin and Shannon were correct in declining the nude photo shoot. The consensus among the group of Explainers was that Robin had contradicted herself and that Shannon had simply followed Robin's poor example. Here is what some of the girls had to say:

> NEEMA: I think Adrianne and Elyse made the best decision because if you really want to pursue a modeling career you have to roll with the punches. If you want to be a model you absolutely have to know that some modeling agency . . . is going to want you to do something that you're not going to want to do. And if that's not what you want to do, then you just need to do something else. And they even gave them an option, they gave Robin and Shannon the option to do the band [covering their breasts] if you don't want to do the band, then you're just really not open-minded.
>
> JOANNA: I feel that Adrianne and Elyse made the right choice because even if they don't want to pose nude, if you want to be a model and walk the runway you going to have to go back stage and people are going to change you [dressers will change your clothes for you]. . . . You're going to be there with titties out and a thong on, mad naked. So if you can't take pictures in front of three people, how you feel you're ready to become a model?
>
> KELLY: I had a different answer, but it was basically the same reason. I said they all made the best decision for themselves because it shows the girls what will be demanded of them in the modeling world and it forces them to decide whether or not they can handle it . . . and then obviously Robin and Shannon couldn't handle what was expected of them. So they eventually got sent home.

In this instant, the girls seemed to accept the basic messages and intentions of the episode. They went on to stress that Robin's downfall lay in the fact that she contradicted herself. Neema and Amanda remarked that Robin had flashed her breasts to Mr. Jay; and, according to Amanda, in a previous episode Robin was seen "droppin' it like it's hot" and "she did it with ease!" "Drop it like it's hot" is a phrase popularized by rapper Snoop Dogg that refers to a female dancer's making a quick, low squat and "dropping" her butt close to the floor. "Droppin' it like it's hot" is regarded as a hypersexualized dance move, practiced not only in dance clubs but also by strippers. Amanda recalled that Robin had "dropped it like it's hot" and remarked, "What [she did] is kinda stupid because how can you be reading your Bible? How can you be doing that and then in one of the episodes you're droppin' it like it's hot?" In light of the historic fascination with Black women's butts, it is especially significant that Amanda focuses on Robin's "drop it like it's hot" move. Moreover, Amanda suggests that modest, Bible-reading girls do not "drop it like it's hot," nor do they flash their bare breasts at men.

Religion was not a topic that readily came up with the teens, so I was intrigued that the episode sparked a conversation about faith and morality. The group brought religion up again at the end of our conversation when I asked them if there was anything else they would like to add. The program framed Robin's religiosity as disingenuous, with the teens' agreeing and using this representation not only to critique Robin's contradictory behavior toward posing nude but also to reproach her for her attitude during the dinner with French society men.

AMANDA: I thought, being that Robin is African American, I think she should be more open. She seemed so like, closed off. I forgot what she said about the young men, but it seems as though she was having *the worst* time of her life. She just didn't want to have anything to do with it. Then she lost the challenge, and she's all mad and stuff. That's not how you should act, you know? You should at least be happy for somebody if they won because she didn't even want it in the first place because she was acting like that.

JOANNA: I feel in the part where they had to go with the French men that Robin should have at least taken a little taste of the food. . . . She just totally like shut down. Like somebody just killed her grandmother or something. And she just sat there like she was at a funeral and was about to cry. It was like she just stuck to her Bible and didn't look at nothing else, didn't make no contact with nobody. You're trying to win, so you have to be like a lady. You want to win so you can be in the presenters seat, and she's acting like she don't want to be there.

Interestingly, Amanda linked being African American with being "open" to trying new things and accepting in novel situations, while Joanna suggested that being ladylike is not only about sticking to your Bible. Joanna's reasoning that ladylike behavior is necessary in order to win mirrors the BCM teen girls' approach to achieving success at the museum; they knew that they would receive their stipends only if they behaved "properly." Nadine followed Joanna's comment, offering insights about her own pastor and her own ideas about "Godliness," while Amanda and China weighed in on notions of African American identity and Christianity.

> NADINE: To me, [Robin] spent too much time trying to be Godly, but she's just missing the whole point. . . . She's trying to switch everything to the Bible. I think even if my pastor was to go with them, he wouldn't act like that. He wouldn't, because he knows what everything is about. She spent too much time fiendin' to just be this Godly person. I know when she gets home, she's not really like that. She just wants the world to see her like that because she's on TV. She's not really like that. And if she was out with some people, without cameras there, she would have been a little laid back. She's spending too much time trying to be this Godly Black person to me.
> AMANDA: I agree with what Nadine was saying because it was in another episode I can't remember who, I think she went into the room and told Elyse to read a passage from the Bible and it was kinda thrown off [inaudible] because the girl was atheist or something, [Elyse] was totally going to get on [Robin's] bad side. I think that being that people are Christian, a Christian is supposed to be open-minded to everything. I could understand a Christian that's like homophobic or that's basically that threatened or that scared of it. But she was *so* closed-minded about it. She didn't open up her mind to it. She didn't at least try to get any taste of it [referring to the French food] to know.
> CHINA: Because as a Christian you're not supposed to tear people apart and treat them negatively you're supposed to understand what you believe, believe what you believe and understand where you're coming from. By her acting the way she was acting, it was like, she ain't no real Christian, please.

The girls saw Robin's antics as pretentious posturing, affected solely for the cameras. In a revealing dialogue, they sketch Blackness and religiousness as conjoined identities, both predicated on realness. These ideologies draw from the girls' schema for authentic femininity and from American and West Indian notions of female respectability. As we saw earlier, Caribbean women have since colonial times been linked to the "respectable" arenas of home and church. In this exchange, when Joanna criticized Robin for "sticking to her Bible and not caring for anything else," she was problematizing the notion that ideal femininity should be based exclusively on religious piousness. Here the girls also touched on well-known polemics surrounding homophobia in the Black community. Revealingly, Amanda excused homophobia in the name of Christianity but could not accept other forms of close-mindedness from a Black Christian. The teens listened regularly to a number of dancehall artists who espouse homophobia, including Buju Banton. And, as we saw at the start of chapter 2, the BCM educators regularly admonished them for using "gay" as a derogatory term. Yet, the youth also accepted the authority of the two gay experts on *Top Model*. In the exchange, when Amanda mentioned homophobia in the Black church, the teens did not directly address the fact that two gay men, Miss J. and Mr. Jay, are prominently featured on the program. While both Tyra Banks and the teens saw Robin as contradicting herself by flashing her breasts at Mr. Jay, it is arguably one thing to show your breasts to a gay man and quite another to pose for nude pictures that will be seen by countless others. Robin's act of exposing herself to Mr. Jay can also be read as an awkward attempt to strike up some form of camaraderie with a man who Robin knew would not be interested in her sexually. And, considering that Robin was positioned as a "plus-size" contestant on the program, it is plausible that she exposed herself to Mr. Jay in a misfired ploy for approval from an industry authority. However, the teens did not see it this way. China concluded the girls' musings on religious faith by asserting that true Christian behavior is predicated on holding true to one's own beliefs while treating others respectfully.

"Who Are You to Judge That?": Achievement, Gendered Success, and Racial "Difference"

The *Top Model* contestants' quests for success resonated with the BCM teens in unexpected ways. When I pressed them to consider whether the show accurately presents all of the different kinds of young women in America, Kelly said, "I think they're portraying the type of people who want to become models." This demonstrated that the youth were well aware of the limited ways in which femininity was defined on the program. Still, members of the group empathized with the "setbacks," as Amanda put it, experienced by the would-be models. Mark, who had not been nearly as outspoken as the girls during our discussion, offered the following:

I don't like the whole thought of the show. Because the way I see it, who are you to tell this person that they can or cannot model? How you going to tell that to somebody? That's like saying I can't go to school. Who are you to judge that?

Mark equated the contestants' efforts to succeed in modeling with his own struggles to succeed in high school and go on to college. While his words were confrontational—"How you going to tell that to somebody?"—Mark's delivery was heartbreaking. I glimpsed this form of despair in the face of challenges to their success again and again among the boys. As we have seen, there was an achievement gap, with the girls outperforming boys in the BCM internship, that mirrored the gender disparity Nancy López has identified between minority girls and boys at both the high school and the college levels (López 2003, 2004). However, when Mark said, "That's like telling me I can't go to school," he was alluding to more than the gendered achievement gap; his comment can also be applied to racialized and gendered barriers that police minority boys' access to education. López documents "physical and symbolic violence directed toward young men" in a New York public school, arguing that "the prevailing assumption that low-income youth who are racialized as Latino and black, especially young men, are prone to aggression has resulted in the normalization of violence as well as the threat of violence against them in urban schools nationally" (Stanton-Salazar 1997 in López 2004: 39). For boys like Mark, attending school was akin to going to prison, and security policies were tantamount to telling these youth that school was not a safe place for them. Still, Mark's stirring comment fell on somewhat unsympathetic ears, eliciting the following retorts from Anton and Neema:

> ANTON: Well, somebody can tell you that if you're going into a certain profession. Like if you can't count, you're not gonna be an accountant [laughter]. Or if you're unattractive and somebody tells you you can't model, then you can't model. That's different than going to school.
>
> NEEMA: Going on what Anton said, it's not like they telling you you can't model, it's that maybe your video that you sent in wasn't good enough. Maybe you can try in the next season and if you improve your skills maybe you can get in. But honestly it's week after week after week, and you're improving your skills. They're giving you classes, they're telling what to do to improve this or that. If you choose not to adhere to what they're telling you, then that's your loss. That's when you're getting kicked off. They're not telling you that you can't model, it's that they're telling you that at this particular time and moment you do not have what they're looking for.

While Anton advocated brutal honesty, Neema emphasized the BCM girls' philosophy: If you follow the rules, work hard, and apply yourself to what you're being taught, then you will succeed. As Mark's comment suggests, however, and as is the case both for the BCM boys and for the contestants who get "kicked off" *Top Model*, sometimes one's personal setbacks and disadvantages *are* barriers to success. Both the BCM boys and girls regarded their own chances for success with trepidation, expressing anxiety and fear about whether they would get into college and/or become gainfully employed. Nadine weighed both Anton and Neema's remarks alongside Mark's and offered a balanced middle ground.

> In a way, I agree with what Anton and Neema is saying by you going on this show, you know what you're going there for. You're going there to be judged. So if you don't want to be judged, don't go. But in a way, I kinda understand what Mark is saying, too, because, especially in the last season, Season Six, they told Danielle that she had to close up her gap [between her two front teeth] and change her accent.

Nadine continued and launched the group into a rousing discussion of how *Top Model* attempted to correct both the southern accent and the dental "defects" of a contestant named Danielle, a favorite among the girls.

> NADINE: That has nothing to do with modeling. . . . She *can* have a gap [between her teeth], that can be her signature thing that makes somebody love her. . . . Nobody's telling Tyra [Banks] to pull her hairline further down on her forehead [laughter] so I understand where Mark be coming from. Nobody's perfect and everything about somebody makes them different. So I don't think Danielle should have to change her accent because they didn't tell the African girl to change her accent. What, it's okay to have an African accent but not okay to have a southern accent? And her teeth? It wasn't like her teeth was doing Crips signs and stuff in her mouth [uproarious laughter]. It was a little space in her tooth and I thought she was pretty with the gap and they didn't have to take off the gap. So in a way I understand where Mark is coming from.
> OL: So did she change her face by the end of the show?
> NADINE: She had to.

NEEMA: But she still won.

NADINE: Yes, she won, but she was forcing herself with this accent. She got better than when she first started. In a way you still couldn't understand her, but Tyra was always telling her, "You gotta get rid of that accent cause it's not gonna work." . . . But she did close up her gap. I mean her gap is still a little bit there, but they closed it up.

KELLY: I was actually disappointed because yesterday I was reading *People* [magazine] and there was an article about her and it said that she did close the gap and she doesn't have as much of an accent because she speaks slower. But I think that necessarily the whole "you must conform to this". . . some of it was "You need to do this because it's the part of a model" if you're walking down the red carpet and they're like "How does it feel to be a model" and you're like "blah, blah, blah" and nobody can understand you then it defeats the whole purpose and like the gap I'm a little bit unsure on, but like the accent is something I can understand. But the gap, I don't know. Maybe they'll think that everybody will focus on the gap and not be able to view the whole picture, I don't know.

Standard American Speech and West Indian Youth

The teens' ruminations about Danielle closing the gap between her teeth and changing her accent are related to their own struggles with the awkward physical changes all adolescents experience and to more specific racialized definitions of beauty and standardized speech with which Black adolescents contend. Their discussion can also be applied to the politics surrounding speech and national identity that Caribbean teenagers negotiate. While having a gap between one's two front teeth is in no way a sign of Blackness, not being able to afford orthodontics is certainly an indication of one's class status. And, for the girls, the idea that Danielle's natural features were not good enough to ensure her victory on the program undermined the idea that a "real" person, someone cosmetically unchanged, could become a symbol of beauty. When Nadine asked, "What, it's okay to have an African accent but not a southern one?," she was emphasizing that Danielle is an American. The underlying ideology here is a marginalization of African American vernacular; on the program, Danielle's speech was not deemed as legitimate as a foreign accent. The issue of Danielle's accent proved to be even more meaningful when China reentered the conversation.

CHINA: I disagree with Tyra on the accent because I have an accent. But I know how to turn it off and turn it on. Yes, I do. Because if I'm talking to people, honestly if I'm going out for a job interview in America, I'm gonna have an American accent. Because I'm not going to be like [using Bajan accent] "How ya' doin'? Wha' goin' on?" [laughter] and having a Bajan accent. They're gonna be saying to me, "What are you saying? What are you doing?" But if I'm with my family or I'm with my friends, I'ma' talk like I just got off the boat! I just disagree with Tyra, you gotta know how to turn it off and turn it on. If you're gonna be on a broad scale talking to a lot of people around the world, you need to have a kinda thing that you can portray to everybody. Not just people who live down in wherever she from.

OL: China is making a really interesting point. She's saying that we all have things that we do or ways of behaving in one context that might be different in a different context, right?

CHINA: Yeah.

China describes the act of using one's accent to code-switch or move back and forth between two identities, in this case American and West Indian. While we all code-switch in one form or another by presenting different versions of ourselves in distinct contexts according to our notions of propriety, scholars of West Indian migration have documented how language and accent are used to code-switch as immigrants maneuver between being perceived as African American and being seen as foreigners (Butterfield 2004; Waters 1999).

Based on her extensive interviews, Mary Waters has noted that "the accent and the type of patois or Creole slang or language spoken by the immigrants [are] important markers of identity for them" (Waters 1999: 76). West Indians are sometimes initially surprised to learn that their accent or use of West Indian patois can be advantageous or disadvantageous depending on the situation. Waters recounts an example of a Trinidadian woman who consciously decided to keep her accent because it garnered her preferential treatment at work (her employer preferred to hire West Indians over Black Americans because of negative stereotypes of African Americans) and positive reactions in school (teachers commented on her "nice accent") (Waters 1999: 124–125). Waters goes on, however, to assert that, while the West Indian accent elicits praise from White Americans, whether they be educators or employers, it is often seen negatively by African Americans, who can interpret it "as a source of annoyance and distance between the two groups" (Waters 1999: 135). I witnessed all of these reactions and motivations with the teens.

While in the dialogue China suggests that turning off her Bajan accent is appropriate when she is "going out on a job interview in America," there were times when the teens described receiving better treatment from their White public school teachers if they asserted their West Indianness by speaking with an accent. And, as China articulated, the teens also knew that playing up their accents in the company of West Indian relatives and friends was an important way to emphasize closeness and help maintain kinship ties. I followed up China's comment by asking her when she thought it was good to use her Bajan accent, and she responded, "When I'm home or when I'm with my friends." Intriguingly, China did not distinguish between her African American and her West Indian friends. These findings add to the scholarship on West Indian migration by offering insight into how language and accent are used in leisure and consumer spheres as opposed to work and schools. Teens both at BCM and at the Flatbush YMCA utilized their West Indian accents in leisure settings when they wanted to assert difference from their African American peers. Since so many of the teens at BCM were West Indian, I did not see any indication that sounding West Indian won them better treatment from the educators there. However, beyond the museum and the YMCA, at local West Indian eateries, for example, the immigrant teens showed off for their African American peers and hoped to receive better service by ordering in West Indian patois. African American teenagers in Flatbush and Crown Heights sometimes turned the tables on their West Indian friends, however, by affecting a West Indian accent in order to sing along with the latest popular dancehall hit. And, on one fascinating occasion, when a Jamaican Flatbush YMCA teen ordered lunch at a roti shop using a Jamaican accent, her African American friend, who was next on line, stunned the Jamaican youth and elicited uproarious laughter by also ordering in a perfectly delivered Jamaican accent. I witnessed such examples of African American teens adopting West Indianness either through the use of language or by appropriating music on numerous occasions and thus came to see the formation of West Indian and African American identities as a "bidirectional process" (Butterfield 2004).

Accents, Class, Generation, and Race

Mary Waters notes:

> Many of the working-class immigrants were proud of their Island patois language and talked about how they would use it to speak to each other on the job, so outsiders could not understand them. The middle-class immigrants were more conflicted about the use of the patois. They all

said they could speak it, and often did speak it at home, but they also described how their parents had tried to discourage their use of it, and how they in turn did not want their children speaking it outside of the home. The middle-class immigrants tended to call the patios [sic] a separate language. They were very proud of their use of standard English, and they saw the use of the patios [sic] in any public situation as a lower-class thing to do (Waters 1999: 77).

In this passage, from her interviews with New York's West Indian immigrants in work and school settings, Waters notes a distinction between how working-class and middle-class West Indians utilized and regarded patois. Class identity was, however, for my interviewees, not a hard and fast label. Some teens' parents were professionals "back home" who had been forced into working-class jobs once they emigrated. Additionally, there was diversity among the BCM teens and, to a lesser extent, among the YMCA youth, with most teens coming from working-class homes and some from poor or middle-class households. Nor was the teens' use of accents and patois readily attributable to their class identity. For teens such as China, whether they were first- or second-generation immigrants and age at migration were more significant indicators of how and whether they employed a West Indian accent. China migrated to Brooklyn when she was ten years old, and she was seventeen when I first interviewed her. For youth like China, speaking in Bajan patois was a recent cultural practice that she did not fully abandon. Yet, China acknowledged that she can choose to speak "like [I] just got off the boat" or to use standard American English. Still, for the youth in my study, the choice was less between Standard American English and West Indian patois and more between the latter and African American vernacular. China astutely articulates this when she asserts that both she, an immigrant from Barbados, and Danielle, the African American contestant from *Top Model*, have accents. While some research on West Indian migration has been framed to suggest that only West Indian immigrants have accents, China asserted that African Americans also have accents (in fact, of course, regional speech patterns are identifiable among White American ethnic and geographic groups, as well). For teenagers, then, identity formation is such a slippery process and code-switching is so prominent that the teens can readily see commonality among ethnic groups other than their own and can claim a sense of African diasporic belonging with African Americans who also employed a distinctive or marginalized form of speech.

Real Beauty, Real Black, and Reality TV

Nadine's and Kelly's disappointment that Danielle's "natural beauty" had to be altered demonstrated the girls' desire for a "real" contestant to win *Top Model*. China's acknowledgment that accents are advantageous in some contexts but a hindrance in others indicates that these teens learned that identity is, as Stuart Hall argues, "a production" and never as static as we may think (Hall 1990). Notions of "real" or authentic Blackness, particularly in relation to beauty and femininity, permeated the teens' conversations and surfaced several times vis-à-vis critiques of *Top Model* in particular and reality television more generally speaking. Mark interrupted China's and Nadine's exchange regarding China's accent to criticize the program's reliance on artificiality.

> MARK: I think the show would be better if it was more stuff based on their natural beauty. I'm not a big fan of makeup and stuff. So all those pounds and pounds of makeup and that airbrushing stuff, that makes you look awkward.

Recall that Mark equated the ways in which *Top Model* judges its contestants with the way others "judge" one's ability to succeed in school. With this second critique, on the heels of China's comment regarding her accent and Kelly and Nadine's contestation of altering Danielle's teeth, the teens underscored the idea that natural or "real" Black beauty was not rewarded on the program. Nadine and Neema interjected in response to Mark, however, in a revealing if not unproblematic defense of how the program portrays "real" beauty.

> NADINE: They do that, too. They do a lot of photo shoots without make up.
> NEEMA: Yes, they do photo shoots without makeup.
> NADINE: A lot of them are without makeup—or just Vaseline. I remember one where they used Vaseline.
> NEEMA: Yeah, when they were crying. I mean the only thing they had on was mascara to make it run. Like that episode when they were doing a photo shoot on the things that make them stand out, the features, they didn't even have on makeup. But guess what? It's not going to be a natural thing because they retouch photos. Jade could be taking a picture and have a big pimple right here in the middle of her forehead [pointing to Jade], but when they take that picture they will retouch that picture so that the pimple is gone! So it doesn't matter if she have on makeup or not, they're gonna retouch it.

The girls tried to rebut Mark's critique by suggesting that *Top Model* did present natural or "unmade-up" beauty. Interestingly, however, what they described is the staging of naturalness; a Vaseline-covered face is presented as one in its natural state, and displaying real emotion, crying, is enhanced— it is visible only if mascara is running down one's cheek. Neema further suggested that in the modeling industry, "a natural thing" is nonexistent because all photographs will be retouched to minimize models' flaws and blemishes. Here, the teens not only offered a critique of the artificiality of the beauty industry and of *Top Model* but also articulated a criticism of reality television in general.

Our group discussion about *Top Model* continued, with the teens growing more and more eager to share their insights. One of the most pressing issues for me was a desire to get at the teens' thoughts regarding how *Top Model* portrayed young women in general and Black women in particular.

> OL: The next question I have is how would you describe the way young women are depicted on the show?
>
> TYRONE: Very diverse.
>
> OL: So what kinds of images of young women did you see?
>
> TYRONE: I mean black, white, [pause as if he can't think of anything else].
>
> CHINA and others: [Laughter]
>
> TYRONE: /Skinny, medium, large=
>
> UNIDENTIFIED Girl: [Whispering] Asian.
>
> TYRONE: Asian, Asian, yes.
>
> JARLEN: They're mostly looking for blond, brown-eyed, green-eyed, twenty-five, thirty-eight, thirty-two/
>
> GROUP: [Laughter]
>
> JARLEN: /looking women.
>
> MARK: I think the ones that have like some kinda backbone are the ones that get booted off.

Here Tyrone interpreted my question to mean the racial identities and physical images of women depicted on the program, while Mark's response focused on the contestants' character. Nadine and Mark continued, unearthing how "reality" shows distort reality by editing footage to tell a particular story and going on to astutely propose that *Top Model* portrays a *certain type* of woman.

NADINE: I think really it depends on the girl. It's not really how—'cause a lot of shows can cut and paste stuff to depict to make you somebody that you're not. This show, I really think it's like straight up. A girl depicts herself. Whatever comes off is based on how she acts. If I go there being mad rude and stink it's gonna be that. That's what they're gonna get from me. To me it's based on the girl.

OL: So you think the show reflects accurate personalities.

NADINE: Yeah.

OL: And when you say there are other shows where they cut and paste and edit, what kinda shows are you talking about?

NADINE: (Sighs and laughs) I don't know—

TWO boys loudly: *Real World*! *Real World*!

NADINE: Yeah! Like they would cut and paste to like make you out to be somebody that you're not or maybe, sometimes you have your bad days, but they only show your bad days rather than your good days, like that.

UNIDENTIFIED Boy: That's true. Yeah.

NADINE: I thought this show was much, you know, about putting it the way it is.

OL: All right, anybody else want to answer this question about how the show depicts young women?

MARK: I think some of them have more to offer than just modeling. I mean usually when you see a model she's like a dumb blond. But some of them could probably go run their own business. And some of them are uncomfortable with modeling. Some of them don't wanna do it because they are uncomfortable doing a certain pose because they're worried about what their boyfriend will think if he sees it. So why model? Teach or something like that. Why put yourself in that position?

By interpreting *Top Model* as presenting more accurate depictions of the contestants' personalities than other reality shows that she felt edit footage in order to portray individuals in a negative light, Nadine addressed the ideological crux of "reality" programming—is it really for real? Her interpretation suggests that Banks succeeded in presenting *Top Model* as a show that "put[s] it the way it is." Mark, however, rather insightfully suggested that the program presented young women who might have other skills and might be better suited for other professions. Mark also positioned modeling as a nontraditional profession that may expose young women to compromising positions and fear of disapproval from male partners. His proposed solution was that women enter the more traditional profession of teaching. I pressed Mark to elaborate on his analysis and tried to get the teens to speak specifically to how Black women are depicted on the program.

> OL: So do you think that's just what's on the show, or do you think the show allows us to see different things that young women can do?
>
> MARK: I just think that some of the things they do seem stupid. Like just now, she don't wanna pose nude. So why, like they know they're gonna be asked to do stupid things every once in a while. If you know you don't want to do certain things, say that in the beginning. Why you gonna' wait till the last second to say, "I don't want to do this," and then look stupid? And while I'm talking about that, I think they *both* should've gotten booted off.
>
> UNIDENTIFIED Boy: Word! I agree with that.
>
> OL: Okay. How do you think Blacks are depicted on the show, in general?
>
> NEEMA: I think it's very diverse because I could come on the show and act ghetto but Nadine could come on the show and she could be civilized. And that's just what you see you see me being ghetto and Nadine acting like she's been someplace. And that's just how it is. It's not showing or picking on nobody or anything like that, it's just showing the intelligence you had coming into the show with.

While Mark lambasted the contestants' "stupid actions," his previous comment laid blame on both the contestants and the program for framing the women solely within the limited world of modeling. Neema's response suggests a telling dichotomy between "ghetto" and "civilized." She argued that *Top Model* portrayed Blacks as "very diverse" but then offered only two polar opposites, "ghetto" and "civilized," as ways of being Black. In this instance, Neema conceptualized Blackness in spatial terms: either "being ghetto" or "acting like she's been someplace." This reemphasizes the salience of place-making and stresses the significance of spatialized notions of race and gender. While Neema and Nadine argued that *Top Model* depicted Blacks as they really are, Amanda chimed in to complicate the discussion and offer insights on Black identities within and beyond *Top Model*.

> AMANDA: So far what I've seen on this show for like the past I forget how many seasons there were, but I could take from Tiffany or Camille or Kenya, they depicted them kinda tough . . . the way they depict them is in a more tough tone. They're more determined.

OL: So you think the Black contestants you've seen on the show have been depicted as more determined than the other contestants. Do you think that's coincidental, or do you think that Blacks *are* more determined?

AMANDA: You know they have that kind of a setback. They know they have a setback, so they're going to act like they really need it, like they care about it. They're going to act way more determined. But some of the other ethnicities are going to be a little bit more laid back.

TYRONE: I think Blacks on shows in general have a more—because maybe Black people on shows are seen to act real crazy, so I think certain Black people go on the show and try to prove that they do have sense. So I think they work harder than other contestants because it's kinda hard [pause] being Black.

GROUP: [Laughter]

Amanda interpreted several Black contestants, Tiffany, Camille, and Kenya, as more determined than others and reasoned that, having experienced social inequalities or "setbacks," Black contestants have had to "act way more determined." Amanda got to the heart of what I was attempting to ascertain: How did *Top Model* portray female Black identities? And did the teens see these portrayals as true to life? Tyrone shrewdly reminded us that Blacks are typically portrayed in stereotypical ways on television in general and so perhaps some contestants on the program felt obliged to counter stereotypes. Finally, although his comment elicited nervous laughter, Tyrone brought out what the teens know all too well—Blacks have to work hard because being Black in America is not easy.

Michelle Obama and Tyra Banks: Role Models "Keepin' It Real"

The teens' responses to my questions about the program exposed their daily challenges and anxieties as young people struggling to define themselves within a larger cultural context that marginalizes their identities. Often, in popular critiques of media representations, these challenges are framed around whether or not girls are offered "positive role models." Ideas about proper "role models" for young minority girls were a "hot topic" in the news media as I sat down to write about the fast-paced, conflicted, and passionate discussion the screening of *Top Model* sparked with the BCM teens. On April 2, 2009, during President and Mrs. Obama's first official trip to Europe, in which President Obama attended the G-20 submit, Mrs. Obama spoke during a surprise visit to a North London school. The one hundred or so British schoolgirls Michelle Obama addressed mobbed the First Lady after her emotional speech. She said, in part:

If you want to know the reason why I am standing here, it's because of education. . . . I never cut class. I loved getting "As." I liked being smart. I liked being on time. I thought being smart is cooler than anything else in the world. You, too, with these values, can control your own destiny. You, too, can pave the way. . . . For nothing in my life ever would have predicted that I would be standing here as the first African-American First Lady. I was not raised with wealth or resources or any social standing to speak of. I was raised on the South Side of Chicago-that's the real part of Chicago.[13]

Michelle Obama's speech and the subsequent "hugfest" between her and a multiracial group of London schoolgirls prompted me to reflect on America's first Black First Lady as a role model for minority adolescent girls. CNN and other American news channels broadcast the British girls' reactions immediately following the First Lady's speech. They screamed as if they had just met Beyoncé Knowles or Jay-Z. Some cried. Mrs. Obama high-fived one of the girls before taking the stage and hugged many of them afterwards. The appearance, in which Mrs. Obama seemed to be utilizing her potential as a role model to champion the importance of education, underscored the First Lady's singular influence as a political figure. I had never seen teenage girls react this way to a public figure who was not a musical artist, actor, or athlete. The teens typically named performers such as R&B singers Mary J. Blige and Alicia Keys as role models. Some named more obscure recording artists, but none of them named Oprah Winfrey or any other public figure who was not an actor or musical artist. And, although *The Tyra Show*'s website offered up the supermodel-turned-talk-show queen as a role model, none of the girls with whom I worked ever volunteered Banks as a role model.

Yet, the online television media routinely position figures such as Banks as "role models," especially for minority girls and young women. A CBS *The Early Show* online article in 2007 reported, "Banks sees herself as a role-model now that she's launched her career as a talk show host."[14] In 2009, the official Warner Brothers website for *Tyra* described the program as "giv[ing] young women the 'girlfriend' they want to hang out with, and the role model they need. With hot, young, celebrity guests. . . ."[15] While the BCM teenage girls certainly expressed great interest in "hot, young, celebrities," none explicitly named Tyra Banks as a role model. They constantly talked about *Top Model* and watched *Tyra* when their school and extracurricular schedules permitted. Yet, they seemed decidedly ambivalent about Banks as a role model. When I asked them what they thought of Banks, they said, "Yeah, I like Tyra," or "She's for real." "She's for real" is the second-highest compliment the girls could have given Banks; they reserved the utmost, "she's *mad real*," for the likes of Mary J. Blige. Therefore, "she's for real" notwithstanding, it was perplexing that they at once seemed heavily focused on Banks, yet were reluctant to designate her as a role model.

The "Real" and the Political

Returning to Mrs. Obama, it was also intriguing that she had co-opted the term "real" in her address to the London schoolgirls, saying she was from the South Side of Chicago, "the real part of Chicago." It was not too long before Mrs. Obama's speech that Alaska governor and Republican vice presidential nominee Sarah Palin had caused controversy by referring to "pro-American" "real parts of America," which she proclaimed consisted only of small towns.[16] Here, political discourse, both in Governor Palin's and Mrs. Obama's speeches, co-opted the teens' term "real" to bolster very different agendas. While Governor Palin was suggesting that Washington, D.C., and other metropolitan areas were not as "pro-America" or as full of hardworking folks as small towns, Mrs. Obama was mapping realness within the Chicago metropolitan area and arguing that the working-class, largely minority South Side was the "real part of Chicago." For Governor Palin, "real" conjured images of small-town, hardworking, conservative, largely White America. For Mrs. Obama, "real" signified inner-city, hardworking, largely minority America. Mrs. Obama was also utilizing Black vernacular; the term "real" is certainly not exclusively used by the BCM teens but, rather, is a common African American vernacular term used in a number of contexts. And, in fact, Tyra Banks has regularly used the term on both *Top Model* and her talk show, where she routinely champions "real women's" bodies.

While it is tempting to conclude that no valid comparison between Tyra Banks and Michelle Obama is possible, with one a fashion icon and the other a political figure, fashion and politics collide in popular representations of both of these Black women in the public eye. Notions of "realness" or "authentic Blackness" were a recurrent theme throughout the 2008 presidential campaign and came to a head in July 2008 when the cover of *The New Yorker* featured a caricature of Michelle Obama wearing a large Afro, camouflage pants, and military boots and holding a machine gun as she fist-bumped her husband, portrayed in a turban, long robes, and sandals. The controversy surrounding the cover marked a new level of scrutiny of Mrs. Obama's personal style and self-presentation. For the duration of the campaign, fears and commentary regarding whether Mrs. Obama was "an angry Black woman" abounded, a signal of the media's preoccupation with the "mad Black woman" as opposed to the teen's fascination with "mad real" Black women. After her husband took office, far more attention turned to the First Lady's "sense of style" and to her fashion choices. For example, *The New Yorker* subsequently featured Mrs. Obama on the cover of its biannual "Style" issue, and analyses of her clothing were prominently featured in both the fashion industry press (e.g., *Women's Wear Daily*) and the mainstream news media (e.g., the *New York Times*).

As I reflected on our focus group discussion of *America's Next Top Model*, I began to replay Mrs. Obama's speech in my mind, juxtaposed with the ways in which popular cultural figures such as Banks used the term "real," and keeping in mind how both women construct themselves and are constructed by the media. While we can certainly critique Mrs. Obama for falling into the same authenticating trap as Palin, that is, proclaiming parts of Chicago as "real," thereby implying that other areas were not, Mrs. Obama's characterization of herself as an educationally oriented "real" South Side girl was in sharp contrast to how the term was usually used by Black popular figures. Tyra Banks's brand of realness, for example, is more often than not couched in terms of physical beauty. At best, Banks can be heralded for influencing girls to feel comfortable in their own bodies (whatever shape they may take). Her sassy, self-professed "fierce" attitude can also be viewed as relying on hegemonic racialized and gendered norms that focus girls around body image and beauty rather than on education, as Mrs. Obama had so explicitly done. My fieldwork with the BCM teens uncovered that, as much as some girls looked up to Banks, others, although they enjoyed her programs, were deeply critical of the staged gestures Banks made toward "redefining beauty."

Bankable Productions:
Commodifying Race, Gender, Body Image and Beauty

Tyra Banks is not only the creator and host of *Top Model*. Before retiring from modeling in 2005 and segueing into television, Banks was a highly visible and enormously successful print and runway model and television spokesmodel for CoverGirl cosmetics. She was also a principal model in Victoria's Secret's advertising campaigns. Additionally, she hosted her daytime talk show, *Tyra*.[17] In 2009, Tyra Banks's official website boasted that *Tyra* was "number one among eighteen to thirty-four-year-old females." As we have seen, all of the teens were extremely familiar with Banks, and talk about her two programs permeated the girls' daily conversations. The girls also knew about Tyra Banks's TZone camp, which the model began in 1999 as a week-long sleepover camp outside Los Angeles designed "to reinforce positive values and encourage girls to resist social pressures through a fierce, self-esteem building adventure."[18] By 2005, Banks had transformed Tzone into The Tyra Banks Tzone Foundation, aimed at supporting community nonprofits "recognized for their impact on girls and young women."[19]

On one hand, Banks can be viewed not only as an African American woman who has achieved the highest levels of accomplishment in the modeling world but also as a shrewd businesswoman who has executive produced, created, and hosted two extremely successful television programs while prioritizing the empowerment of girls and young women. Moreover, as of 2009, Banks's empire was steadily growing with the debut of another reality program, *True Beauty*, which she coexecutive produces with actor/producer Aston Kutcher.[20] On the other hand, however, Banks's talk show can be criticized for portraying stereotypical representations of African Americans reminiscent of *The Jerry Springer Show* format, replete with rowdy African American female guests whose sexual reproduction and social skills seem "out of control." Her modeling career, bookended by an appearance on the cover of the *Sports Illustrated* swimsuit issue (she was the first African American woman to do so) and a long-standing contract with the Victoria's Secret lingerie empire, can be seen as channeling in the objectification of women.

Thus, Banks's public persona can perhaps best be characterized as paradoxical—potentially empowering to young girls of color but also trading in hegemonic definitions of women in general as sex objects and Black women in particular as hypersexualized, "fierce" vixens. Such representations, or "controlling images," in the parlance of Patricia Hill Collins, including the sexually aggressive Jezebel image (which can arguably be applied to Banks), originated during slavery as a way to control Black women's sexuality and to justify sexual assaults by white men (Collins 1991: 77).

Two examples of Banks's forays into discourses surrounding body image and sexual identity are meaningful in relation to the teens' interpretations of *Top Model*. Conceptions of body image, discrimination against overweight individuals, and celebrity narcissism were dramatically played out when Banks aired an episode of *Tyra* in which she donned a fat suit. The episode was highly publicized even before it aired, with several online and televised news outlets running promotional stories. The episode, focusing on an issue that frequently comes up in today's teenagers' conversations, was a hot topic in the blogosphere for days leading up to its airing and remained a much-viewed video on YouTube for months afterwards. Abcnews.com, for example, ran the following headline: "Tyra Banks Experiences Obesity through Fat Suit: Supermodel Wears Suit on Blind Dates."[21] In an interview for this article, Banks lamented how horribly she was treated as she shopped and went on blind dates as a 350-pound woman. However, the article foreshadowed the backlash Banks would soon experience by stating, "At the end of her 15-hour suit stunt, Banks had the luxury of taking off her costume and returning to her supermodel figure." In an interview for the same article, Banks argues that women are much more approving of overweight men than men are of larger women. Yet, when asked what kinds of men she preferred, Banks responded,

> I like 'em all, child! A while ago I said that, "you know, I like a guy—he doesn't have to be rich and famous—he can be normal." And I remember I was walking in the mall and this guy was like, "Tyra, I'm normal. I live with my mama. I ain't got a car and I ain't got a job! I'm real normal." And I'm like, "that's not normal—that's a loser!"

This quote illustrates the pernicious racialized and gendered conundrums Banks embodies. Punctuating her comments with "child!," Banks employs racialized speech markers to "talk Black." And, while she makes gestures in support of those who are marginalized and discriminated against either because they are overweight or because they're just not "rich and famous," she reveals with brutal irony how she would view an unemployed man: as a "loser." Banks's narrative of her encounter with the man in the mall employs racialized linguistic codes such as, "child," "mama," and the repeated use of "ain't" to position both her and her male suitor as African American. Yet, her flippant comment that such an individual is not "normal" but, rather, "a loser" disregards obdurate racial and class-based forms of discrimination that leave African American men disproportionately susceptible to homelessness, unemployment, and disenfranchisement. Furthermore, with the National Urban League reporting that unemployment rates among African American men reached 16 percent in 2009, one can argue that the man who approached Banks in the mall certainly is not abnormal but, rather, is at least somewhat representative of the all too common hardships Black men face.

In 2007, Banks's actual weight (as opposed the temporary weight she literally "put on" by wearing the "fat suit") became a controversial topic when tabloids printed unflattering photographs of her in a bathing suit accompanied by headlines reporting that she had gained forty pounds. The story occupied the tabloids and television entertainment news magazines for weeks, and

Banks retaliated in interviews, saying that not only had the tabloids exaggerated her weight gain but also that "I get so much mail from young girls who say, 'I look up to you, you're not as skinny as everyone else, I think you're beautiful.' So when they say my body is 'ugly' and 'disgusting,' what does that make those girls feel like?"[22] On February 1, 2007, Banks also responded on *Tyra* by appearing in the same bathing suit beside a life-size photograph of her heavier self, as she had appeared on the tabloid cover. In an impassioned monologue, to which China alluded earlier, Banks admonished the tabloids and championed women everywhere by saying:

> The bottom line is that people are used to seeing me looking like this [striking model poses], and like this and all that. And everyone seems to be pretty okay with that. But for some reason people have a serious problem when I look [posing in profile with her stomach extended and rear protruding], like that. All right, when I look like that [slapping herself on the behind as the audience giggles]. But luckily I'm strong enough and I have a good support system in me and I love my mama because she helped me to be strong woman so I can overcome these kinds of attacks. But if I had lower self-esteem, I would probably be starving myself *right now*. But that is exactly what is happening to other women all over this country. So I have something to say, to all of you that have something nasty to say about me, or other women that are built like me. Women that sometimes or all the time look like this [sticking her stomach out], women whose names you know [speaking directly to the camera and gesturing emphatically with her fist], women's whose names you don't, women who've been picked on! Women whose husbands put them down! Women at work or girls in school! I have one thing to say to you [bursting into tears and then slapping herself on the behind]: kiss my fat ass!

Banks's in-studio audience cheered and leapt to their feet as she concluded, wiping tears from her eyes. The YouTube posting of Banks's "Kiss my fat ass" soliloquy logged 136,602 viewings as of April 2009. Banks appeared to give the tabloids a much-deserved tongue-lashing while standing up for other women who bear the brunt of weight-related insults. Yet, as I watched (and rewatched, thanks to the power of YouTube) Banks's diatribe, I could not help but notice that Banks's physique seemed to have slimmed in the time between the unflattering tabloid photographs and her televised rebuttal. I wondered if she *had* dieted in preparation for the televised retaliation. Although Banks's words allied her with countless women and girls who suffer because of unattainable definitions of "the perfect weight," Banks's long, straight, blond hair extensions, relatively fair skin, and flawless makeup, which make her look like anything but an average African American woman, separate her from the women on whose behalf she claimed to be fighting. Banks did not stack up to the BCM girls' criteria of looking "real." And, while her weight-gain controversy positioned Banks as an underdog, in 2006 she had been ranked on askmen.com, alongside singers Beyoncé and Ciara and actress Gabrielle Union, as one of the "top ninety-nine most desirable women" (Sharpley-Whiting 2007: 28).

Banks has openly discussed how, after she gained post adolescent womanly curves, she was pressured by the modeling industry to lose weight. Rather than change her body to fit the standards of runway and editorial industry decision makers, Banks pursued modeling for commercial clients such as *Sports Illustrated* and Victoria's Secret because they favored more voluptuous models. Still, at five feet ten inches tall, with long limbs, full breasts, and blond hair extensions, Banks is hardly an "everywoman." These facts perhaps underscore Banks's point: If *she* faces harsh criticisms about her weight, what hope do "regular" women have? On the official website for her talk show, Banks states, "It is so important to me to redefine beauty and to make sure that everyone gets a fair chance to pursue their dream."[23] To this end, with each ensuing season or "cycle," *Top Model* has made attempts at "pushing the envelope" of how the modeling industry defines beauty. These attempts include casting "plus-size" contestants, casting a transgender model, and opening the competition to contestants under five feet seven inches tall.

In addition to championing weight and body-image-related issues, Banks has become known for her support of the gay, lesbian, bisexual, and transgender communities. As noted earlier, *Top Model* stars two openly gay men, J. Alexander, or "Miss J," a Black gay man who often dresses in women's clothing and who serves as the contestants' runway coach (he skillfully walks the catwalk in mile-high pumps, making turns and spins look like child's play), and Jay Manuel, or "Mr. Jay," a bleached-blond makeup artist who serves as the program's photo shoot director. Also, in 2008, the show featured a transgender contestant, Isis, whom Banks reportedly had found living in a homeless shelter the previous season when the show visited the shelter to do a shoot with disadvantaged girls. Banks's support for gay, lesbian, bisexual, and transgender causes was recognized when she was presented with the Excellence in Media Award at the Twentieth Annual GLAAD (Gay and Lesbian Alliance against Defamation) Media Awards. Banks's support of gay causes adds complexity to her aim of "redefining beauty." One issue to consider is how the BCM teens exposed contradictions in this agenda by deconstructing *Top Model's* problematic representations of Blackness. Yet another consideration must be how the youths' homophobia underscores the necessity for a media more attuned to how gay, lesbian, bisexual, and transgender people are represented.

Conclusion

The BCM teens' interpretations of *Top Model* unmask complex identity negotiations, revealing shrewd critical analyses of how race and gender are commodified in mass culture. The youth grapple with tenacious stereotypes that have historically portrayed African American and Caribbean women's bodies as hypersexualized, illicit, and aberrational. Alternatively accepting and denying these stereotypes but always interrogating them, the young people demonstrate that they are critical social agents who are well aware of the ways in which their own identities are at once marginalized and offered up as profitable commodities.

Girls who participated in this focus group maneuvered between American and West Indian notions of femininity. They were hopeful that "real" Black beauty would be rewarded on *Top Model*, rooting for the Black contestants and simultaneously defending their own bodies as legitimate sites of power and beauty. By identifying with Danielle's marginalized speech, while conceding that there was a proper time and place for "talking like you just got off the boat," the girls demonstrated their ability to succeed within a hegemonic system that undermines their cultural practices. Still, they sought to define "real Blackness" as "open-minded," "determined," and "beautiful."

Boys who spoke out in this discussion utilized sensitive discourse patterns and illustrated that they identify with females on the program in unexpected ways. The boys face a different set of challenges from the girls, with stereotypes of young minority men as aggressive and prone to violence restricting their chances for educational achievement. BCM boys' views of success are darkened by the harsh realities they confront, and the insights uncovered about minority boys here beg for further scholarly attention.

Although they mediated their comments through humor, all of the teens acknowledge the "setbacks" they encounter as Blacks negotiating their identities within American consumer culture, where they are portrayed as either "civilized" or "ghetto." Interrogating these dichotomies proved to be a challenge for the teens as they demonstrated they were at once adept and acerbic social critics *and* somewhat impressionable recipients of the contradictory and limited definitions of racialized femininity offered on television. They alternatively argued that *Top Model* "shows Black bodies more" and that "Blacks got more body to show." These are exposed as painfully limited choices, and the fact that the youngsters are able to extract some margin of hope, pleasure, and power underscores their determination to claim America as their own. We turn to these limited choices, especially in relation to the girls, in the conclusion.

Conclusion

Placing Gendered and Generational Notions of West Indian Success

Every afternoon she walked from the college to the center of the city, and only during these long reckless walks did she rouse a little. Holding her books like a shield, she weaved down through the East Side, past the sedate brownstones and the tall apartment houses thrusting into the sky, glancing in her swift walk, into the richly appointed lobbies. At Fifth Avenue she walked almost cautiously past the luxurious displays in the tall windows and covertly watched those to whom the street belonged: the meticulously groomed, mink-draped women, who tapped out their right to possession with their high heels, who moved secure in an aura of wealth, with ennui like a subtle blue shading under their cold eyes and a faint famished touch to their pallid cheeks. They made her rage inside, for she knew, walking amid them in her worn coat and tam, that she was non-existent—a dark intruder in their glittering inaccessible world.
—Paule Marshall, *Brown Girl, Brownstones*

Amanda's Story

Amanda scribbled in a stenographer's notebook—she was busy organizing her interview questions when I approached her at a Harlem cafe in March 2009. She shouted "Miss Oneka!" and rose to throw her arms around me. When I told her (for the hundredth time now) to drop the "Miss" and just call me "Oneka," she said, "Okay, that's just how I was raised. You always show respect."

Amanda and I have been in sporadic touch since 2007. She is now nineteen years old and a sophomore at a branch of CUNY (City University of New York) in Manhattan. She still lives at home with her mother in Crown Heights and remains, in many respects, the shy young woman I knew at BCM. Clearly struggling to gain autonomy from her mother, she seems on a quest to understand what "independence" means and to figure out how one goes about claiming it—to come to terms with whether she has the stuff to be independent.

Amanda was excited about seeing me because she wanted to interview me for her journalism class. I was fascinated by the idea of the "informant" turning the tables on the anthropologist. Telling me that the assignment was very open-ended and that she had already interviewed one of her former educators from BCM, Amanda added that she was intrigued by the fact that Kiara, the BCM teacher, had moved, by herself, from Virginia to New York City when she was eighteen years old. "I'm nineteen now and I can't imagine moving to another city all by myself. How did she get to be so independent? What was that experience like? That's what I want to write about." Amanda asked me to tell her my life story and directed me to focus on "life-changing events and experiences in which [I] gained independence."

Although Amanda was ostensibly interviewing me, ironically the interview revealed much more about her. As I told her about various events from my childhood, she interjected, "That reminds me of my mother's experience!" As I proceeded, she added, "Yeah, that's like what happened to me when I was a kid." Since her mother is much older than the mothers of the other girls we've met in this book, Amanda's mother's experiences did mirror those of my mother. And, I think, because we were both academically successful, slow social bloomers, and daughters of protective West Indian mothers, Amanda and I shared much in common. I felt indebted to Amanda; she and the other girls had revealed so much to me. Feeling the need to reciprocate, I answered all of her questions truthfully and in detail (I share excerpts from Amanda's essay about me later in this conclusion).

In turn, Amanda opened up even more. I wanted to get a deeper sense of how Amanda had managed a conflict between her mother and her over whether she should go away to college. In 2007, while still at BCM and a junior in high school, Amanda won a summer fellowship to go to an Ivy League university outside New York and take college-level classes. The fellowship entailed living at the university for several weeks during the summer months, but Amanda's mother had to be convinced to allow Amanda to participate. Amanda's mom didn't want her daughter staying out of state and away from home at that age. Amanda recalled, "My mom said to me, 'You're sixteen years old; why are you trying to live in another state? Why are you trying to get away from me?'" Her mother interpreted the desire to attend the summer program as a plot to "get away from her." With help from the BCM educators, Amanda finally convinced her mother to let her attend, but every step of getting to the summer program proved a battle: "She was annoyed because I needed to bring all of this stuff with me for the summer. Like I needed a fan. And she thought it was a lot of work to take all of that stuff up there for a few weeks."

After she completed the summer program, Amanda's grades were high enough to garner her an invitation to apply to the college, but her mother would not have it. She insisted that her daughter attend a college within New York City. Amanda's round, full face usually features a broad smile. However, her mouth dropped when she discussed this period when her mother basically forbade her to apply to the prestigious school. Her eyes darkened, and she seemed to be holding her breath, as if part of her wanted to scream in anger against her mother and the other part was biting her tongue. "I was angry," she told me, "but I had to listen to my mother. And I had to stay strong." Eventually, Amanda did not apply to the Ivy League school. She was accepted at a CUNY school and has been a student there for two years. She is majoring in journalism.

As a commuter student (it takes one and one-half hours by subway to get to her school), Amanda has found it hard to make any friends. Her older brother also attends the same school: "He has been a student there for three years and doesn't have a single friend from the city." Amanda takes the subway, attends class, then often immediately gets back on the subway to return home. I thought back to how Amanda had described the two-bedroom apartment on the ground floor of a brownstone in Crown Heights in which she, her mother, and her brother lived. When I initially interviewed her, I had asked Amanda if she had posters of any musical artists in her room at home. Amanda had responded:

> I have pictures of Alicia Keys. I have a poster of Usher. I don't really have
> my own space or room to have posters or anything like that, but when I get
> their CD case, I take care of it really well and their books, I look at it all the
> time. I like the little books [in the CD cases] with the lyrics in it.

With no personal space of her own, Amanda situated her celebrity icons within the words and lyrics in their CD cases. She valued music and books from a young age—sources of escape from the confines of life at home. She recently joined the school newspaper as a way to gain experience in her major and, she hopes, to meet friends. But her mother makes it difficult. "I have a class that starts at 6:30 p.m. and ends at 8:30. So I don't get back home until around 10 p.m. and Mom is always like, 'Why are you coming home at 10 p.m.!?!? Where have you been?' and I keep reminding her I have a night class, but it's like she doesn't hear me or doesn't believe me. She thinks I'm out with people she wouldn't want me hanging out with. She thinks I'm up to no good."

Amanda now has an opportunity to apply to be a summer Resident Advisor at the Ivy League school. Her mother doesn't want her to apply to the program. When she was fifteen years old, Amanda's mom immigrated from a rural village in Jamaica to Toronto, Canada, where she joined her three sisters. Later, she moved to Brooklyn and worked as a domestic, cleaning houses. She was thirty-nine years old when Amanda was born. As a young child in Jamaica, Amanda's mother had been the victim of a hit-and-run car accident that left her in critical condition and took the life of her younger sister, who was only four years old. Amanda's parents are now divorced, but she sees her father often. Her mother works as an adult care nurse practitioner, and her father works for the Department of Education's school lunch program. Her mother disapproves of Amanda's brother's girlfriend (who is now pregnant) because "she's not West Indian." The "tactless and disapproving" things her mother says in the presence of her brother's girlfriend routinely embarrass Amanda and her brother.

While she is doing well at her CUNY school, Amanda received her first C ever in astronomy. I laughed upon hearing this, telling her that I had received my first C in astronomy as an undergraduate. Laughing, and in unison, we both added, "There's a lot of math in astronomy!" Still, Amanda had been maintaining a 3.50 GPA until then. She received a B+ on her last journalism assignment, and the professor said, "If I give you an A it means your work is publishable, so a B+ is pretty good." Amanda describes herself as a perfectionist, partially driven by her mother's demands. She laments that her mother won't let her experience life and adds, "It just makes you want to rebel more when someone is controlling you that much."

I felt saddened by the thought that Amanda's mother's protectiveness was prohibiting her from pursuing the elite education she wanted. Amanda said, "[The Ivy League school] is a part of me now. That experience really changed me. I'll always have [it] as a part of me." Interestingly, after she returned from the Ivy League summer program, a tenant in her building remarked about how proud Amanda's mother was of her and told Amanda that her mom had been boasting about her during her absence.

I felt compelled to advise Amanda but simultaneously constrained by disciplinary norms. And I also did not want to cause further conflicts for her at home. I ended up telling her that there comes a time when we have to decide to take charge of our own lives. We have to love and respect our parents but also know that sometimes part of being an adult is knowing when your own judgment is better than that of your parents. I suggested that she read Paule Marshall's book *Brown Girl, Brownstones,* in which the protagonist, a young Barbadian girl, eventually defies her strong-willed mother.

Certainly, aspects of Amanda's story are coming-of-age universals. Youth everywhere struggle to define themselves, to find, as Erik Erikson put it, "something to be true to" and to become autonomous adults (Erikson 1968). Some of the details of Amanda's story, that a mother who experienced the violent loss of a sibling at a young age might hold tighter to her own children, are not unique to the West Indian experience. Yet, there are many aspects of Amanda's narrative that can be linked to West Indian cultural norms and Caribbean social realities. The trauma Amanda's mother experienced at a young age, part of the social realities of so many children in Africa, Latin America, and the Caribbean, is a result of the sociostructural factors to which China alluded in chapter 3. Young children traverse busy intersections as they fetch water, walk miles to school, and chaperone their younger siblings. The significance Amanda attaches to respect, a reflection of how she was raised, is considered a mainstay of West Indian femininity. Also, Amanda's emotional work, how she managed the conflict with her mother, and her use of the words "staying strong" to describe both her mother's way of surviving childhood trauma and her own manner of accepting her mother's prohibitions have been ascribed to West Indian culturally defined ways of managing depression (Schreiber et al. 2004). My trepidation about intervening, especially when Amanda was still a high school student, was influenced by my own understanding of the role corporal punishment plays in West Indian parenting; I worried that, if Amanda disobeyed her mother, she might be subject to physical discipline. Elements of Amanda's story also resonated with the other girls. The degree to which *place* factors into Amanda's strivings surfaced again and again with the girls, many of whom did not have their own rooms. Amanda slept on a daybed in the family's living room. For adolescents who are already displaced from and marginalized in the public spaces into which they venture, such lack of privacy, of personal space, is especially difficult. Amanda's mother saw the city streets as treacherous places for her daughter, a fear shared by other mothers and by the educators at BCM. From Amanda's perspective, however, home was constricting and equally troublesome. And, given the opportunity to let her daughter leave the city streets behind and attend college beyond its confines, Amanda's mother chose to keep her close. Although BCM prepared them for and helped them gain admissions to college, Amanda and her peers faced difficult choices and limitations, not all of which stemmed from parental control but many of which centered on the complex negotiation of place.

China's Story

While I was well aware of Amanda's conflicts with her mother and thus was not entirely surprised when she was prohibited from attending the Ivy League school, I expected China, a confident, already self-reliant girl, to rise to all the opportunities life after high school might afford her. I began, around the time of China's high school prom, however, to get an inkling that China was not as self-assured as she appeared. China, Nadine, Neema, and Mariah had spent weeks preparing for the prom. China and Nadine had designed their own dresses and commissioned a West Indian seamstress in Flatbush to execute their visions. The day before the prom, they all went for manicures, with Nadine's Grenadian boyfriend paying for hers. China's date was a boy she had been "talking to" for three months, Mariah had just been asked by a boy one week before the prom, and Neema was going on a blind date with China's prom date's best friend. The girls, especially Neema and Mariah, whose prom preparations predated their securing dates, put far more salience on the girl-centered process of preparing for the prom than they did on the prom ritual as a vehicle for heterosexual courtship and a rite of passage (Best 2000). All four girls were paying for their dresses and their prom tickets with money they had earned from BCM and from other part-time jobs.

China, Nadine, and Neema attended the same high school, and their prom was to take place at a restaurant on Long Island. As I chatted with the girls the night before the prom, China's dress was still incomplete, and I could see concern on her face. Working with the seamstress, whom the girls described as "a little crazy," had been a challenge for all of them, but especially thorny for China. "I'm copying the Beyoncé dress from the Grammys," she told me, describing the singer's ornate strapless dress with a mermaid shaped train. "You know, the two-tone one? Hers had shades of gold, but mine will be iridescent turquoise." "Yeah! *If you have a dress by tomorrow!*" Neema blurted. China appeared, for the first time since I had met her, to be on the verge of tears. I assured her that her dress would be ready on time, but I did not sleep well that night. I lay awake considering why, instead of modeling her dress after something worn by her idol, Mary J. Blige, China had opted for emulating a dress worn by Beyoncé. Blige symbolized the everyday, authentic self, while Beyoncé represented fantasy. Had China traded in her "mad real" individualism for conventional femininity? And would her choice bite her in the butt if the dress was not completed? I could certainly understand why China aspired to a fantastic and glamorous prom night. But

China's confidence waned as she wondered if the glamour Beyoncé so effort-lessly embodied could be hers, even for one night.

The seamstress came through, the prom went off without a hitch, and the girls gleefully showed me pictures the following week. But the uncertainty China displayed around the prom seemed to characterize the eleventh hour of her high school career. All of the BCM seniors were admitted to colleges, and all of them, save China, planned to attend. Mariah would teach for a semester before starting at a CUNY school in the spring. Nadine had been admitted to her first choice, a college in the south, close to where her mom had resettled for work. In the weeks following receipt of her acceptance let-ter, Nadine was jubilant as she thought about reuniting with her mom after their long separation. China's first choice had been a CUNY school located in Manhattan, but she had not been accepted. She did, however, get into a respected State University of New York (SUNY) school upstate and into a college on Long Island that offered open admissions. With her heart set on the Manhattan school, China decided that she would not go to college at all. She tried to convince Nadine to put off school, too, hatching a plan for the two girls to move into a housing project in Brooklyn. Alarmed, the BCM educators and I tried to dissuade the girls from this plan. China told me that she had ruled out the SUNY school "because it's too far away." I tried to persuade her that going away to college was a wonderful opportunity and that she would meet new people and thrive from fresh experiences. China looked me squarely in the eyes and said, "Sometimes people aren't so nice." In that moment, I saw China not as the take-charge, attention-seeking girl I had come to know but as a vulnerable young woman who was frightened at the prospect of moving beyond her comfort zone. Too many of China's expe-riences beyond the museum had taught her that "sometimes people aren't so nice"; these experiences included moments of racialized discrimination at her job and on the subway. China had also astutely deciphered the ways in which Black girls were undervalued in the larger popular culture. She did not want to hear about meeting new friends. Nadine, who had essentially become her sister, was the only friend with whom she was concerned. Since she did not want to leave the city, I asked China why she would not consider attending the school on Long Island. "I failed the Regents math test," she told me. "I failed by one point."

I was determined to help China go to college. The next day, I called the admissions office of the school on Long Island and explained China's situa-tion. I found out that China needed to pass the Regents exam only in order to avoid taking another placement test at the college. The school provided applicants with the opportunity to retake the math test on their campus; the test was scheduled for June 14. I put China in touch with the admissions officer. When I saw China again, she said, "I'm supposed to go there on June 14 to retake it—but I don't want to go. The test is at 6 p.m., and it will be dark by the end of the test, and I don't have any way to get home from Long Island." I smiled, thinking that this was a problem I could easily solve. "I'll drive you there," I said. "And I'll wait until you're done with the test and drive you home afterward." China reluctantly agreed to this plan, but, when I called her the night before the exam, she flatly told me that she was not going. Previously, China had reveled in her own self-reliance and looked askance at American parents' apprehension at letting their children stay out after dark. China negotiated a transnational identity from a young age and held two jobs, purchasing her own clothes and contributing to her household income. She had also posed as an eighteen year old in order to acquire her own cell phone calling plan. A girl who had, alone and at the age of nine, dodged oncoming traffic on the streets of Barbados and who traveled on her own between New York and her island home was daunted by the prospect of commuting to and from Long Island. I surmised that China's refusal to attend the Long Island school had more to do with her fear that "people are not so nice" than with the logistics of commuting or anxiety about retaking the test. And China's proposed solution, that she and Nadine move into the projects, suggested that a predominantly Black housing project represented a "safer," "friendlier" place than a college on Long Island where people "were not so nice." After my attempt to intervene and drive her to the math exam, China stopped returning my calls. We fell out of touch.

The Politics of Help

China's decision not to go to college and my inability to help change her mind haunted me for months. Implicit in BCM's teachings was the notion that if the teens could claim the museum as their own, they would, in turn, claim other elite spaces, like college campuses. This came to fruition for most of the teens. But, for both China and Amanda, the complexities of negotiating place and West Indian feminine identity erected obstacles to fully realizing their potential and to journeying beyond the confines of Crown Heights and the museum. I felt compelled to "help" both girls but grappled with the politics of help, in Amanda's case worrying about how her mother would react if I intervened and in China's case questioning whether my ideal trajectory for China's life (one that included college and avoided life in the projects) should supersede China's agency and ability to set the parameters of her future. Recognizing that pathologizing labels like "at risk" should not be applied to *any* teens, I also wanted to intervene and influence both girls to make "the right" decisions in the face of what I saw as risky choices. Months after wrestling with both girls' stories, I still felt a sense of failure on my part and strove to critically consider my own ideas about what entailed "a good life" for these girls. In December 2009, I joined a group of researchers presenting at an American Anthropological Association panel titled, "Youth and Childhood Researchers as Cultural Critics." There, I heard accounts from similarly positioned scholars who had faced parallel challenges (although, as the only native anthropologist who participated in the panel, I felt that for me, the politics of help were further complicated). In a paper titled, "Undoing Goodness Itself: A Proposal for a Critical Look at the Work of Helping Troubled Youth," Julia Kirst examined the conflicting interpretations of intervention by youth researchers, youth parents/guardians, and adult service providers, applying the literature on the politics of help between "developed" and "underdeveloped countries" to understand the politics of help between youth and adults. Kirst observed that in the United States, "helping children" is protected from public criticism because it is considered, by definition, benign. "Ideas about helping" and "the perception that help is not needed" were, according to Kirst, common currents in the relationships between youth researchers and "at-risk" youth. In relation to my experiences with China, Amanda, and the other teens, this framework exposes how even well-meaning anthropologists employ age-based and classed interpretations of "children in need" when they intervene in the lives of urban youth.

The Museum Revisited

I considered the politics of help, my own as a youth researcher, the museum's as a "community-oriented" institution, and that of the museum's funders, as I strove to unpack the problematics of how offering "help" was intricately connected to designating youth as "at risk." Between 2003 and 2008, BCM underwent a renovation at a cost of more than $43 million. I had hoped that the museum's renovations would transform it into a space that was more teen friendly and that, along with other changes to its pedagogical approaches, a program that was already successful would address the gender disparity and better serve both male and female teens. Returning to BCM in the summer of 2008, I observed that its sociospatial construction as a women's sphere and as a Black space had in fact been renegotiated. I encountered two male educators (previously all of the teachers had been females) and activities that might be more appealing to boys, such as a Capoeira class and a website design workshop. Previously, the teens had had limited computer access, sharing cubicle space with the Museum Team educators. Now, a sprawling new teen area lay before me, with six computers and an open space for physical activities like Capoeira; adult-size tables and chairs for teaching and lounging had replaced the kiddy furniture. Teens and educators alike seemed to thrive in this new space and on the thrill of the revamped, state-of-the-art museum.

The summer of 2008 was a hopeful time for BCM youth and for politics in America. Just a few days before my visit, Senator Barack Obama, the Democratic party hopeful for president, had given a momentous speech in Berlin. I was eager to hear what the group of eighth and ninth graders who were sitting waiting their turns at the new BCM computers thought of the speech and about the prospect of electing the nation's first Black president.

> OL: Did you watch Obama's speech last night?
> GROUP: Yes!
> OL: What did you think?
> ALLISON: [Smiling broadly and nodding] It was good!
> JAMES: It was [pause] interesting.
> OL: Why?
> JAMES: Because politicians love to promise you stuff, so he made a lot of promises, and it will be interesting to see if he can keep them.
> CAROLINE: But if he becomes president it will be easier to get loans to go to college!

Caroline suggests that the hope on which Obama built his presidential campaign signaled, for BCM teens, additional opportunities to attend college. But James's apprehension, that promises might go unrealized, came back to me later like a sinister foreshadowing of the tough times BCM would face between 2008 and 2010. The museum's grand reopening came on the heels of increasing gentrification in Crown Heights and coincided with the national economic crisis. The sparkling new facility was better suited to adolescent bodies, but it also reflected and encouraged gentrification. When I asked Shelly, a Trinidadian BCM administrator, to reflect on the changing neighborhood, she said:

I worked at the museum for twenty-four years. The other day I got off the bus in the late summer, in the late afternoon. When I got off the bus, I encountered seven people, none of them looked like me. There was a young man on a skateboard, a mother with a cute redheaded boy, people around the corner and a couple, all of them were White, all using the park and living in the area. Wow! What a tremendous change! A lot of the brownstones have not been chopped up, so if you have the money if you're coming in now, you have a lot of house for your money.

For Shelly, these changes occurred at a time when, in her mid-forties and after close to twenty-five years, she had just been laid off from her administrative position at BCM. Shelly described the slew of layoffs that precipitated hers:

The economic situation that we're in has hit most institutions, and it hit the museum. It started when we reopened. And that was a tough thing to happen at that particular time. Here we reopen and bam! Some fundraising was not as robust as we expected. There were pay cuts and changes. The former [BCM] president wanted to retain jobs. The president took the highest pay cut. We all took a pay cut. Then another. In May, we had to lay off people because we couldn't pay people. The DYCD [Department of Youth and Community Development] was not going to renew our funding. Can you imagine? The City Council and mayor said they wouldn't let that happen. We were cut down to four days a week. The new president looked at the cumulative. Before, we had laid off people who didn't make enough to make a difference. So she [the new president] cut the vice presidents of three departments and full-time and part-time staff in other departments. She gave back cuts in salaries to remaining staff. For me, I was like, I'm not fifty. I won't be fifty for a few years. I couldn't take early retirement. For many years I wanted to make a change and got comfortable at museum. All of my attempts [to leave] would light a fire, and the burner would go down. I think this is my year to change. And this is the change I've wanted. I don't feel bad about it. I can't worry about it.

Shelly did worry, though, about BCM's funding and the security of the Museum Team program:

I hope the museum recovers and gets in a better place. My efforts [before I left were] to make sure funding continues—that our funders know our program will continue. My priority before leaving was so that everybody had an agenda for this program. . . . The fact that these kids go on to college really excites funders. They can see progression of change. They can track it, it's easy to track. I'm sure change and restructuring are imminent, but it's a marvelous program. I smile because these kids who are going to do marvelous things.

BCM receives a mix of public and private funding. It is part of the Cultural Institutions Group, composed of thirty-four arts organizations, including the Metropolitan Museum of Art, Lincoln Center for the Performing Arts, and the Brooklyn Museum, all of which occupy land owned by New York City and which receive major funding from the city (Taylor 2008).[1] I told Shelly that in reviewing the literature on urban youth and afterschool programming, I repeatedly encountered the phrase "at risk." I asked Shelly if she would define the BCM interns as "at risk."

No. Hell, no! It think it's a ridiculous label that allows society at large and funders and people less familiar to put a label on giving money to the [Museum Team] program. It's come up since I've been overseeing the program. Also other terms like "underserved" or "poor." Some of the kids might be all of those things or none of those things. They may be poor or they may not know, the younger ones especially, that they are considered "poor." If my needs are being met as I know them, how is that poor or at risk? Whether they're in the suburbs of Michigan or Milwaukee or the suburbs of Long Island, teens can be "at risk." . . . Most kids in the Museum Team program are from working- or middle-class environments. It depends on their backgrounds. Some live in a house, some in an apartment. It might be a two-parent house or a single mother. Some parents have professional jobs, or some have three or four jobs. They are doing what they have to do to provide for their kids. Some kids, I know, use their stipend from the program to assist in their household. For other kids, it's just pocket change, or they buy their clothes or whatever they need with it.

Shelly is usually a mild-mannered and professional woman, and her outburst of "Hell, no!" was uncharacteristic. She forcefully rejects the "at-risk" label, yet, in her experience, labeling the BCM interns as such has gone hand-in-hand with receiving funding for the program. Shelly acknowledges the importance of the BCM teens going on to college because it is a progression that funders "can track"; in order to be deemed worthy of funding, the BCM teens must achieve success that funders can measure. And, like the museum funders, I had ascribed my own notion of quantifiable success onto Amanda and China's life choices. Shelly emphasizes the diversity of the teens' socioeconomic backgrounds and suggests that the dangers they face are no different from those faced by teens across America. Still, she notes the demographic changes in Crown Heights, observing that "if you have money and you're coming in now, you can get a lot of house for your money." Shelly's assessment of the range of economic backgrounds from which the teens came is accurate. Still, I encountered only one BCM teen whose family owned a home in Brooklyn. Aspiring to home ownership, which provided the central conflict in Paule Marshall's *Brown Girl, Brownstones*, was a dream that went unfulfilled for my interviewees' parents. Therefore, both parents and teens struggled, in the face of economic inequalities, to claim their own place. What additional barriers would accompany gentrification if Crown Heights' spaces, both public and private, increasingly became the property of those who "have the money"? In the same conversation, Shelly told me that, after the renovation and reopening, the Museum Team remained predominantly West Indian and African American, and that it included some new arrivals, a few immigrant youth from Africa. The museum's toddler program, however, reflected the changes in the neighborhood and included a growing number of White toddlers. Knowing that many of the BCM youth with whom I worked had started frequenting the museum when they were young children, I imagined, ten years into the future, a program that included increasing numbers of affluent White youth. In such a future, could West Indian and African American youth continue to claim BCM as their own?

"New Ethnicities" and "Different, Youthful Subjectivities"

How can the difficult choices Amanda and China faced be reconciled with the identity assertions the girls made throughout their time at BCM? In our earlier consideration of China's subjectivity formation, we saw that she, like many of the other girls, routinely oscillated between "keeping it real" and projecting a version of herself that was conducive to "getting paper," or earning money. She knew when it was advantageous to speak in a Bajan accent and when employing her accent would limit her chances for success. China drew strength from Mary J. Blige's "mad real" persona but also understood that the modeling industry was "just looking for a skinny chick." Until the last weeks of her high school career, China seemed to effortlessly manage these often contradictory and always contingent identifications. However, when it came time to design her prom dress, China's self-fashioning seemed contrived. China and Amanda favored "real" artists like Blige and Kelly Rowland of Destiny's Child (as opposed to the now-defunct group's more popular lead singer, Beyoncé Knowles). Of course, recalling Lacan's theorizations, neither Blige nor Beyoncé is "real"; both are representations of reality. Still, here, I refer to the girls' perceptions of the artists' representations. The girls' preferences for these artists, we have seen, stake claims to an "authentically Black" femininity defined outside mainstream norms. Although Blige has enjoyed enormous popularity for more than a decade, her success does not match that of the more conventionally feminine Beyoncé. Therefore, the girls have explicitly chosen less celebrated star personae, underdogs whose femininity was not representative of the epitome of beauty and style. These alliances speak both to the barriers and the limitations the girls themselves faced and to their attempts to claim Americanness. Like Amanda and China, Blige and Rowland have faced restrictions and limitations; they are not unabashedly celebrated for embodying pleasure, fashion, fantasy, and beauty the way mega-successful performers like Beyoncé are (the singer/actress is a darling of the red carpet who has won numerous Grammys and starred in multiple films, owns her own clothing line, and is married to hip-hop mogul Jay-Z). Constricted by age, class, gender, ethnicity, and race, Amanda had never been on a date and China dared to embody Beyonce's style only at the prom. And both girls faced complex challenges as they graduated from high school and transitioned into womanhood.

As we witnessed in conceptualizing West Indian girls as "dual citizens in the hip-hop nation," these young women straddle West Indian and African American, hip-hop-inspired and dancehall-derived contradictory notions of femininity. These gender articulations navigate false dichotomies between "African American" and "West Indian" and between "hip-hop" and "dancehall," within which African American social productions are interpreted as corrupt while West Indian forms escape parental criticism. Sunaina Maira exposes similar false dichotomies when she writes, "The dichotomy that second-generation youth create between 'pure' Indian traditions and an 'inauthentic,' mixed aesthetic overlooks the reality that hybridity has shaped even so-called authentic cultural traditions on the subcontinent, which has a long history of multiple cultural influences and cross-fertilization with other cultural traditions" (Maira 2002: 190). Although Maira is writing about the Indian diaspora, her theorizations engage with the cultural politics of hip-hop and draw on scholars of the Afro-Caribbean diaspora such as Paul Gilroy and Stuart Hall, who have grappled with Caribbean hybridity. Like Maira, I have reworked Hall's notion of "new ethnicities" to shed light on how first- and second-generation immigrant youth negotiate notions of self vis-à-vis popular culture and public spaces. Following Hall, Maira writes, "A 'non-coercive and more diverse conception of ethnicity' would be based on a reconceptualized notion of difference as 'positional, conditional, and conjunctural' but also as facilitating 'struggle and resistance'" (Hall 1996: 447, cited in Maira 2002: 192). For China and her peers, ethnic identity is truly "positional, conditional and conjunctural." In Brooklyn, first-generation West Indian girls like China identify with African American singers such as Mary J. Blige, and African American girls like Christina identify with West Indian public figures like Roger Toussaint. And, as evidenced in their conversation about beauty, body image, and notions of "authentic Blackness," these youth simultaneously contest and re-create false oppositions between West Indian and African American, between authentic and inauthentic Blackness. Just as Maira finds, the girls in this book moved into and out of identities, creating "new categories between spaces" (Battaglia 1999, cited in Maira 2002: 195). This vision of "new ethnicities" derived from Hall and revamped to account for gender in Angela McRobbie's "different, youthful subjectivities" allows us to understand how China can admire Mary J. Blige but still aspire to Beyoncé's glamour. West Indian migration scholars have neatly categorized first- and second-generation immigrant youth as "American-identified," "immigrant-identified," and "ethnic identified" (Waters 1999) but have not fully engaged with the intricate ways individual youth might move among these categories. These discursive movements are evidenced not only in the fluidity that girls demonstrate as they accept and reject Tyra Banks's version of "real Black" but also in the ways they choose to negotiate place, race, and gender at different points in their lives.

Shelly's Story and West Indian "Success"

Amanda's and China's stories offered important lessons for me, lessons I did not fully appreciate until long after. Central to the "failure" I felt in my ability to convince China to go to college was a conception of the West Indian immigrant's ideal trajectory toward achieving the American dream. Shelly, the BCM administrator, alluded to this when, in her account of the Trinidadian girl who was sent home after becoming pregnant, she lamented, "The whole idea of her coming here [to America] was to have her go to college, to finish high school and to go to college." To my mind, this, too, was the whole point of China's coming here. In fact, China herself listed the opportunity to go to college as one of the primary reasons her mother had brought her to

Brooklyn. In relation to Amanda, the BCM educators and I felt that not only should she go to college but that, given the opportunity, she should attend an Ivy League college, as opposed to a less selective local school. These expectations deny the youths' agency and ignore the pressures immigrant teens face when all of the adults around them thrust conflicting "opportunities" upon them, opportunities that they are expected to gratefully accept. China and Amanda forced me to recognize my own positionality; as a dutiful West Indian daughter and a college professor, I bemoaned China's decision to put off college and was confounded by Amanda's mother's refusal to let her attend the Ivy League school.

Shelly astutely pointed out that these expectations are intricately wrapped up in West Indian notions of success. After she noted the high percentage of West Indian youth at BCM, I asked Shelly if she felt the West Indians were more successful in the internship program than their African American peers, although my own research presented evidence to the contrary. In her response, Shelly referred to her own upbringing and to Amanda's story:

> I don't distinguish between the two [West Indians and African Americans]. I think coming into this country [from Trinidad]—I went to high school here— my mother's generation talked about that. I spent so much time fighting against that distinction. What I got from my upbringing is that would pit people against each other. I could see how that could be troubling and divisive. Kids don't see the distinction. I remember at one point that the teens were not identifying as Jamaican. I don't know if they were given a hard time at school, whether they were Haitian, Trinidadian, Jamaican. I would say Museum Team allows kids to shine and see their possibilities. Take the last Inniss award winner [an honor BCM bestows to graduating seniors who excel academically], for example. Do you remember the Inniss winner, Amanda? Well, she's a West Indian young woman; her parents are Jamaican. She won it. But that year there was as well a young man who was African American. [Another year] a young lady won it for academic achievement, she was an African American, a National Merit Scholar. This year [the winners were] an African American and Marcus, whose parents are Jamaican. Some kids, if I didn't ask I wouldn't know [their ethnicity] until parents come and then you're like, oh! Amanda's mom did not want her to go away to school. Would not let her go! Wouldn't let her go! Another child, too, like Amanda, there was another one who just wanted to get away from her mother, took all these dance classes—mother could not let her go! Sometimes parents themselves are not always ready for all the opportunities.

For Shelly, it is important to fight against notions that West Indians enjoy greater success than African Americans. In her personal experience, such distinctions are generational, fostering divisiveness, and in her professional experience they do not hold water. Still, my research contradicts Shelly when she says, "Kids don't see the distinction." Sometimes "kids" either saw or created distinctions between West Indians and African Americans; other times, they borrowed from one another and minimized distinctions. In fact, Shelly contradicts herself when she recalls a historical moment when youth were reluctant to reveal their Jamaican nationality at school. Especially in relation to popular culture, West Indian youth continuously asserted and circumvented distinctions between themselves and African Americans. Still, Shelly implicitly points to the contradiction I struggled to reconcile: Aren't (West Indian) parents supposed to want their children to achieve the highest levels of success? How could Amanda's mother "not let her go"? How could China refuse the opportunity to go to college?

For Shelly, expecting immigrants to naturally gravitate to prescribed notions of success can be linked to good old-fashioned racism:

> To me it would be the same old, same old, which is racism. Race in this country will always be between Black and White, because there's some institutional pain and memory that has to be completed. In a way, it's a way of sticking it the other side. Immigrants have so much obligation. They have no choice, they have so much obligation to their families. Friends of mine from Africa have obligations to do well, send money, get the next family member so they could come here. Even my cousin's children—[my cousin's son] has had the best of everything in Trinidad, he's one of those kids who'll apply to Ivy League schools. He had so much prepping. He's seventh in the world in math or something. What choice does he have?

In order to fully dissect Shelly's insights as they relate to West Indian and African American cultural definitions of parenting and success, we need to revisit one of China's earlier remarks. When I asked China about the differences and similarities between growing up in Barbados and in Brooklyn, recall that she said:

> Similarities is that the people that I—I live in a Black neighborhood and my friends are Black and I know this is common—Most Black houses, you get, you get beat. So you get, you get whipped. So that's a similarity. Because most White families, you know, they don't beat their children, they get spanked.

Here, China uses "Black" to refer to African American *and* West Indian; she later distinguishes this description from life in Barbados. Although West Indian migration researchers, myself included, have conceptualized corporal punishment as a marker of distinctively West Indian approaches to child rearing, China observes that, in "most Black houses, you get beat." China points to commonalities between West Indian and African American approaches to parenting. In her book *Unequal Childhoods*, anthropologist Annette Lareau argues that corporal punishment and the notion that children should not talk back to parents are class-based rather than racialized approaches to parenting (Lareau 2003). Lareau also finds that working-class and poor children are less likely to feel entitled and more readily accept financial limitations than their middle-class peers. While Lareau does not adequately address ethnic differences, framing the book as an analysis of "Black" and "White" families, her findings resonate with the experiences of girls like China and Amanda. Lareau notes that, while middle-class teens might be better prepared for school on the whole, they are also more likely to suffer from stress, whereas working-class and poor children cultivate closer family ties.

Generational Perspectives

The scholarly findings Lareau offers can be fleshed out with regard to West Indian girls and women if we bear witness to the generational stories presented in this conclusion. Here, McRobbie's notion of "different, youthful subjectivities" takes on an additional nuance, as gender, ethnic, racial, class-based, and generational differences color the accounts and perspectives offered by China, Amanda, Amanda's mother, Shelly, and me (and Paule Marshall's protagonist). China is a first-generation Barbadian, Amanda is a second-generation Jamaican, her mother is a first-generation Jamaican, Shelly is a first-generation Trinidadian and I am a first-generation Guyanese. The five of us also represent different age groups, different generations, and distinct moments of incorporation into American society. Jennifer Cole and Deborah Durham have argued, "Age and intergenerational relations are shaped by, but also shape, political and economic processes, and are centrally implicated in economic and political restructuring. . . . Age mediates relationships in the family and household, social cohorts across space, and history and change (Cole and Durham 2007: 2). A consideration of generational and age-based experiences among different West Indian women uncovers "new perspectives on contemporary social processes by highlighting the ways in which people experience the broader social and economic changes associated with globalization in their intimate lives" (Cole and Durham 2007: 2). As Cole and Durham have noted, global economic changes and transnationalism are "reconfiguring the nature of childhood, youth and old age" (Cole and Durham 2007: 2). These reconfigurations are evidenced in the distinct visions of West Indian success imagined by Shelly, Amanda's mother, Amanda, China, and me.

Examining these experiential differences in the context of women's storytelling offers particular rewards for feminist ethnography. Reflecting on an ethnographic approach that incorporates women's storytelling, Lila Abu-Lughod writes,

> If one merit of the textual technique of storytelling is that it draws attention to, even as it refuses, the power of social scientific generalization to produce "cultures" (with their differentiation of selves and others), the other merit has to do with feminism's second lesson: the inevitability of positionality. A story is always situated; it has both a teller and an audience (Abu-Lughod 1993: 15).

Following Abu-Lughod, I considered China's, Amanda's, Amanda's mother's, Shelly's, and my accounts as "stories" offered by positioned subjects. As I sat down to write the conclusion to this book, I asked Amanda to share the assignment she wrote based on her interview with me. With Amanda's permission (she was in fact delighted at the prospect of my including her essay here), and following an approach employed by Abu-Lughod (1993), I am including excerpts from Amanda's essay, titled, "Independence and Rational Success." By linking her quest for independence with notions of success, Amanda proved herself to be a keen anthropologist; scholars have explored success and achievement as defining principles of West Indian identity (Hintzen 2001: 6). As I read Amanda's essay, I was intrigued by her notion of "rational success." Amanda's essay began:

> It is usually in the most unexpected places where you learn the most valuable life lessons. No one ever knows how their life is going to turn out but many people work towards the lifestyle they would like to attain. It was in a fifties themed restaurant located in Harlem where I learned these values. In an interview with my mentor, Oneka LaBennett—a Professor of African American Studies at Fordham University and an Archaeologist by training—several of these factors hit home for me. One being that starting out is never the easiest thing to do and another being that success is somewhat a rationalized benefit.

This excerpt contains a number of striking factors. I was surprised that Amanda referred to me as her mentor and did not expect that the entire essay would be about me, since Amanda had also interviewed a BCM educator for the same assignment. Her referring to me as her "mentor" forced me to think critically about how I had influenced Amanda, even unwittingly. We can also pause at "errors" in Amanda's account, for example, she refers to me as "an archaeologist" when, in fact, I am a social anthropologist. As I encountered more inconsistencies between what I remembered telling Amanda and how my story unfolded in her essay, I hesitated and contemplated how Amanda might view the version of herself presented in this book. Might she see efforts I have made to preserve her anonymity, for example, as "inconsistencies" that do not completely represent her "real" story? With this in mind, I continued reading:

> Oneka LaBennett was born on May 12th, 1971, in Guyana, a modest country located in South America. In 1977, at the age of six, Oneka and her older brother finally migrated to America to live with their mom. She found it to be a completely different world from the one she had already known for most of her life. "I remember when I was little my mom use to send us letters from America all the time," Oneka states after reminiscing on her mother-less time in Guyana. "My grandmother had no phone and my mother never thought it would have taken so long to send for us."

I had, in fact, emigrated to New York in 1978, but, again, I forgave Amanda for this revision and continued reading her essay. She went on to reflect, "Learning about Oneka's ordeal as a six-year-old seemed to enlighten me about how lives use to be. To not have most of the technology we have today did not seem to bother her." Amanda closed her essay by attributing her notion of independence as related to "rational success" to me—another surprise! I do not recall uttering the following sentence, which Amanda quoted in her essay:

> As Oneka enamored about her time in Spain, you could see the fire that blazed from her long awaited success. "The way I see it is independence is what I would call rational success. It's always a sane goal made to create overall stability in one's life, but it's also always up to the person to agree on pursuing it."

As I tried to reconcile my own memory and my own fieldnotes from that day with Amanda's version of my story, I began to see Amanda's retelling of important moments in my life and her re-creation of what comes across as my "philosophy of independence" as an effort to reconcile generational perspectives on West Indian success and female autonomy. Amanda wrote:

> This interview also gave me insight on the lives of today's adolescents. Interviewing her made me realize that today everything is at our fingertips. For instance, Oneka spoke about the hardships of finding independence from her mother as she got older. "I don't know if it's mainly a characteristic of West Indian mothers but they tend to hover over their daughters like a lioness does with her cubs. Finding independence within me was always a harsh reality for my mother; one that she could not take until I up and left for college."

Again, if my memory serves, Amanda's "like a lioness does with her cubs" metaphor was an embellishment, something I do not recall saying. Yet, her literary flourish and her account of my assessment of West Indian mother/daughter relationships were, on the whole, accurate. Amanda pays critical attention to the generational divide between her and me and between my mother and me. West Indian migration scholars have engaged with the differences between first- and second-generations and with generational approaches to parenting, again pointing to strict West Indian parenting that butts heads with American norms and arguing for relatively neat categorizations: "Of the American-identified 66% were born in the United States, as opposed to only 14% of the immigrant-identified or 38% of the ethnically identified" (Waters 1999: 289). These precise categorizations are as much a result of authors' methodological approaches as they are accurate reflections of how West Indian youth form their subjectivities. Such tidy categorizations do not speak to the messy contradictions evidenced in the five different stories offered here, including Amanda's revision of my life story and my reactions to the girls' dilemmas. And, although I have attempted to distinguish between Amanda's voice and my own, between Shelly's perspective and China's, Abu-Lughod warns that such efforts are embedded in structures of authority that have traditionally done violence to marginalized people's accounts:

> I could have distinguished between the women's words and my own commentaries, or interjected reminders of the ways I was using their narratives to produce certain effects. The latter technique might have made for more honesty but would have drawn attention away from the stories. The former would have set up the usual hierarchy between "informants' words"

and expert's explanations, a construct that, even when unintended, is hard to resist because of the habits of reading and the structures of authority" (Abu-Lughod 1993: 31).

Throughout this book, we have witnessed how space and place are always embodied—physically located in cinemas, McDonald's restaurants, museums, neighborhoods, and schools but conceptualized and given meaning within cultural representations and human subjectivities—revealing how racial and ethnic stereotyping and notions of authenticity are particularly enmeshed in youths' understandings of popular culture and the Black female body. All of these issues come to a head in the notions of West Indian authenticity/femininity, class mobility, and cultural citizenship that emerge in the intertwined generational stories offered in this conclusion. And here, authenticity, or being "mad real," takes on another dimension. Percy Hintzen writes, "I consider authenticity to be the most important issue in the social sciences today and one that should be the preeminent concern of scholars presenting and representing social reality" (Hintzen 2001: 1). Hintzen is not referring to ideas about authentic blackness as represented in popular culture. Rather, he is animated by the researcher's endeavor to "see" and "understand," to produce authentic understandings of what his or her subjects are up to. By juxtaposing my findings with stereotypical popular understandings of Black youth, I positioned this text as a representation of the "real" complexities of Black girls' identities. In a passage that can be applied to the ruptures and competing perspectives offered in this conclusion, Hintzen implicates himself, a native anthropologist, as complicit in shaping an authentic representation of West Indians. Distinguishing between "etic" and "emic" approaches, Hintzen follows Abu-Lughod in arguing that, even with the emic approach, the ethnographer selects what is observed and represented (Hintzen 2001: 2). He also reminds us that, in every ethnographic encounter, the "subject" is likely to be influenced by the researcher's interests. These insights speak both to my decision to include Amanda's essay here (I still selected which parts of the essay to include) and to the ways in which I may have influenced Amanda's behavior. Yet, in both Amanda's and China's case, because I am a native anthropologist, it is difficult to tease out how pleasing me is distinct from pleasing their communities, since my ideas of success are also informed by West Indian ideologies. Still, it is important to note that neither girl made the choice she thought I favored. And, for both girls, the choice hinged on the negotiation of place, a process we have seen to be inextricably connected to West Indian notions of female respectability.

Sunaina Maira writes:

> the intense parental concern with young women's sexuality and accounts of intergenerational conflict provide a framework within which to address other issues, such as women's entry into the workforce, future professionalism, and residential arrangements; significant class concerns are embedded in these conflicts that are ostensibly focused on sexuality, and underwrite the ideology of ethnic authenticity (Maira 2002: 197).

The choices and mediations explored here therefore provide a launching pad for confronting how place, gender, and achievement are tied up in West Indian young women's aspirations. And, although our focus has been on youth, these generational accounts relate to West Indian women from different age groups. While Shelly asserted that being laid off from the museum provided the impetus to actualize long-postponed plans for a change in career, she ended the conversation by asking if she could send me her resume and whether I would forward to her any relevant job announcements I encountered. I felt uneasy playing this role with such a seasoned administrator, a woman who had many more years' experience than I. It occurred to me that the country's economic crisis and the subsequent funding cuts to the museum jeopardized not only the youths' road to success but also disrupted the life trajectory of at least one member of another generation of West Indian women. And, considering that BCM employed a number of West Indians, as administrators, security guards, and cleaning staff, Shelly was certainly not alone.

Although my intervention signaled the end of my relationship with China, I was able to learn about her subsequent experiences from other contacts at the museum. I learned that, following high school graduation, China lived with her mother for a year and worked full time. After saving money for college and retaking the Regents math test a year later, China was accepted into a school of her choice in Manhattan. It has become common for middle-class teens to take a "gap year," during which they travel, intern, or work after high school graduation. Granted, middle-class youngsters' "gap years" do not usually include plans to live in a housing project. Still, my fretfulness about China's choice (what did I fear would happen to her if she moved into the projects?) influenced me to discredit her decisions and to try to deny her the freedoms afforded to middle-class youth. While I maintain the interpretation that anxiety about feeling displaced in areas beyond the city's confines where "people are not so nice" colored China's decision, ultimately, China made the choice that was right for her, in her own due time.

A similar interpretation can be attached to Amanda's story. One year after I initially reconnected with Amanda, I checked in with her again. Now she was a junior at the CUNY school, where she continued to excel. She was still living at home with her mother, and her academic schedule, which she e-mailed me, was dominated by English and writing classes. I noticed that one class ended at 9 p.m. and wondered how that sat with Amanda's mother. In an e-mail peppered with exclamation marks, Amanda wrote, "I have been DYING to catch up with you!!" She continued, "Now that I'm in the publishing program at my school, I must say that I'm twice as excited about your book!! And I even purchased the novel you told me about last year, *Brown Girl, Brownstones*. I haven't read it yet." Maybe, I thought, Amanda didn't need to read it after all. She had found a place for herself.

Notes

1. Interviewees' names and identifying characteristics have been changed in order to protect anonymity.

2. As anthropologists Sargent and Harris note, "child fostering" is not an exclusive outcome of migration; rather, it is a "prevalent" and "culturally legitimate" survival strategy in the West Indies, where an urban Jamaican woman, for example, may pass her children to rural kin if she is financially unable to care for them (Sargent and Harris 1998: 212).

3. In the video for "No More Drama," Blige connects what is ostensibly a song about lost love to the dramatic hardships of urban life, including scenes of gang members struggling to break free from violence, a battered woman daring to leave her abuser, and a drug addict grappling with entering rehab.

4. Since the settings of the Brooklyn Children's Museum and Crown Heights are both crucial to my analysis, and would be easily identified based on my descriptions, I have elected not to change the names of these places.

5. Andrew Tiedt, a sociologist and a graduate student in the Department of Sociology and Anthropology at Fordham University, compiled, analyzed, and helped incorporate the 2000 U.S. Population Census, 2008 American Community Survey, and University of Minnesota IPUMS project data presented in this book.

6. Elsewhere, in *Children's Places: Cross-Cultural Perspectives*, which she co-edited with Eva Gullov, Olwig has placed children at the analytical center.

7. Shalini Shankar's book, *Desi Land: Teen Culture, Class and Success in Silicon Valley* (2008), should also be mentioned here. While Maira's New York–based analysis is more relevant for my purposes, Shankar's attention to a diverse group of South East Asian American youth, their uses of popular culture, and their understandings of success represents an important contribution. Also pertinent, especially because it is similarly grounded in an afterschool program, is Angela Reyes's book, *Language, Identity, and Stereotype among Southeast Asian American Youth: The Other Asian* (2006), which shares my concerns with African American popular culture, stereotyping, and the multidimensionality of identity formation.

8. "Emic" refers to the subject's understandings of practices and representations, while "etic" refers to the ethnographer's understanding of how social reality is organized.

9. An example of ethnographers' growing interest in studying children's lives is evidenced in the launching of the Anthropology of Children and Childhood Interest Group of the American Anthropological Association in 2007. Between 2007 and 2010, the group expanded from approximately one hundred members to more than seven hundred members.

10. The Guyanese government introduced laws in 1994 that set the legal age at which children are permitted to work outside the home at fifteen. Recently, however, the Minister of Labor, Manzoor Nadir, publicly voiced his desire to reset the legal age to allow thirteen-year-olds to work. While Nadir related consideration of lowering the legal age in Guyana to the practices of countries such as the United Kingdom, where children twelve and older are permitted to work for limited periods of time, local activists interpreted the minister's aims as encouraging children to drop out of school at younger ages ("Nadir Seeks to Clarify Child Labour Issue," Kaieteur News Online, April 2, 2010, accessed June 4, 2010, www.kaieteurnewsonline.com/2010/04/02/nadir-seeks-to-clarify-child-labour-issue/). Interestingly, Nadir's reported reason for considering lowering the legal age at which work would be permitted was to permit children to do "light work" such as having paper routes and to reap the benefits of the existence of a large population of already truant children. The Guyanese official's proposal and his suspect reasoning speak to hazy, culturally constructed definitions of "work" and to the blurred distinction I am making between "play" and "labor."

11. See, for example, Elizabeth Cohen, "Painful Plight of Haiti's 'Restavec' Children," CNN, January 29, 2010, accessed June 2, 2010, www.cnn.com/2010/HEALTH/01/29/haiti.restavek.sende.sencil/index.html.

CHAPTER 2

1. The release of Morgan Spurlock's popular documentary *Super Size Me*, in which the filmmaker explored the negative health consequences of eating at McDonald's for thirty days straight, prompted some changes in the franchise's menu. In the documentary, Spurlock forced himself to eat everything on the McDonald's menu and to supersize his meal when asked. The film documented his deteriorating health, and subsequently McDonald's removed the phrase "supersize" from its menu options. However, customers could still "make it a large," which essentially amounted to the same quantity as supersizing.

2. See www.cinematreasures.org/theatre/2553, accessed January 2, 2010.

3. Rebecca Webber, "When A Multiplex Moves into the Neighborhood," *Gotham Gazette*, March 18, 2002, accessed January 2, 2010, www.gothamgazette.com/iotw/culture-community/doc1.shtml.

4. This account was shared via e-mail communication on January 3, 2010, under the condition of anonymity.

5. "UA Theater: Nightmare on Court Street," Brooklyn Heights Blog, January 22, 2008, accessed January 2, 2010, http://brooklynheightsblog.com.archives/2104.

6. "Court Street Cinema, Fire Again," Brownstoner, September 14, 2009, accessed January 2, 2010, www.brownstoner.com/brownstoner/archives/2009/09/court_street_ci.php.

7. My research is concerned less with the youths' duties than with the ideologies imparted and revealed in their workshops and their time spent socializing at the museum. It should be noted that, while I designate their time at BCM as "play-labor," BCM is

an educational institution, and a good deal of the youngsters' time there was spent in classroom settings, where they listened to lectures and completed homework assignments for the classes taken at BCM.

8. Joanna handled the museum's Ball Python, not to be confused with BCM's famous twenty-foot-long albino Burmese Python, named Fantasia, who eats whole chickens and is handled by the museum's live-animal curator.

9. Some of the descriptions offered in this section also appeared in my Ph.D. dissertation, "Consuming Identities: Consumption, Gender and Ethnicity among West Indian Adolescents in Brooklyn."

10. Carol Enseki resigned in 2009, and the Museum's Board of Trustees announced the appointment of a new president and CEO, Georgina Ngozi, a Black woman who was born and raised in Brooklyn.

11. In their study of low-income families in Kingston, Jamaica, Sargent and Harris describe mothers' high expectations for girls as including, "hoping that they will pass exams, obtain good jobs, and contribute to the family finances; mothers watched carefully to prevent inappropriate sexual liaisons that might limit their future opportunities" (Sargent and Harris 1998: 207). These expectations for daughters are contrasted with mothers' treatment of sons, who "may roam around the neighborhood and may sometimes not be seen by their parents for most of the day" (Sargent and Harris 1998: 207).

12. It is worth noting, however, that the twenty-first century marked a period of renewed gentrification in Brooklyn, concomitant with the elevated cache of its cultural institutions, not the least of which was the Brooklyn Museum, located on Eastern Parkway, a few blocks west of BCM.

13. Edward Shapiro argues against portraying the riots as an anti-Semitic attack but notes that most of the Blacks who were "caught up in the riot" were teenagers or youth in their early twenties, using the prominence of this age group in the conflict to also dispel the notion that "the economic conditions and the thwarted ambitions" of Blacks are an apt explanation for the riots (Shapiro 2006: xv). Here, Shapiro suggests that youth are less concerned with "economic frustrations" (Shapiro 2006: xv). However, by exposing the centrality of play-labor and the consumer sphere in the lives of Crown Heights youth, *She's Mad Real* places the pursuit of jobs and access to consumer goods squarely within the daily concerns of youth.

14. This incident was covered in local newspaper articles, including Joe Gould et al., "History of Violence Follows Hasidic Teen Beaten in Brooklyn by Thugs," *New York Daily News*, January 22, 2008, accessed February 6, 2010, www.nydailynews.com/news/ny_crime/2008/01/22/2008-01-22_history_of_violence_follows_hasidic_teen.html; "'Tribal' Tension in Crown Heights Keeps Neighborhood from Moving beyond Hate," *New York Daily News*, April 23, 2008, accessed February 6, 2010, www.nydailynews.com/news/ny_crime/2008/04/23/2008-04-23_tribal_tension_in_crown_heights_keeps_ne.html.

15. This incident was also reported on by numerous sources including the *New York Times* and the *Yeshiva World News* who picked up the story from Channel 2, the local CBS station. My descriptions are gleaned from Al Baker and Ann Farmer, "Residents' Help Sought after Man Is Beaten in Crown Heights," *New York Times*, April 19, 2008, accessed January 2, 2010, www.nytimes.com/2008/04/19/nyregion/19crown.html; "Crown Heights Man: I Was Beaten by Hasidic Jews," *Yeshiva World News*, April 24, 2008, accessed January 2, 2010, www.theyeshivaworld.com/article.php?p=17171.

16. This incident received coverage on local news stations and on the CrownHeights.info blog, "Protests Beating in Crown Heights," May 17, 2008, accessed January 2, 2010, www.crownheights.info/index.php?itemid=11976.

17. For a compelling portrait of Hasidic girls in another Brooklyn neighborhood, Borough Park (known as "Boro Park" by residents), see Ayala Fader's 2009 ethnography, *Mitzvah Girls: Bringing up the Next Generation of Hasidic Jews in Brooklyn,* which explores language, the body, and gender as Hasidic girls negotiate their subjectivities in their homes, in schools, and on city streets. For a description of girls within the Lubavitcher community in Crown Heights, see Stephanie Levine's *Mystics, Mavericks, and Merrymakers: An Intimate Journey Among Hasidic Girls* (2003).

18. For an insightful analysis of Black Jewish identity as it relates to police violence and the gendering of public space in Crown Heights, see chapter 4 of John L. Jackson's *Real Black* (2005).

19. For more on West Indian youths' engagement with the horror genre, see "Reading *Buffy* and 'Looking Proper': Race, Gender and Consumption among West Indian Girls in Brooklyn," in which I discuss the invisibility or untimely deaths of Black characters in Hollywood horror (LaBennett 2006). More recent popular culture incarnations of the vampire narrative as a metaphor for youthful angst can be seen in the immensely popular *Twilight* films and in the HBO series *True Blood.* While *Twilight* confirms my observations about Black invisibility (Blacks are nonexistent, save for an evil Black vampire, a secondary character), *True Blood,* set in Louisiana, presents central Black characters as both heroes and villains.

20. John L. Jackson also offers a meaningful discussion of Crown Heights residents' distrust of the police (Jackson 2005).

21. See, for example, Jamie Schram and Reuven Fenton, "Perv in a Pixel: Teen Snaps Subway Sleaze on Cellcam," *New York Post,* October 5, 2010, accessed October 14, 2010, www.nypost.com/p/news/local/brooklyn/perv_in_pixel_RSEYcQRJk3flysqSqFMlkL.

22. Thirty-seven minutes is the official time given in the Department of Education's press release; however, the exact amount of time by which the day was extended varies from school to school.

23. Interviews with one New York City public high school teacher and one middle school teacher revealed that, under the new Department of Education program, an art teacher, for example, was charged with providing tutoring for standardized math tests during the extended school time. The art teacher with whom I spoke lamented that he was not trained for this form of instruction and was therefore of little use to the students.

24. Available at http://pewinternet.org/Reports/2010/Teens-and-Mobile-Phones/Chapter-2/Part-1.aspx, accessed October 14, 2010.

25. See http://cnn.com/video/date/2.0/video/tech/2009/10/08/kwtv.teen.texting.driving.kwtv.html.

26. Amy S. Clark, "School Cell Phone Ban Causes Uproar: NYC Moms and Dads Say They Need Way to Reach Kids in Emergencies," CBS News, May 12, 2006, accessed November 17, 2009, www.cbsnews.com/stories/2006/05/12/national/main1616330.shtml.

27. Michael Bloomberg, quoted by the Associated Press, "Bloomberg Dreams of Jamming Cell Phones in Schools," November 2, 2007, accessed October 14, 2010, www.freerepublic.com/focus/f-news/1920243/posts.

28. The cell phone has become a technological marker of youth in more ways than one. The Associated Press reported that New York City high school students were downloading and using a ringtone that could not be heard by adults because of its high-pitched frequency. Originally created to disperse teenagers hanging out in front of stores, the "Mosquito" tone was audible to children and adolescents but inaudible to aging adult ears, allowing students to receive phone calls and text messages in class unbeknownst to their teachers (Associated Press, "Students Find Ring Tone Adults Can't Hear: High Pitched 'Mosquito' Originally Created to Disperse Youngsters," MSNBC, June 12, 2006, accessed November 22, 2009, http://msnbc.msn.com/id/13274669.

29. Blacks' stereotypical, predatory consumption of fried chicken was dramatized in the critically acclaimed 2009 film *Precious: Based on the Novel* Push *by Sapphire*, when the title character, a pregnant African American teenage girl, steals a bucket of fried chicken from a local fast-food restaurant. Precious escapes with the bucket of chicken under one arm, running down a busy New York sidewalk as she bites into a piece of chicken with her free hand. The film includes a portrayal of a West Indian girl among Precious's cohort of illiterate teenage girls who come together under the tutelage of an inspirational teacher.

30. See Amy S. Clark, "School Cell Phone Ban Causes Uproar: NYC Moms and Dads Say They Need Way to Reach Kids in Emergencies," CBS News, May 12, 2006, accessed November 17, www.cbsnews.com/stories/2006/05/12/national/main1616330.shtml.

31. Rather than presenting an in-depth recount of the details surrounding the strike, I relate the specifics relevant to my respondents.

32. Toussaint's sentence was reduced for good behavior, and he was released after three and one-half days in jail.

CHAPTER 3

1. Some credited Arrested Development, which hailed from Atlanta, with establishing southern hip-hop. However, as Marcyliena Morgan has noted, the group was severely criticized for its goody-goody image and, after it gained crossover success, was viewed as "naive" about the real-life problems facing urban youth (Morgan 2009: 61). Although members of the group tried to defend themselves against such critiques, their second album bombed, and they fell into virtual obscurity.

2. M-1 won teens' respect because Dead Prez's 1990 hit song "Hip-hop" had been used as comedian Dave Chappelle's entrance music on his immensely popular Comedy Central show.

3. For more on *krumping*, see Christina Zanfagna (2009) and the documentary film *Rize*, directed by David LaChapelle (Lions Gate Films, 2005).

4. Although distinctions should be made between rap (which is usually accompanied by recorded music) and spoken-word poetry (which is usually unaccompanied), spoken-word poetry and hip-hop music are thought of as related forms of cultural expression. The hip-hop mogul Russell Simmons's popular television program *Def Poetry Jam*, hosted by rapper Mos Def, illustrates the relationship between the two forms; many of the spoken-word poets who perform on the show are also rap MCs. I should also note here that Urban Word is an overtly community-oriented and political group that, according to its mission statement, "exists to ensure that New York youth have a safe, supportive,

dynamic and challenging community in which to discover their powerful voices" (www.urbanwordnyc.org/uwnyc/index.php?q=MissionVision, accessed June 21, 2010). Urban Word was founded in 1999; in addition to its public performances, the group leads school and community organization workshops. The group has collaborated with a number of New York City institutions that work with youth, including the Brooklyn Children's Museum.

5. I refer to the 2005 edition to Mary Pipher's *Reviving Ophelia*, in which she includes discussion questions about minority girls, and to Carol Gilligan's collaborative volume, *Between Voice and Silence: Women and Girls, Race and Relationship* (Pipher 2005; McLean Taylor, Gilligan, and Sullivan 1995).

6. See, for example, Marisa Meltzer and Julianne Shepherd, "Spitting Fire," in *Spin* 22, no. 3 (March 2006): 77–81, http://books.google.com/books?id=J98LX7jemQC&lpg=PP1&dq="Riot+in+the+streets:+French Rap"&f=false.

7. While John Jackson might read our (both mine as anthropologist and China's as subject) reliance on "realness" as examples of false liberation that ultimately reify the "very terms of power they eschew," realness was an omnipresent emic term that could not be ignored and its ironies and limitations did not escape the girls (Jackson 2005; Shipley 2007). Moreover, in line with Jackson's notion of racial sincerity, the girls' conceptual-izations of realness were not "hard, fast, and absolute" but steeped in "unfalsifiablity, ephemerality, partiality, and social vulnerability" (Jackson 2005: 18).

8. Omi and Winant assert that 1960s-era Black Power consumption practices stem from "ideas that the black community should patronize businesses owned by blacks . . . [and] were concepts which borrowed as much from the tradition of Booker T. Wash-ington as they did from those of Cyril Briggs, Marcus Garvey, or Malcolm X" (Omi and Winant 1994: 102).

9. In her exploration of the "production and performance of violence in dancehall music culture," Donna Hope documents how, for example, Vybz Kartel was arrested after a showdown between him and another artist, Ninja Man, exploded into a violent on stage battle (Hope 2006).

10. This respondent quote appears in a previously published article (LaBennett 2006: 291).

11. This controversy is discussed in Ray Fishman's "Cos and Effect: Bill Cosby Might Be Right about African-Americans Spending a Lot on Expensive Sneakers—But He's Wrong about Why," *Slate*, January 11, 2008, accessed November 1, 2009, www.slate.com/id/2181822. Cosby's public remarks were first made in 2004, and he continued for several years to elicit sharp critiques that he was blaming the victims from many in the Black community. Cosby repeated much of his argument in a 2007 book coauthored with Dr. Alvin Poussaint and titled *Come on People: On the Path from Victims to Victors* (Nashville, TN: Thomas Nelson).

12. Dancehall artists' profanity, unlike that of American hip-hop artists, also often escapes the conservative ears of radio censors who frequently miss "explicit" lyrical content because it is not understood by those not fluent in West Indian patois.

13. Once again, John L. Jackson's brilliant musings prove to be useful here: "As a racial construct, blackness 'represents' (indeed, over-represents) the real. It is decidedly a fiction. In hip-hop culture . . . invocations of 'the real' help to explain how people make sense of the world by combining models based on authenticity with those based on

sincerity, cobbling together these two separate routes to the realness of everyday life—and often using one half of that dyad to challenge and confound the other" (Jackson 2005: 28). My reference to the girls' "most sincere moments" can be likened to Jackson's concept of "racial sincerity," which complicates "materialist and literal readings of racial identity" (Jackson 2005: 21).

CHAPTER 4

1. T. Denean Sharpley-Whiting notes that in 2004, *Top Model* was the UPN network's highest-rated program among eighteen- to forty-nine-year-old female viewers and teenagers (Sharpley-Whiting 2007: 29). Sharpley-Whiting adds, "As the network's cash cow, [*Top Model*] was also one of the top ten programs among African American adults, and the highest-rated reality show among African Americans (Sharpley-Whiting 2007: 29).

2. The first focus group, Explainers, consisted of fourteen teens (seven girls and seven boys). The second group, Volunteers-in-Training, consisted of twelve teens (eight girls and four boys). While I glean general insights from both focus groups, direct quotes are taken from the group of Explainers.

3. The program was initially dubbed *The Tyra Banks Show*, but its title was later shortened to *The Tyra Show* and then *Tyra*.

4. "Go-see" is a modeling industry term for when models meet with potential clients.

5. See www.topmodelfan.com/c1shannon.html, accessed June 15, 2009.

6. For more on the Eva/Yaya controversy, see chapter 1 in Sharpley-Whiting 2007.

7. "Obesity in Children and Adolescents," American Association of Child and Adolescent Psychiatry, Facts for Families, No. 79, May 2008, accessed June 17, 2009, www.aacap. org/cs/root/facts_for_families/obesity_in_children_and_teens.

8. Editorial: "Selling Obesity at School", *New York Times*, April 26, 2009, accessed June 18, 2009, www.nytimes.com/2009/04/27/opinion/27mon2.html.

9. Public reactions to the film *Precious: Based on the Novel* Push *by Sapphire* brought attention to these issues in the winter of 2009. Coproduced by Oprah Winfrey and Tyler Perry, the film garnered critical acclaim and mixed reviews from Black communities. Many Black teenage girls reportedly identified with the overweight, abused protagonist, with *Essence* magazine heralding the film for "exorcising the demons" of the Black community (Michaela Angela Davis, "The Film 'Precious' Exorcises Our Demons," *Essence*, November 23, 2009, accessed June 21, 2010, www.essence.com/entertainment/ commentary_4/madvision_the _politics_of_beauty_and_sty.php). However, the author, Sapphire, voiced her own fears that the movie might reinforce earlier film stereotypes of Black women as "obese maids" (Bonnie Davis, "Does 'Precious' Movie Stereotype Big Black Women?," *The Grio*, November 6, 2009, accessed June 21, 2010, www.thegrio. com/2009/11/does-precious-movie-stereotype-big-black-women.php).

10. Available at http://www.cdc.gov/NCCDPHP/publications/AAG/obesity.htm, accessed June 18, 2009.

11. I have encountered various spellings of Baartman's name, including "Baartman" (Maseko 1998) and "Bartmann" (DuCille 1996). Her first name has been presented as "Saartjie," "Sara," and "Sarah."

12. See www.brownpride.us/forum/armenian-vs-puerto-rican-jennifer-lopez-vs-kim-kardashian-t11858.html, accessed July 20, 2009.

13. Michelle Obama, as quoted in Sam Coates, "First Lady Michelle Obama Gives Schoolgirls a Pep Talk," (London) *Times*, April 3, 2009, accessed April 3, 2009, http://www.timesonline.co.uk/tol/news/politics/article6025234.ece.

14. Caitlin A. Johnson, "Tyra Banks Responds to Weight Critics," CBS News, January 25, 2007, accessed June 10, 2009, http://www.cbsnews.com/stories/2007/01/25/earlyshow/leisure/celebspot/main2397891.shtml.

15. See http://tyrashow.warnerbros.com, accessed April 22, 2009.

16. Palin is quoted in the Huffington Post as saying, "We believe that the best of America is not all in Washington, D.C. We believe that the best America is in these small towns that we get to visit, and in these wonderful little pockets of what I call the real America, being here with all of you hard working very patriotic, um very, um, pro-America areas of this great nation." Sam Stein, "Palin Explains What Parts of the Country Not 'Pro-America,'" *Huffington Post*, October 17, 2008, accessed August 30, 2009, www.huffingtonpost.com/2008/10/17/palin-clarifies-what-part_n_135641.html.

17. In December 2009, after five years on the air, Banks announced that she would end *Tyra* in the spring of 2010.

18. See http://tzonefoundation.org/tzone-story/, accessed March 20, 2009.

19. See http://tzonefoundation.org/tzone-story/, accessed April 22, 2009.

20. Debuting on ABC in January 2009, *True Beauty* is a reality program premised on contestants who believe they are competing on the basis of their outer beauty when in fact they are being judged on inner beauty.

21. This headline was posted on November 4, 2005.

22. "Cover Story: Tyra Banks Speaks Out About Her Weight" *People*, January 24, 2007, accessed April 27, 2009, www.people.com/people/article/0,,20009611,00.html.

23. See http://tyrashow.warnerbros.com/2009/03/top_model_audition.php, accessed October 14, 2010.

CHAPTER 5

1. BCM also receives significant funding from the Department of Youth and Community Development (a city government organization that distributes city, state, and federal funds) and additional aid from other sources such as the Department of Juvenile Justice, which was recently linked with the Administration for Children's Services; the Career Internship Network, a program of the Youth Development Institute; and corporations such as Verizon.

Bibliography

Abu-Lughod, Lila. 1993. *Writing Women's Worlds: Bedouin Stories.* Berkeley: University of California Press.

Alexander, Jacqui M. 2005. *Pedagogies of Crossing: Meditations on Feminism, Sexual Politics, Memory, and the Sacred.* Durham, NC: Duke University Press.

Appadurai, Arjun, ed. 1986. *The Social Life of Things: Commodities in Cultural Perspective.* Cambridge: Cambridge University Press.

Appiah, Kwame Anthony. 1996. "Race, Culture, Identity: Misunderstood Connections." In *Color Conscious: The Political Morality of Race*, ed. Kwame Anthony Appiah and Amy Gutman. Princeton: Princeton University Press.

Augé, Marc. 1997. *Non-Places: Introduction to an Anthropology of Supermodernity.* Translated by John Howe. London and New York: Verso.

Bailey, Wilma. 1988. "Child Morbidity in the Kingston Metropolitan Area, Jamaica, 1983." *Social Science and Medicine* 26, no. 11 (June): 1117–24.

Barboza, David. 2000. "Rampant Obesity, a Debilitating Reality for the Urban Poor." *New York Times*, December 26, section F, p. 5.

Basch, Vilna. 2001. "Transnational Social Relations and the Politics of National Identity: An Eastern Caribbean Case Study. " In *Islands in the City: West Indian Migration to New York*, ed. Nancy Foner. Berkeley: University of California Press.

Baudrillard, Jean. 1981. *Towards a Critique of the Political Economy of the Sign.* St. Louis: Telos Press.

———. 1988. "Consumer Society." In *Jean Baudrillard: Selected Writings*, ed. Mark Poster. Oxford: Polity Press.

Bennett, Andy, M. Cieslik, and S. Miles. 2003. *Researching Youth.* London: Palgrave.

Best, Amy. 2000. *Prom Night: Youth, Schools and Popular Culture.* New York: Routledge.

———. 2007. Introduction to *Representing Youth: Methodological Issues in Critical Youth Studies*, ed. Amy L. Best. New York: New York University Press.

Bohannon, Laura. 1966. "Shakespeare in the Bush." *Natural History*, August-September, 45–49.

Bonilla-Silva, Eduardo. 2010. *Racism without Racists: Color-Blind Racism and Racial Inequality in Contemporary America.* Latham, MD: Rowan and Littlefield.

Brennan, Denise. 2004. *What's Love Got to Do with It? Transnational Desires and Sex Tourism in the Dominican Republic.* Durham, NC: Duke University Press.

Brown, Jacqueline Nassy. 2005. *Dropping Anchor, Setting Sail: Geographies of Race in Black Liverpool.* Princeton: Princeton University Press.

Bryce-Laporte, Roy S. 1972. "Black Immigrants: The Experience of Invisibility and Inequality." *Journal of Black Studies* 3: 29–56.

Burrell, Jackie. 2009. "What's That 'Tap Tap Tap' in the Night? Teens' Texting Causes Sleep Problems." *Chicago Tribune*, November 9, 25, accessed October 25, 2010, http://articles.chicagotribune.com/2009-11-01/features/0910290560_1_texting-teens-adolescent-health.

Butcher, Kristin F. 1994. "Black Immigrants in the United States: A Comparison with Native Blacks and Other Immigrants." *Industrial and Labor Relations Review* 47 (January): 265–84.

Butterfield, Sherri-Ann P. 2004. "'We're Just Black': The Racial and Ethnic Identities of Second-Generation West Indians in New York." In *Becoming New Yorkers: Ethnographies of the New Second Generation*, ed. Philip Kasinitz, John H. Mollenkopf, and Mary C. Waters. New York: Russell Sage Foundation.

Cahill, Caitlin. 2007a. "The Personal Is Political: Developing New Subjectivities through Participatory Action Research." *Gender, Place & Culture: A Journal for Feminist Geography* 14, no. 2 (June): 267–92.

———. 2007b. "Negotiating Grit and Glamour: Young Women of Color and the Gentrification of the Lower East Side." *City & Society* 19, no. 2: 202–53.

Campbell, Colin. 1995. "The Sociology of Consumption." In *Acknowledging Consumption: A Review of New Studies*, ed. Daniel Miller. London: Routledge.

Chin, Elizabeth M. 2001. *Purchasing Power: Black Kids and American Consumer Culture.* Minneapolis: University of Minnesota Press.

———. 2007. "Power-Puff Ethnography/Guerilla Research: Children as Native Anthropologists." In *Representing Youth: Methodological Issues in Critical Youth Studies*, ed. Amy L. Best. New York: New York University Press.

Christensen, Pia, and Allison James, eds. 2000. *Research with Children: Perspectives and Practices.* London: Falmer.

Codrington, Raymond. 2006. "The Homegrown: Rap, Race, and Class in London." In *Globalization and Race: Transformations in the Cultural Production of Blackness*, ed. Kamari M. Clarke and Deborah A. Thomas. Durham, NC: Duke University Press.

Cole, Jennifer, and Deborah Durham, eds. 2007. *Generations and Globalization: Youth, Age, and Family in the New World Economy.* Bloomington: Indiana University Press.

Collins, Patricia Hill. 1991. *Black Feminist Thought: Knowledge, Consciousness, and the Politics of Empowerment.* New York: Routledge.

Cooper, Bruce S., and John W. Lee. 2006. "Cellphones in Schools?" *Education Week* 24, no. 42 (July 12): 44–45.

Cooper, Carolyn. 1995. *Noises in the Blood: Orality, Gender, and the "Vulgar" Body of Jamaican Popular Culture.* Durham, NC: Duke University Press.

———. 2004. *Sound Clash: Jamaican Dancehall Culture at Large.* Oxford: Palgrave Macmillan.

Cosby, Bill, and Alvin F. Poussaint. 2007. *Come On People: On the Path from Victims to Victors.* Nashville, TN: Thomas Nelson.

Daniels, Lee, dir. 2009. *Precious: Based on the Novel* Push *by Sapphire.* 109 min. Lions Gate Films.

Dimitriadis, Greg. 2001. "'In the Clique': Popular Culture, Constructions of Place, and the Everyday Lives of Urban Youth." *Anthropology and Education Quarterly* 32, no. 1 (March): 29–51.

Docksai, Rick. 2009. "Teens and Cell Phones." *The Futurist*, (January-February): 10-11, accessed November 27, 2009, www.wfs.org/node/1123.

Douglas, Mary, and Baron Isherwood. 1979. [1996]. *The World of Goods: Towards an Anthropology of Consumption*. 2nd ed. New York: Basic Books.

duCille, Ann. 1996. *Skin Trade*. Cambridge, MA: Harvard University Press.

Erikson, Erik H. 1968. *Identity: Youth and Crisis*. New York and London: W. W. Norton.

Fader, Ayala. 2009. *Mitzvah Girls: Bringing Up the Next Generation of Hasidic Jews in Brooklyn*. Princeton: Princeton University Press.

Farley, Christopher. 1999. "Hip-Hop Nation." *Time*, February 8, 54–64.

Fears, Darryl. 2002. "A Diverse—and Divided—Black Community: As Foreign-Born Population Grows, Nationality Trumps Skin Color." *Washington Post*, Sunday, February 24, A01, accessed October 4, 2010, www.washingtonpost.com/ac2/wp-dyn/A57951-2002Feb23?language=printer.

Fine, Gary A., and Kent Sandstrom. 1988. *Knowing Children: Participant Observation with Minors*. Qualitative Research Methods, Vol. 15. Newbury Park, CA: Sage.

Fishman, Steve. 2006. "Anger Management: Why TWU Honcho Roger Toussaint Still Blames Bloomberg—and Still Believes Striking Was the Only Possible Course." *New York*, January 9.

Fleetwood, Nicole. 2005. "Authenticating Practices: Producing Realness, Performing Youth." In *Youthscapes: The Popular, the National and the Global*, ed. Sunaina Maira and Elizabeth Soep. Philadelphia: University of Pennsylvania Press.

Flores, Juan. 2000. *From Bomba to Hip-Hop: Puerto Rican Culture and Latino Identity*. New York: Columbia University Press.

Foner, Nancy. 1978. *Jamaica Farewell: Jamaican Migrants in London*. Berkeley: University of California Press.

———. 2001. "Introduction: West Indian Migration: An Overview." In *Islands in the City: West Indian Migration to New York*, ed. Nancy Foner. Berkeley: University of California Press.

———. 2005. *In a New Land: A Comparative View of Immigration*. New York: New York University Press.

Forman, Murray. 2004. Introduction to *That's the Joint!: The Hip-Hop Studies Reader*, ed. Murray Forman and Mark Anthony Neal. New York: Routledge.

———. 2005. "Straight outta Mogadishu: Prescribed Identities and Performance Practices among Somali Youth in North American High Schools." In *Youthscapes: The Popular, The National, The Global*, ed. Sunaina Maira and Elizabeth Soep. Philadelphia: University of Pennsylvania Press.

Foucault, Michel. 1975. *Discipline and Punish: The Birth of the Prison*. New York: Vintage Books.

Fraser, Sandy, V. Lewis, S. Ding, M. Kellet, and C. Robinson, eds. 2004. *Doing Research with Children and Young People*. London: Sage.

Freeman, Carla. 2000. *High Tech and High Heels in the Global Economy: Women, Work and Pink Collar Identities in the Caribbean*. Durham, NC: Duke University Press.

Gaunt, Kyra D. 2006. *The Games Black Girls Play: Learning the Ropes from Double-Dutch to Hip-Hop*. New York: New York University Press.

George, Nelson. 1998. *Hip-Hop America*. New York: Penguin Books.

Gewertz, Catherine. 2006. "N.Y.C. Schools Take Hard Line on Cellphones: Parents, Advocates Say District's Rules Ignore Safety Concerns." *Education Week*, July 12 accessed November 17, 2009, www.edweek.org/login.html?source=http://edweek.org/ew/articles/2006/07/12/42cell.h25.html.

Gilligan, Carol. 1993. *In a Different Voice: Psychological Theory and Women's Development.* Cambridge, MA: Harvard University Press.

Gilroy, Paul. 1993. *The Black Atlantic: Modernity and Double Consciousness.* Cambridge, MA: Harvard University Press.

———. 1995. "'. . . To Be Real': The Dissident Forms of Black Expressive Culture." In *Let's Get It On: The Politics of Black Performance*, ed. Catherine Ugwu. Seattle: Bay Press.

———. 2000. *Against Race: Imagining Political Culture Beyond the Color Line.* Cambridge, MA: Harvard University Press.

"The Girls Get Really Naked." 2003. *America's Next Top Model.* UPN. Originally aired July 1.

Giroux, Henri. 1996. *Fugitive Cultures: Race, Violence, and Youth.* New York: Routledge.

Glazer, Nathan, and Daniel Patrick Moynihan. 1963. *Beyond the Melting Pot: The Negroes, Puerto Ricans, Jews, Italians, and Irish of New York City.* Cambridge, MA: MIT Press.

Goldschmidt, Henry. 2002. "Suits and Souls: Trying to Tell a Jew When You See One in Crown Heights." In *Jews of Brooklyn*, ed. Ilana Abramovitch and Sean Galvin. Hanover, NH, and London: Brandeis University Press and the University Press of New England.

———. 2006. *Race and Religion among the Chosen Peoples of Crown Heights.* New Brunswick, NJ: Rutgers University Press.

Goodman, J. David. 2009. "Making Money Foot over Hand." *New York Times*, January 28, accessed January 5, 2010, www.nytimes.com/2009/01/29/nyregion/29breakdance.html.

Goodwin, Marjorie Harness. 1990. *He-Said-She-Said: Talk as Social Organization among Black Children.* Bloomington: Indiana University Press.

Graue, M. Elizabeth, and Daniel Walsh. 1998. *Studying Children in Context: Theories, Methods, and Ethics.* Thousand Oaks, CA: Sage.

Gray, Herman. 1995. *Watching Race: Television and the Struggle for "Blackness."* Minneapolis: University of Minnesota Press.

Guevara, Nancy. 1996. "Women Writin', Rappin', Breakin'." In *Droppin' Science: Critical Essays on Rap Music and Hip-Hop Culture*, ed. William Erick Perkins. Philadelphia: Temple University Press.

Gupta, Akhil, and James Ferguson. 1997. *Culture, Power, Place: Explorations in Critical Anthropology.* Durham, NC: Duke University Press.

Hall, Stuart. 1990. "Cultural Identity and Diaspora." In *Identity: Community, Culture, Difference*, ed. Jonathan Rutherford. London: Lawrence and Wishart.

———. 1993. "What Is This 'Black' in Black Popular Culture." In *Black Popular Culture*, ed. Gina Dent. Seattle: Bay Press.

———. 1995. "Negotiating Caribbean Identities." *New Left Review* 209 (January-February): 3–14.

———. 1996. "New Ethnicities." In *Stuart Hall: Critical Dialogues in Cultural Studies*, ed. D. Morley and K. H. Chen. London: Routledge.

Handler, Richard. 1993. "An Anthropological Definition of the Museum and its Purpose." *Museum Anthropology* 17, no. 1 (February): 33–36.

Harvey, David. 1990. *The Condition of Postmodernity: An Enquiry into the Origins of Cultural Change*. Malden, MA: Blackwell.

Hayden, Dolores. 1995. *The Power of Place: Urban Landscapes as Public History*. Cambridge, MA: MIT Press.

Hawkswood, William. 1996. *One of the Children: Gay Black Men in Harlem*. Berkeley: University of California Press.

Hebdige, Dick. 1976. "Reggae, Rastas and Rudies." In *Resistance through Rituals*, ed. Stuart Hall and T. Jefferson. New York: Routledge.

Hintzen, Percy C. 2001. *West Indian in the West: Self-Representations in an Immigrant Community*. New York: New York University Press.

Hirschberg, Lynn. 2008. "Banksable." *New York Times Magazine*, June 1, www. nytimes. com/2008/06/01/magazine/01tyra-t.html.

Hodges, David Julian. 1978. "Museums, Anthropology, and Minorities: In Search of a New Relevance for Old Artifacts." *Anthropology and Education Quarterly* 9, no. 2, *New Perspectives on Black Education* (Summer): 148–57.

Holmes, Robyn. 1998. *Fieldwork with Children*. Thousand Oaks, CA: Sage.

Honwana, Alcinda, and Filip de Boeck, eds. 2005. *Makers and Breakers: Children and Youth in Postcolonial Africa*. Trenton, NJ, and Asmara, Eritrea: Africa World Press.

Hope, Donna. 2006. "Dons and Shottas: Performing Violent Masculinity in Dancehall Culture." *Social and Economic Studies* 55, nos. 1 & 2: 115–31.

Horst, Heather, and Daniel Miller. 2006. *The Cell Phone: An Anthropology of Communication*. Oxford: Berg.

HoSang, Daniel. 2006. "Beyond Policy: Ideology, Race and the Re-Imagining of Youth." Paper presented at the Society for the Anthropology of North America Conference, April 22, New York, New York.

Huq, Rupa. 2006. *Beyond Subculture: Pop, Youth and Identity in a Postcolonial World*. London: Routledge.

Ifekwunigwe, Jayne O. 2006. "Recasting 'Black Venus' in the 'New' African Diaspora." In *Globalization and Race: Transformations in the Cultural Production of Blackness*, ed. Deborah A. Thomas and Kamari M. Clarke. Durham, NC: Duke University Press.

Jackson Jr., John L. 2005. *Real Black: Adventures in Racial Sincerity*. Chicago: University of Chicago Press.

James, Allison, and Alan Prout, eds. 1990. *Constructing and Reconstructing Childhood: Contemporary Issues in the Sociological Study of Childhood*. New York: Routledge.

Julien, Isaac, dir. 1994. *The Darker Side of Black*. Drift Releasing.

Kasinitz, Philip. 1992. *Caribbean New York*. Ithaca: Cornell University Press.

———. 2001. "Invisible No More? West Indian Americans in the Social Scientific Imagination." In *Islands in the City: West Indian Migration to New York*, ed. Nancy Foner. Berkeley: University of California Press.

Kasinitz, Philip, J. H. Mollenkopf, M. C. Waters, and J. Holdaway. 2008. *Inheriting the City: The Children of Immigrants Come of Age*. New York: Russell Sage Foundation; Cambridge, MA: Harvard University Press.

Kasinitz, Philip, J. H. Mollenkopf, and M. C. Waters, eds. 2004. *Becoming New Yorkers: Ethnographies of the New Second Generation*. New York: Russell Sage Foundation.

Katz, Cindi. 2004. *Growing Up Global: Economic Restructuring and Children's Everyday Lives*. Minneapolis: University of Minnesota Press.

Kaufman, Jonathan, and Gary Fields. 2008. "Black in a New Light: Sen. Obama's Candidacy Has Sparked a Debate about Identity in the African-American Community." *The Wall Street Journal*, August 23, A1.

Kaushal, Neeraj, and Lenna Nepomnyaschy. 2009. "Wealth, Race/Ethnicity, and Children's Educational Outcomes." *Children and Youth Services Review* 31, no. 9, (September): 963–71.

Kelley, Robin D. G. 1997. *Yo Mama's Disfunktional!: Fighting the Culture Wars in Urban America*. Boston: Beacon Press.

Keyes, Cheryl L. 2004. "Empowering Self, Making Choices, Creating Spaces: Black Female Identity Via Rap Music Performance." In *That's the Joint!: The Hip-Hop Studies Reader*, ed. Murray Forman and Mark Anthony Neal. New York: Routledge.

Kirst, Julia. 2009. "Undoing Goodness Itself: A Proposal for a Critical Look at the Work of Helping Troubled Youth." Paper presented at the Annual Meeting of the American Anthropological Association, December 2, Philadelphia, Pennsylvania.

Kleinfield, N. R. 2000. "Guarding the Borders of the Hip-Hop Nation." *New York Times*, July 6, accessed October 23, 2010, www.nytimes.com/200/07/06/us/guarding-the-borders-of-the-hip-hop-nation.html.

Kozol, Jonathan. 2005. *The Shame of the Nation: The Restoration of Apartheid Schooling in America*. New York: Crown.

LaBennett, Oneka. 2002. *Consuming Identities: Consumption, Gender and Ethnicity Among West Indian Adolescents in Brooklyn*. Unpublished Ph.D. dissertation, Harvard University, Cambridge, MA.

———. 2006. "Reading Buffy and 'Looking Proper': Race, Gender and Consumption amongst West Indian Girls in Brooklyn." In *Globalization and Race: Transformations in the Cultural Production of Blackness*, ed. Deborah A. Thomas and Kamari M. Clarke. Durham, NC: Duke University Press.

———. 2009. "Histories and 'Her Stories' from the Bronx: Excavating Hidden Hip-Hop Narratives." *Afro-Americans in New York Life and History* 33, no. 2 (July): 109–31.

Lacan, Jacques. 1974. *Télévision*. Paris: Editions du Seuil.

Lady Saw, featuring Beenie Man. 1997. "Healing." *Passion*. New York: VP Records.

Lancy, David. 2008. *The Anthropology of Childhood: Cherubs, Chattel, Changelings*. Cambridge: Cambridge University Press.

Lareau, Annette. 2003. *Unequal Childhoods: Class, Race, and Family Life*. Berkeley: University of California Press.

Lefebvre, Henri. 1991. *The Production of Space*, tr. Donald Nicholson-Smith. Malden, MA: Blackwell.

Leamy, Elisabeth. 2008. "Don't Buy Candy from . . . Children: The Sales Are Often Scams; the Kids Are Underpaid and Exploited." ABC News, June 23, accessed January 5, 2010, http://abc.news.go.com/Business/story?id=5213468&page=1.

LeVine, Robert, and Rebecca New, eds. 2008. *Anthropology and Child Development: A Cross-Cultural Reader*. Malden, MA: Blackwell.

Levine, Stephanie Wellen. 2003. *Mystics, Mavericks, and Merrymakers: An Intimate Journey among Hasidic Girls*. New York: New York University Press.

Lewis, Amanda. 2003. *Race in the Schoolyard: Negotiating the Color Line in Classrooms and Communities*. New Brunswick, NJ: Rutgers University Press.

Lipsitz, George. 1994. *Dangerous Crossroads: Popular Music, Postmodernism and the Poetics of Place*. London: Verso.

López, Nancy. 2003. *Hopeful Girls, Troubled Boys: Race and Gender Disparity in Urban Education*. New York: Routledge.

———. 2004. "Unraveling the Race-Gender Gap in Education: Second-Generation Dominican Men's High School Experiences." In *Becoming New Yorkers: Ethnographies of the New Second Generation*, ed. Philip Kasinitz, John H. Mollenkopf and Mary C. Waters. New York: Russell Sage Foundation.

Low, Setha M. 1996. "A Response to Castells: An Anthropology of the City." *Critique of Anthropology* 16, no. 1 (March): 57–62.

———. 2005. "Spatializing Culture: The Social Production and Social Construction of Public Space in Costa Rica." In *Theorizing the City: The New Urban Anthropology Reader*, ed. Setha M. Low. New Brunswick, NJ: Rutgers University Press.

MacCormack, Carol P. 1988. "Health and the Social Power of Women." *Social Science and Medicine* 26, no. 7 (April): 677–83.

MacCormack, Carol P., and Alizon Draper. 1987. "Social and Cognitive Aspects of Female Sexuality in Jamaica." In *Cultural Construction of Sexuality*, ed. Pat Caplan. London: Travistock.

Maira, Sunaina Marr. 2002. *Desis in the House: Indian American Youth Culture in New York City*. Philadelphia: Temple University Press.

Maira, Sunaina, and Elizabeth Soep, eds. 2005. *Youthscapes: The Popular, the National and the Global*. Philadelphia: University of Pennsylvania Press.

Marshall, Paule. 1981. *Brown Girl, Brownstones: A Novel*. New York: The Feminist Press at CUNY.

Maseko, Zola, dir. 1998. *The Life and Times of Sara Baartman*. Icarus Films.

Massey, Douglas S., Margarita Mooney, Kimberly C. Torres, and Camille Z. Charles. 2007. "Black Immigrants and Black Natives Attending Selective Colleges and Universities in the United States." *American Journal of Education* 113 (February): 243–71.

McBride, James. 2007. "Hip-Hop Planet." *National Geographic* 211, no. 4 (April): 100–19.

McLean Taylor, Jill, Carol Gilligan, and Amy Sullivan, eds. 1995. *Between Voice and Silence: Women and Girls, Race and Relationships*. Cambridge, MA: Harvard University Press.

McRobbie, Angela. 1994. "Different, Youthful Subjectivities: Towards a Cultural Sociology of Youth." In *Postmodernism and Popular Culture*, ed. Angela McRobbie. London: Routledge.

———. 1999. *In The Culture Society: Art, Fashion and Popular Music*. London: Routledge.

Miller, Daniel. 1994. *Modernity: An Ethnographic Approach (Dualism and Mass Consumption in Trinidad)*. Oxford: Berg.

———. 1998. *A Theory of Shopping*. Cambridge: Polity.

Miller, Daniel, and Don Slater. 2001. *The Internet: An Ethnographic Approach*. Oxford: Berg.

Miller, Jody. 2008. *Getting Played: African American Girls, Urban Inequality, and Gendered Violence*. New York: New York University Press.

Model, Suzanne. 1991. "Caribbean Immigrants: A Black Success Story?" *International Migration Review* 25 (Summer): 248–76.

———. 1995. "West Indian Prosperity: Fact or Fiction?" *Social Problems* 42, no. 4 (November): 535–52.

Molotch, Harvey. 2003. *Where Stuff Comes From: How Toasters, Toilets, Cars, Computers, and Many Other Things Come to Be as They Are*. New York: Routledge.

Montgomery, Heather. 2009. *An Introduction to Childhood: Anthropological Perspectives on Children's Lives*. Malden, MA: Wiley-Blackwell.

Morgan, Joan. 1992. "Artists of the Year Runners Up: Arrested Development." *Spin* 8, no. 9 (December): 64–65.

———. 1999. *When Chickenheads Come Home to Roost: My Life as a Hip-Hop Feminist*. New York: Simon and Schuster.

Morgan, Marcyliena. 2009. *The Real Hip-Hop: Battling for Knowledge, Power, and Respect in the LA Underground*. Durham, NC: Duke University Press.

Nathanson, Constance A. 1991. *Dangerous Passage: The Social Control of Sexuality in Women's Adolescence*. Philadelphia: Temple University Press.

Neal, Mark Anthony. 2004. "No Time for Fake Niggas: Hip-Hop Culture and the Authenticity Debates." In *That's the Joint!: The Hip-Hop Studies Reader*, ed. Murray Forman and Mark Anthony Neal. New York: Routledge.

New York City Department of Education. 2006. "Regulation of the Chancellor, Category: Students; Subject: Security in Schools." No. A-412 (November 8): 1–9.

Niang, Abdoulaye. 2006. "Bboys: Hip-Hop Culture in Dakar, Sénégal." In *Global Youth? Hybrid Identities, Plural Worlds*, ed. Pam Nilan and Carles Feixa. New York: Routledge.

Nilan, Pam, and Carles Feixa. 2006. "Introduction: Youth Hybridity and Plural Worlds." In *Global Youth? Hybrid Identities, Plural Worlds*, ed. Pam Nilan and Carles Feixa. New York: Routledge.

Ogbar, Jeffrey O. G. 2009. *Hip-Hop Revolution: The Culture and Politics of Rap*. Lawrence: University of Kansas Press.

Ogbu, John. 1990. "Cultural Model, Identity, and Literacy." In *Cultural Psychology: Essays on Comparative Human Development*, ed. James W. Stigler, Richard Schweder, and Gilbert Herdt. New York: Cambridge University Press.

Olwig, Karen Fog. 2007. *Caribbean Journeys: An Ethnography of Migration and Home in Three Family Networks*. Durham, NC: Duke University Press.

Olwig, Karen Fog, and Eva Gullov, eds. 2003. *Children's Places: Cross-Cultural Perspectives*. New York: Routledge.

Omi, Michael, and Howard Winant. 1994. *Racial Formation in the United States: From the 1960s to the 1990s*. New York: Routledge.

Ong, Aihwa. 1999. "Cultural Citizenship as Subject Making: Immigrants Negotiate Racial and Cultural Boundaries in the United States." In *Race, Identity, and Citizenship: A Reader*, ed. R. D. Torres, L. F. Miron, and J. X. Inda. Malden, MA.: Blackwell.

Perry, Imani. 2004. *Prophets of the Hood: Politics and Poetics in Hip-Hop*. Durham, NC: Duke University Press.

Perry, Marc D. 2008. "Global Black Self-Fashionings: Hip-Hop as Diasporic Space." *Identities: Global Studies in Culture and Power* 15 (November): 635–64.

Pipher, Mary. 1994. *Reviving Ophelia: Saving the Selves of Adolescent Girls*. New York: Ballantine.

Portes, Alejandro, and Rubén Rumbaut. 1990. *Immigrant America: A Portrait*. Berkeley: University of California Press.

———. 2001. *Legacies: The Story of the Immigrant Second Generation*. Berkeley: University of California Press.

Pough, Gwendolyn D. 2004. *Check It While I Wreck It: Black Womanhood, Hip-Hop Culture and the Public Space*. Boston: Northeastern University Press.

Ragland-Sullivan, Ellie. 1986. *Jacques Lacan and the Philosophy of Psychoanalysis*. Urbana: University of Illinois Press.

Reid, Ira De A. 1939. *The Negro Immigrant: His Background, Characteristics, and Social Adjustments, 1899–1937*. New York: Columbia University Press.

Reyes, Angela. 2006. *Language, Identity, and Stereotype Among Southeast Asian American Youth: The Other Asian*. London and New York: Routledge.

Rimer, Sara, and Karen W. Arenson. 2004. "Top Colleges Take More Blacks, but Which Ones?" *New York Times*, June 24, accessed October 10, 2010, www.nytimes.com/2004/06/24/us/top-colleges-take-more-blacks-but-which-ones.html.

Rivera, Ray. 2010. "Man is Arrested in Shootings from a Crown Heights Rooftop." *New York Times*, April 17, accessed October 23, 2010, www.nytimes.com/2010/04/17/nyregion/17roof.html.

Rogers, Reuel. 2001. "'Black Like Who?' Afro-Caribbean Immigrants, African Americans, and the Politics of Group Identity." In *Islands in the City: West Indian Migration to New York*, ed. Nancy Foner. Berkeley: University of California Press.

———. 2006. *Afro-Caribbean Immigrants and the Politics of Incorporation: Ethnicity, Exception, or Exit*. Cambridge: Cambridge University Press.

Rose, Tricia. 1994. *Black Noise: Rap Music and Black Culture in Contemporary America*. Middletown, CT: Wesleyan University Press.

———. 2004. "Never Trust a Big Butt and a Smile." In *That's the Joint! The Hip-Hop Studies Reader*, ed. Murray Forman and Mark Anthony Neal. New York: Routledge.

Sargent, Carolyn, and Michael Harris. 1998. "Bad Boys and Good Girls: The Implications of Gender Ideology for Child Health in Jamaica." In *Small Wars: The Cultural Politics of Childhood*, ed. Nancy Scheper-Hughes and Carolyn Sargent. Berkeley: University of California Press.

Scheper-Hughes, Nancy, and Carolyn Sargent, eds. 1998. Introduction to *Small Wars: The Cultural Politics of Childhood*. Berkeley: University of California Press.

Schwartzman, Helen B., ed. 2001. *Children and Anthropology: Perspectives for the 21st Century*. Westport, CT: Bergin and Garvey.

Schreiber, Rita, Phyllis Noerager Stern, and Charmaine Wilson. 2000. "Being Strong: How Black West Indian Canadian Women Manage Depression and Its Stigma." *Journal of Nursing Scholarship* 32, no. 1 (March): 39–45.

Seifman, David. 2009. "Mike's Message on School-Cellphone 'Danger.'" *New York Post*, September 2, accessed September 19, 2009, www.nypost.com./p/news/regional/mike_message_on_school_cellphone_dv9NyTM2eoUWbncdBSljpL.

Shankar, Shalini. 2008. *Desi Land: Teen Culture, Class and Success in Silicon Valley*. Durham, NC: Duke University Press.

Shapiro, Edward S. 2006. *Crown Heights: Blacks, Jews and the 1991 Riot in Brooklyn*. Lebanon, NH: Brandeis University Press.

Sharpley-Whiting, T. Denean. 1999. *Black Venus: Sexualized Savages, Primal Fears, and Primitive Narratives in French*. Durham, NC: Duke University Press.

———. 2007. *Pimps Up, Ho's Down: Hip-Hop's Hold on Young Black Women*. New York: New York University Press.

Shipley, Jesse Weaver. 2007. "Real Black: Adventures in Racial Sincerity" (Review). *Anthropological Quarterly* 80, no. 1 (Winter): 271–76.

Soep, Elisabeth. 2005. "Making Hard-Core Masculinity: Teenage Boys Playing House." In *Youthscapes: The Popular, the National and the Global,* ed. Sunaina Maira and Elizabeth Soep. Philadelphia: University of Pennsylvania Press.

Skelton, Tracey. 1996. "'I Sing Dirty Reality, I Am Out There for the Ladies,' Lady Saw: Women and Jamaican Ragga Music, Resisting Patriarchy." *Phoebe* 7, no. 1-2 (Spring/Fall): 86–104.

Skelton, Tracey, and Gill Valentine, eds. 1998. *Cool Places: Geographies of Youth Cultures.* London: Routledge.

Sowell, Thomas. 1981. *Ethnic America: A History.* New York: Basic Books.

Smith, Raymond T. 1987. "Hierarchy and the Dual Marriage System in West Indian Society." In *Gender and Kinship: Towards a Unified Analysis,* ed. Jane Collier and S. J. Yanagisako. Palo Alto: Stanford University Press.

Stanley-Niaah, Sonjah. 2009. "Negotiating a Common Transnational Space: Mapping Performance in Jamaican Dancehall and South African Kwaito." *Cultural Studies,* Vol. 23, nos. 5-6 (September-November): 756-774.

Stanton-Salazar, Ricardo. 2009. "A Social Capital Framework for Understanding the Socialization of Racial Minority Children and Youths." *Harvard Educational Review* 67, no. 1 (Spring): 1–41.

Stephens, Sharon, ed. 1995. *Children and the Politics of Culture.* Princeton: Princeton University Press.

Straus, Martha. B. 2007. *Adolescent Girls in Crisis: Intervention and Hope.* New York: W. W. Norton.

Sutton, Constance, and Elsa Chaney, eds. 1987. *Caribbean Life in New York City: Sociocultural Dimensions.* New York: Center for Migration Studies.

Taylor, Kate. 2008. "Adding Yellow and 'Green' to the Brooklyn Children's Museum." New York Sun, June 16, www.nysun.com/arts/adding-yellow-and-green-to-the-brooklyn-childrens/80039/ .

Thomas, Deborah A. 2004. *Modern Blackness: Nationalism, Globalization, and the Politics of Culture in Jamaica.* Durham, NC: Duke University Press.

Thomas, Deborah A., and Tina M. Campt. 2007. "Diasporic Hegemonies: Popular Culture and Transnational Blackness." *Transforming Anthropology* 15, no. 1 (June): 50–62.

Thomas, Mary E. 2004. "Pleasure and Propriety: Teen Girls and the Practice of Straight Space." *Environment and Planning D: Society and Space* 22 (October): 773–89.

Vickerman, Milton. 1999. *Crosscurrents: West Indian Immigrants and Race.* New York: Oxford University Press.

Waksler, Frances C., ed. 1991. *Studying the Social Worlds of Children: Sociological Readings.* London: Falmer.

Waters, Mary C. 1999. *Black Identities: West Indian Immigrant Dreams and American Realities.* Cambridge, MA: Harvard University Press.

———. 2001. "Growing Up West Indian and African American: Gender and Class Differences in the Second Generation." In *Islands in the City: West Indian Migration to New York,* ed. Nancy Foner. Berkeley: University of California Press.

Watkins-Owens, Irma. 1996. *Blood Relations: Caribbean Immigrants and the Harlem Community 1900–1930.* Bloomington: Indiana University Press.

———. 2001. "Early-Twentieth-Century Caribbean Women: Migration and Social Networks in New York City." In *Islands in the City: West Indian Migration to New York,* ed. Nancy Foner. Berkeley: University of California Press.

Watson, James L. 1997. Preface to *Golden Arches East: McDonald's in East Asia*, ed. James L. Watson. Palo Alto: Stanford University Press.

West, Cornel. 2001. *Race Matters*. Boston: Beacon Press.

Wilson, Peter J. 1973. *Crab Antics: A Caribbean Case Study of the Conflict between Reputation and Respectability*. Prospect Heights, IL: Waveland Press.

Yardley, Jim. 1998. "Lights, Camera, Lots of Action: Multiplex Plan Raises Concerns in Brooklyn Heights." *New York Times*, December 28, http://select.nytimes.com/gst/abstract.html?res=F70D17F73C5B0C7B8EDDAB0994D0494D81&scp=2&sq=.

Zanfagna, Christina. 2009. "The Multiringed Cosmos of Krumping/Hip-Hop Dance at the Intersections of Battle, Media, and Spirit." In *Ballroom, Boogie, Shimmy Sham, Shake: A Social and Popular Dance Reader*, ed. Julie Malnig. Urbana: University of Illinois Press.

Index

Black teenagers: Black youth culture, 3; as "combat" or "predatory" consumers, 89, 101, 109–110; eating patterns, 45; hip-hop music and culture, 110; stereotypes of, 3–4, 69

Black women: bodies of, 153–159; hip-hop music and culture, 106–107, 112; stereotypes of, 152–153, 154–155, 158

Black youth culture: authenticity in, 4–5; Black teenagers, 3; diasporic belonging, 13; *place* and, 4; West Indian girls, 12; West Indian youth, 3

Blackness: Black femininity, 122–123; Christianity, 161–162; hip-hop music and culture, 25–26; large butts, 155–158; markers of, 92; "real" or "authentic" Blackness, 65–66, 115–117, 122–123, 169–172, 175–176, 181, 197, 212n13

Blacks in United States: BCM as "place for Blacks," 53, 65, 102, 192; foreign-born among, 11–12; and Hasidim in Crown Heights, 71–75; heteromasculinity, 65–66; homophobia, 162; stereotypes of, 92

Blige, Mary J.: China (interviewee) and, 1–3, 4–5, 6, 114–115, 120, 188, 195–196, 197; dress, 114; feminine style, 117, 132; as "*mad* real," 2, 4, 5, 114, 115; "No More Drama," 1–2, 207n3; personal struggles, 2; upbringing, 114

The Blind Side (film), 3

Bloods (gang), 76–77

Bloomberg, Michael, 84, 87, 88, 93, 94

Bohannon, Laura, 44

Bonilla-Silva, Eduardo, 48–49

"Boom Bye Bye" (song), 126

"Bootylicious" (song), 155

Brennan, Denise, 158

Brooklyn Academy of Music (BAM) outing, 103–106, 113

Brooklyn Children's Museum (BCM), 41–102, 191–194; appearance, 57, *58*, 69; cell phone usage, 54, 82–83, 89–90; Cultural Institutions Group, 194; expansions and renovations, 57, 70, 191–192; extracurricular activities, 53; founding, 57; funding, 193–195; gang activity near, 77; gendered as female, 53, 54, 64–66, 101, 191–192; gentrification of Crown Heights, 192–193, 195; heterosexualized space, 65–66; hip-hop music and culture, 83, 114; as home for youth, 35, 58, 62; identity formation, 53–54, 60, 62–68; interviewees at, 32–33, 35; Jewish Museum (New York) compared to, 71, 73; keeping "at-risk" teens off streets, 67–68; live animals, 56; locations, 57, 69–70; mission, 61–62; performing obedience within, 52; place making at, 69; play-labor, as site of, 24–25; programs (*see* —Museum Team program; —other programs); racialized as Black, 53, 65, 102, 192; as "safe" space, 54, 67, 76, 77–78, 80, 81, 83, 89, 101; as social space, 59; structured environment, 59; Urban Word, 211n4; visitors, children, 58–59; visitors, Jamaican, 30; visitors, race/ethnicity of, 62; visitors, school groups, 70

—exhibits: "Global Shoes," 61; "World Brooklyn," 61

—library, 70

—Museum Team Internship Program: Explainers (high school seniors), 51, 55, 95, 96, 98–99, 136, 143; Mardi Gras celebration, 54, 65, 68, 95–100, 99–100; Peer Mentors (eleventh graders), 55, 95, 96, 136; play-labor, 55–57; teen pregnancy, 127–128; Volunteers (tenth graders), 55, 91, 95, 96; Volunteers-in-Training (ninth graders), 55, 91, 96–97, 99

—Museum Team program, 55–57; admittance into, 55; bookbinding project, 51–52, 65; college admissions, 55, 194–195; dismissals from, 52–53, 68; funding, 193–194; gender disparity in performance, 66–67; goals, 75; identification cards, 89; leadership, 65, 67, 74; participant observation of, 33; pay for participation, 52–53, 55, 101; pedagogical approaches, 37; popularity, 55; racial identity role playing exercises, 91–92, 94; SAT prep courses, 59; school time *vs.* museum time, 81–82; snack time, 89–90, 122–123; temporal barrier to attending, 81–82

—Museum Team program outings: Barnes and Noble, 41–43, 46–47, 51, 118; "best behavior" on, 43, 51, 143; Chinatown, 44, 68–69; Court Street multiplex, 50–51, 118; hip-hop concert, 103–108, 113; Jewish Museum (New York), 74–75; McDonald's, 43–45, 51, 118
—other programs: afterschool program, 4, 24, 32–33, 62, 73, 81–82 (*see also* Museum Team program); Inniss award, 198; "Kids Crew," 56, 59; preschool and elementary school children, 55, 59; Sukkot festival, 73; "Totally Tots," 59, 195
—staff: author's helping, 37; Kiara (educator), 74, 95–96, 99, 103–105, 113, 184; male educators, 192; Neru (educator), 103–106, 113; Rebecca (educator), 74, 91, 128; security guards, 89; Shelly (administrator) (*see* Shelly)
—"the Tank," 95
Brooklyn Heights, response to Court Street multiplex, 46–49
Brooklyn Museum, 194
Brower Park, 57–58, *117*
Brown, Jacqueline Nassy, 18–19
Brown Girl, Brownstones (Marshall), 63, 183, 186, 195, 206
BrownPride.us, 156
Bryce-Laporte, Roy, 13–14
Buffy the Vampire Slayer (television program), 139
Buju Banton (musician), 126, 162
Butterfield, Sherri-Ann, 17, 23, 34, 98

Cahill, Caitlin, 102
Campbell, Clive (DJ Kool Herc), 112
Caribbean Diaspora Studies, 13
Caribbean gender ideologies, 62–64, 66–67
Caribbean music. *See* West Indian dancehall music
Cato, Gavin, 71, 72, 74, 98
cell phones, 82–95; Bloomberg and, Michael, 84, 87; Brooklyn Children's Museum, use in, 54, 82–83, 89–90; Canada, schools in, 88; Caribbean region, usage in, 85–86; as detriment to performing in work or

school, 92; driving hazards, 87; Great Britain, schools in, 88; Internet accessibility compared to, 86; Jamaica, schools in, 88; Jamaica, usage in, 86; Klein and, Joel, 84, 87; as markers of style, 90; minority students' rights to personal property, 84; minority youths' usage, 83; moral panics about use of, 86; music, listening to, 90; New York City Department of Education (DOE) ban, 83–84, 88, 92–93, 94, 110; pathologizing of minority youths' consumption, 88, 94; protection against racialized discrimination, 87; public school students, criminalization of, 84; racializing popular culture as "corruptive," 88; ringtones, 90, 211n28; sleep deprivation, 87; texting, dangers of, 86–87; tracking children, 87; United Federation of Teachers (UFT), 84; wealth and ownership of, 87; West Indian youth, 86
Center for Contemporary Cultural Studies (CCCS), 20
Centers for Disease Control (CDC), 150, 151
Chaney, Elsa, 14
Charles, Andrew, 72
Chicago Tribune (newspaper), 87
Children's Museum (Boston), 61
Chin, Elizabeth, 36, 155, 156–157
China (interviewee; Barbadian), 114–117, 129–131, 188–191, 195–198; accent, turning on and off, 165–167, 168, 169; African American popular culture, 133; *America's Next Top Model*, behavior while watching, 143; *America's Next Top Model*, Black women's bodies on, 153–154, 157; *America's Next Top Model*, favorite contestant on, 114–115, 135; *America's Next Top Model*, plus-sized women on, 146–149, 150; *America's Next Top Model*, portrayal of women on, 170; *America's Next Top Model*, Robin on, 161–162; appearance, 41; BCM afterschool program, 4–5; BCM Barnes and Noble outing, 41–42; BCM Court Street multiplex outing, 50–51; BCM hip-hop concert outing, 103; BCM Mardi Gras

Cultural Institutions Group, 194
culture theorists, 111
Curry, Adrianne, 139, 140–144, 159
Cuvier, Georges, 155

DaCosta, Yaya, 145
dancehall music. *See* West Indian dancehall music
Danielle (contestant on *America's Next Top Model*): accent and dental "defect," 164–166, 169, 181; attitude, 145; Blackness of, 135; as favorite of West Indian youth, 135, 145, 146
Def Poetry Jam (television program), 211n4
Delirious (film), 50
Desis in the House (Maira), 20–21
Destiny's Child (musicians), 155, 196
Dickerson, Janice, 142–143
Diggs, Taye, 145
Dimitriadis, Greg, 67, 108
DOE. *See* New York City Department of Education (DOE)
Douglas, Mary, 109
Dropping Anchor, Setting Sail (Brown), 18–19
duCille, Ann, 155
Durham, Deborah, 200–201

education: extended school days, 81–82, 102, 110; foreign-born Blacks, 29; minority boys' access to, 163; minority women, 66; wealth and outcomes, 94; West Indians, 29–32
Education Week (magazine), 83–84, 87
El Museo del Barrio (New York), 61
Enseki, Carol, 61–62
Erikson, Erik, 187
ethnic identity, 197

Ferguson, James, 54, 69
Fishman, Ray, 212n11
Flatbush (Brooklyn): economic and social power, lack of, 54; gentrification, 54–55; as marginalized place, 54; minority population, 54; movie houses, 46; police brutality, 76

Flatbush YMCA: cheerleaders, 32, 35, 113, 121; cheerleaders' mothers, 123–124; hip-hop music and culture, 113, 121–122; keeping "at-risk" teens off streets, 67–68; as play-only site, 121; as social space, 123
Fleetwood, Nicole, 115–116
Flores, Juan, 26
Foner, Nancy, 14
Forman, Murray, 26
Foxy Brown (musician), 121–122, 126, 158
Frankfurt School, 108

gang violence, 76–77
Gates, Henry Louis, Jr., 31
Gaunt, Kyra D., 118
gender: Brooklyn Children's Museum, 53, 54, 64–66, 101, 191–192; Caribbean gender ideologies, 62–64, 66–67; commercials, 144; discourse styles, 137–138; gender propriety, West Indian notions of, 119–120; heteromasculinity, 65–66; hip-hop music and culture, 112; hypermasculinity, 121, 125; labor market differences, 14; performance in BCM Museum program, 66–67; play-labor, definition of, 10; public space, definition of, 10; stereotypes, 79–80; subway performers, 9
gentrification: Brooklyn Children's Museum (BCM), effect on, 192–193, 195; Crown Heights, 54–55, 58, 102, 192–193, 195; Flatbush, 54–55
Gilroy, Paul, 25, 115–116, 196
Glazer, Nathan, 14
Global Youth? (Nilan and Feixa), 111
globalization: literature on, 21; of McDonald's, 45; West Indian migration scholarship, 22; youth culture, 26; youth culture studies, 111
Goodwin, Marjorie Harness, 137–138
Guinier, Lani, 31
Gupta, Akhil, 54, 69
Guyanese child labor laws, 208n10

Hall, Stuart, 20, 25, 169, 196–197
Handler, Richard, 59–60
Harris, Michael, 66–67, 207n2, 209n11

Harvey, David, 54, 82, 98
Hasidim, 71–75
Hayden, Dolores, 62, 113
"Healing" (song), 124–125
"Heart Attack" (song), 90, 95
Hebdige, Dick, 19–20
Heritage Museum, 61
Hill, Lauryn, 122–123, 132
Hintzen, Percy, 15, 119–120, 204
hip-hop music and culture, 103–133;
  African American girls, 131; alternative
  hip-hop, 105–106; in anthropology,
  26–27; Black girls, 107; Black teenagers,
  110; Black women, 106–107, 112, 158;
  Blackness, 25–26; Brooklyn Children's
  Museum (BCM), 83, 114; CD sales, 121;
  "corruptive" nature, 83, 110, 121, 123–124;
  discourses about, 106; Flatbush YMCA,
  113, 121–122; as *the* hegemonic African
  diasporic youth culture, 26; hypersexualized femininity, 158–159; ideas about
  gender and nationhood, 112; "keeping it
  real," 115; *krumping*, 106; misogyny, 107;
  as "negative," 126; parents' view of, 121,
  123–124; political activism, 106; popularity, 112; profanity, 121; rap, 115, 211n4;
  "realness," 212n13; sexist lyrics, 122;
  spoken-word poetry, 211n4; transnationalism, 12, 112; videos, 107; West Indian
  dancehall music compared to, 126; West
  Indian girls, 12, 131; West Indian youth,
  33–34, 112; White youth, 121
"hip-hop nation," 112, 122, 131, 196
"hip-hop planet," 111–112
Hodges, David Julian, 60–61
Holdaway, Jennifer, 16 –17, 26–27
homophobia, 125–126, 161, 162
Hope, Donna, 26, 125, 126
Hopeful Girls, Troubled Boys (López), 84–85
Horst, Heather, 85–86, 88, 90
Huq, Rupa, 26

"I Like Big Butts" (song), 155
identity formation: accents as markers of
  identity, 166; adolescent transnational
  identities, consumer culture in, 110;

African Americans, 17, 98; "American
  identified" personalities, 16, 197, 203;
  American social constructions of race, 12;
  association of becoming American with
  access to consumer goods, 16; British
  West Indian youth, 19; Brooklyn Children's Museum (BCM), 53–54, 60, 62–68;
  code-switching between identities, 166,
  168; consumer and leisure culture, 19–20,
  109; critical agency in Black youth and
  parents, 126, 132; "ethnic identified"
  personalities, 16, 197, 203; ethnic identity,
  197; "identity work" of goods, 109;
  "immigrant identified" personalities, 16,
  197, 203; music in, 25–26; racial identity
  role playing exercises, 91–92, 94; stereotypes, role of, 32; West Indian girls, 5, 11;
  West Indian identity, 74–75; West Indian
  youth, 16, 17, 112; West Indians, 17
Indian American youth, 20–21
"informant" (the term), 37–38
Inheriting the City (Waters, Kasinitz, Mollenkopf, and Holdaway), 16
"interviewees" (the term), 38
interviewees: awareness of "at-risk"
  stereotypes, 28; at Brooklyn Children's
  Museum, 32–33, 35; college admission,
  levels of, 32; demographic profile, 27–28;
  at Flatbush YMCA, 32, 35; gender-based
  violence, experience of, 27; identification with the author, 35–36; intimate
  relationships, 35; minority schools, 45;
  movie going, 46, 50–51, 76; neighborhood turfs, unwritten rules about, 51;
  schools attended by, 85, 93; shopping/
  spending habits, 43, 57
—BCM staff: Kiara (educator), 74, 95–96,
  99, 103–105, 113, 184; Neru (educator),
  103–106, 113; Rebecca (educator), 74, 91,
  128; sexual harassment by, accusation of,
  77–81; Shelly (administrator) (*see* Shelly)
—boys: Anton, 144, 163–164; James, 82–83,
  192; Jarlen, 145–146, 153, 170; Kareem,
  52–53, 66, 68, 70; Kevin, 52, 66; Malik,
  146; Mark, 136–137, 162–164, 169–172;
  Tyrone (*see* Tyrone)

McDonald's outing, 43–45, 51, 118
McRobbie, Angela, 26, 110, 197, 200
Metropolitan Museum of Art (New York), 69–70, 194
Metropolitan Transit Authority (MTA), 7, 97
Miller, Daniel, 85–86, 88, 90, 109
Miller, Jody, 27, 80
The Miseducation of Lauryn Hill (album), 122
Missy Elliot (musician), 122, 132
Model, Suzanne, 14
model minority myth, 29–32
Mollenkopf, John H., 16 –17, 26–27
Molotch, Harvey, 108–109, 111
Montana, Marshall (musician), 121
Morgan, Marcyliena, 112, 118, 211n1
Mos Def (rap MC), 211n4
Moynihan, Daniel Patrick, 14
Murphy, Eddie, 50
Museum of Modern Art (New York), 69–70
museums: minority children, 60–61; "new museums," 60–61; possessive individualism, 59–60; as social spaces, 59
"Museums, Anthropology, and Minorities" (Hodges), 60–61
My Fair Brady (television program), 139

Nadine (interviewee; Trinidadian): *America's Next Top Model*, artificial beauty on, 169–170; *America's Next Top Model*, commercials on, 144; *America's Next Top Model*, contestants' accents on, 164–165; *America's Next Top Model*, favorite contestant on, 135, 145; *America's Next Top Model*, plus-sized women on, 146–151; *America's Next Top Model*, portrayal of women on, 171; *America's Next Top Model*, Robin on, 161; appearance, 41; BCM Barnes and Noble outing, 41–42; BCM Chinatown outing, 69; BCM Court Street multiplex outing, 50; BCM Jewish Museum outing, learning from, 74–75; Black femininity, 123; China and, 1, 2, 24, 52, 188; college, decision to

forgo, 33; college acceptance, 189–190; dress as an ethnic marker, 74–75; housing project, moving to, 33, 189; Kareem's dismissal from Museum program, 52–53, 66; mother, separation from, 2, 24, 148–149; music for Mardi Gras celebration, 99; personality, 41–42, 149; prom preparations, 188; self-reliance, 2; shopping, 2, 24; subway performance, 1; weight, 149, 150; White adults, 1, 3
Nadir, Manzoor, 208n10
National Urban League, 178
Neal, Mark Anthony, 26
Neema (interviewee; Jamaican): *America's Next Top Model*, artificial beauty on, 169–170; *America's Next Top Model*, contestants' accents on, 165; *America's Next Top Model*, contestants' quest for success, 163–164; *America's Next Top Model*, favorite contestant on, 135; *America's Next Top Model*, plus-sized women on, 148; *America's Next Top Model*, portrayal of Black women on, 172; *America's Next Top Model*, Robin on, 159–160; BCM Barnes and Noble outing, 42; prom preparations, 188; subway performance, 1
The Negro Immigrant (Reid), 14
Nepomnyaschy, Lenna, 93–94
New, Rebecca, 22
New Childhood Studies, 35
"new ethnicities," 196–197
New York City: movie houses per capita, 47; "safe" places in, 52–53
New York City City Council, 193
New York City Department of Cultural Affairs, 61
New York City Department of Education (DOE), 81–82, 83–84, 92–93, 94
New York City Department of Youth and Community Development (DYCD), 193
New-York Historical Society, 69
New York Police Department (NYPD), 75, 76
New York Post (newspaper), 77, 88
New York Sun (newspaper), 57

New York Times (newspaper): break-dance crews (b-boy crews), 8, 9; Court Street multiplex, 46–47; gang activity near BCM, 77; hip-hop and White youth, 121; obesity epidemic, 150, 151
The New Yorker (magazine), 175–176
Niang, Abdoulaye, 26
Nielsen Company, 86
"No Child Left Behind" program, 93
"No More Drama" (song), 1–2
Notorious B.I.G. (musician), 122

Obama, Barack, 12, 30, 31–32, 150, 192
Obama, Michelle, 150, 173–174, 175–176
obesity epidemic, 150–152
Olwig, Karen Fog, 14, 69
The Omen (film), 50, 76
Oneka (musician), 121
Ong, Aihwa, 113
oral-kinetic lessons, 118

Palin, Sarah, 175, 176
Passion (album), 124
Perry, Marc, 26
Perry, Tyler, 213n9
Pew Internet and American Life Project, 87
Pigford, Eva, 145–146
Pimps Up, Ho's Down (Sharpley-Whiting), 106–107
Pipher, Mary, 109
place making, 69
play-labor, 8–9, 24–25, 55–57
"Poison" (song), 155
Portes, Alejandro, 29–30
possessive individualism, 59–60
Precious: Based on the Novel Push by Sapphire (film), 3, 211n29, 213n9
Public School 289 (George V. Brower school), 58
Public Use Microdata Area (PUMA) data, 55, 102

Quillian, Beau, 142, 147

racial identity role playing exercises, 91–92, 94

racism: belief in racial difference, 155; color-blind racism, 48–49; conformance to prescribed notions of success, 199
Ragland-Sullivan, Ellie, 116
rap, 211n4. See also hip-hop music and culture
Ray J (musician), 156
Reflections: A Retrospective (album), 115
Reid, Ira De A., 14
research methodology, 34–35
Robin (contestant on America's Next Top Model): appearance, 139; Banks and, Tyra, 141, 142–143, 147, 152, 162; butt, 143, 152; closed-mindedness, 160–161; "Droppin' it like it's hot," 160; flashing breasts at Mr. Jay, 141, 162; French food, sneering at, 141, 160; in "Girls Get Really Naked" episode, 139–143; job, 139; larger women, 143, 147, 149; religiosity, 139, 161–162; simulated nude shoot, refusal to participate in, 141–143, 159–162; voted off the show, 143
Rogers, Reuel, 14, 97
Rose, Tricia, 108
Rosenbaum, Yankel, 71
Rowland, Kelly, 116, 196
Rumbaut, Rubén, 29–30

Sargent, Carolyn, 66–67, 207n2, 209n11
Scary Movie 2 (film), 50
Sewell, Elyse, 140–144, 159
Sex and the City (television program), 132
sexuality: Black heteromasculinity, 65–66; citizenship and heterosexuality, 125; heterosexualized space, 65–66; hypersexualized femininity, 158–159; sexually explicit lyrics, 124–125; spatializing practices, 65
"Shakespeare in the Bush" (Bohannon), 44
Shani (Black doll), 155
Shapiro, Edward, 72, 209n13
Sharpley-Whiting, T. Denean, 106–107, 152–153
Shelly (BCM administrator; Trinidadian): "at-risk" youth, 194; gentrification of Crown Heights, 192–195; immigrants, success of, 199–200; laid off, 193, 205; sending troubled girls home to the Caribbean, 129, 197

West Indian dancehall music: Black women, stereotypes of, 158; Hill and, Lauryn, 122; hip-hop music and culture compared to, 126; homophobia, 126, 162; hypermasculinity, 121, 125; hypersexualized femininity in, 158–159; as "positive," 126; profanity, 212n12; sexually explicit lyrics, 124–125; West Indian youth, 34

West Indian Day Parade, 54, 65

West Indian girls, 62–67, 76–81; abandonment of, 67; academic success, mothers' demands for, 63–64, 209n11; advances from adult men, 78–81; African American popular culture, 133; *America's Next Top Model*, watching, 137–138; aspirations, 205; beauty, definitions of, 116; "being mad real," reliance on, 5, 115; cheerleaders, 35; consumer and leisure culture, 4, 11, 12, 132; "coolness," 68; discourse style, 137–138; dual citizenship in hip-hop nation, 113, 196; false nails, 122; favorite female artists, 131; favorite musicians, 121–123; female identity and space, 62–63; femininity, view of authentic, 116–117, 132; gangs, fear of, 76–77; hair weaves, 122–123; hip-hop music and culture, 12, 131; identification with the author, 35–36; identity formation, 5, 11; makeup, lack of, 117; marginalization of, 4; mortality rates, 66–67; mothers, separation from, 2, 24, 129, 148–149; police, fears of, 76; policing of, 4; "*real* Black people," identification with, 4–5, 115–116, 131; reprimands of boys, 136, 146; sexism, recognition and criticism of, 107–108; skin color, 123; staying home, 63–64, 67, 114, 183, 190–191, 206; teen pregnancy, 127–128

West Indian identity, 74–75

West Indian in the West (Hintzen), 15

West Indian migration, scholarship about, 13–27; accents in, 168; "child fostering" in, 207n2; children in, 21–22, 97, 208n9; comparisons of West Indians with African Americans in, 14; consumer and leisure culture in, 13, 17, 111; corporal punishment in child rearing, 200; globalization in, 22; Liverpool as field site, 18–19; second-generation youth in, 15–17, 26–27; "voluntary" *vs.* "involuntary" minorities in, 29; work and school, focus on, 17

West Indian transnationalism: consumer and leisure culture, 12; youth culture-centered approach to, 11, 18, 111

West Indian youth, 16–25, 29–34; African American youth, 29–34; African Americanness, 25, 120; African Americans, 5, 97; "American identified" personalities, 16, 197, 203; Americanness, 34; *America's Next Top Model*, interpretations of, 181–182; association of becoming American with access to consumer goods, 16; Black youth culture, 3; British West Indian youth, 19–20; Caribbean musical artists, 34; cell phones, 86; class identity, 168; critical thinking about consumer culture, 136, 151; domestic labor, entry into, 22–23; "ethnic identified" personalities, 16, 197, 203; gangs, fears of, 75; hip-hop music and culture, 33–34, 112; homophobia, 181; identity formation, 16, 17, 112; "immigrant identified" personalities, 16, 197, 203; interethnic neighborhood conflicts, 71; interpretations of *America's Next Top Model*, 138; jobs held by, 24; in Liverpool, 18–19; as museum workers, 24–25; play-labor, 24–25; police, fears of, 75; "realness," 5–6; from "respectable" households, 24–25; Restavek children, 23; second-generation, 16–17, 20; West Indianness, 25, 34, 120

West Indians: African Americans, 14, 17, 29–32, 98, 119–120, 167, 199; American Dream, 197; as "Black," 72; "child fostering," 207n2; citizenship and heterosexuality, 125; corporal punishment in child rearing, 200; differential treatment of boys and girls at home, 66–67; educational successes, 29–32; gender divisions in the labor market, 14; gender propriety, notions of, 119–120; Guyanese child labor laws, 208n10; hiring of, 29; identity formation, 17; in Miami, 11–12; middle-class migrants, 30; model minority myth, 29–32; in New York City, 12; in New York compared to California, 15; percentage of foreign-born Blacks in U.S., 11; political activism in home and host countries, 15; respectable feminity, notions of, 63–64, 119–120, 122, 125, 161–162, 181, 204; social networks, 14, 29; success, notions of, 119–120, 198, 201; transnational social practices, 14–15; as "voluntary minority," 29

Winfrey, Oprah, 213n9

YMCA. *See* Flatbush YMCA
"youth" (the term), 37
youthscapes, 21, 34
"You've Got Me Working Day and Night" (song), 6

About the Author

ONEKA LABENNETT is Assistant Professor in African and African American Studies, Anthropology, and Women's Studies at Fordham University. She is also Research Director of the Bronx African American History Project (BAAHP).

CPSIA information can be obtained
at www.ICGtesting.com
Printed in the USA
LVHW08s0006010818
585563LV00002B/249/P